I0814461

‘Reflecting Kuruvilla’s homiletical and hermeneutical expertise, *From Glory to Glory* traces the biblical story line, wonderfully framed from sin to salvation to spirit to Scripture. It contains expected emphases on, for example, Scripture, which the author both brilliantly exegetes and clearly communicates through helpful visuals, but also less anticipated yet greatly appreciated treatments on, for example, the Holy Spirit as the necessary doctor-director of our sanctification. This book is readily accessible to church members, and its depth of insight will additionally attract the attention of pastors and Christian educators. Highly recommended!’
Gregg R. Allison, Professor of Christian Theology, Southern Baptist Theological Seminary, Louisville

‘Deeply scriptural, deeply pastoral, deeply honest and sensitive, Abe Kuruvilla’s *From Glory to Glory* is a homily to the children of God in the likeness of a book. It should draw the ears, eyes and hearts of those who struggle against sin and the flesh; who believe that the Bible reveals God’s guidance and consolation; who desperately feel their need for the Spirit’s ministry; and who yearn to worship God by their holiness.’
D. Jeffrey Bingham, Jesse Hendley Professor of Biblical Theology, Southwestern Baptist Theological Seminary, Forth Worth

‘The story of sanctification is a journey in the restoration of what sin cost humanity. God in his goodness and grace did not give up on humanity but worked to restore us. This work traces the theology of God doing this amazing work. It is a serious topical study of both glory lost and restored, all through Christ. It is a read that will instruct, encourage and guide for the growth not just of us as individuals, but also as a Church.’
Darrell L. Bock, Senior Research Professor of New Testament Studies, Dallas Theological Seminary, Dallas

‘In this classic yet contemporary study of the glory of God, Abraham Kuruvilla compellingly argues that the glory of God is also the very goal of God. Written with a light touch but drawing on deep resources of biblical and theological insights, Kuruvilla demonstrates that through intervention to put right humanity’s predicament, God not only restores individuals so they might offer praise but also shows that all things work towards

displaying the glory of the ever-loving God. This book is essential reading for all seeking a deeper understanding of the purpose and goal of God.'
Paul Foster, Professor of New Testament and Early Christianity, School of Divinity, University of Edinburgh, Edinburgh

'An engaging overview of redemptive history from biblical origins to ultimate destiny. A thorough-going biblical theology well worth careful study. Highly commendable!'
Timothy George, Distinguished Professor, Beeson Divinity School, Samford University, Birmingham, Alabama

'Someone, somewhere suggested that the reading of many books brings consternation, even bewilderment. While that perception may be valid, I also find what I would call "a pearl of great price" often. This one is an exceptional gem. It offers an overarching metanarrative of the meaning of holy Scripture through the lens of divine redemption accomplished in our ultimate sanctification, the divine purpose being to gather a people to dwell in his presence, glorifying him for ever. The clarity of the literary composition is excellent, the exegesis of relevant passages precious, the depth of insight rare, the structure of the chapters easily grasped, the methodology executed throughout that of a seasoned homiletical practitioner. I think it is one of the best books I have ever read and seriously recommend it to you.'
John D. Hannah, Distinguished Professor of Historical Theology, Dallas Theological Seminary, Dallas

'In a work hermeneutically sensitive and homiletically shaped, Kuruvilla again shows himself a masterful expositor and communicator, drawing the reader in and expounding his theme with many valuable insights.'
Craig S. Keener, F. M. and Ada Thompson Professor of Biblical Studies, Asbury Theological Seminary, Wilmore

'Thanks be to God, the Creator intervened and provided an unnatural solution to the natural condition of sinfulness. God not only cured the disease of sin, but he also positively added health to these sin-sufferers so that their latter state is infinitely better than their life in the original

creation. Kuruvilla tells the biblical story of this redemption, from glory to glory, as the narrative of sanctification by grace alone through faith alone in Christ alone. Readers will be challenged by this book to be conformed increasingly to the image of Christ and to be more appreciative of the extent to which a gracious God will go to save his creatures.'
Glenn R. Kreider, Professor of Theological Studies, Dallas Theological Seminary, Dallas

'Informed by careful biblical exegesis but also accessible and engaging, *From Glory to Glory: An unnatural history of sanctification* will inform and inspire readers to worship the God who is transforming them progressively into the image of his Son.'
Robert L. Plummer, Collin and Evelyn Aikman Professor of Biblical Studies, Southern Baptist Theological Seminary, Louisville

'How should we understand sanctification as Christians? What does it mean to live the Christian life? Abraham Kuruvilla takes us on a scriptural tour in this beautifully written and biblically faithful book, showing us what it means to be disciples of Christ. As believers we desire to glorify God, and Kuruvilla unpacks for us what glorifying God looks like in our daily lives. Highly recommended for pastors, students and all who aspire to grow in Christ.'
Thomas R. Schreiner, James Buchanan Harrison Professor of New Testament Interpretation, Southern Baptist Theological Seminary, Louisville

'In this book Abraham Kuruvilla, both a theologian and medical doctor, examines the malady of sin and its known prescription – a spiritual remedy through Incarnational intervention. Using his excellently honed analytical tools, he creates a theological tapestry weaving the threads of canonicity and redemptive history; creation and the new creation; sanctification and glorification; and revelation and application to present a prescription accessible by laity and clergy, relevant to scholars and students, and applicable in the academy and the Church. It is my privilege to highly endorse this masterpiece.'
Robert Smith Jr., Distinguished Professor of Divinity, Beeson Divinity School, Birmingham, Alabama

'Abraham Kuruvilla in *From Glory To Glory: An unnatural history of sanctification* has written a superb defense of the biblical doctrine of sanctification. *From Glory to Glory* is nothing less than a *coup d'etat* against the many contemporary books on discipleship which effectively renders sanctification as nothing more than "sin management". Kuruvilla reminds us afresh that God has a divine destiny for us which is nothing less than the full restoration of his glory in us. I recommend this book – you will find it clear, helpful, hopeful and inspiring!'
Timothy C. Tennent, Methodist Chair of Divinity and Professor of World Christianity, Beeson Divinity School, Birmingham, Alabama

'With his usual astute eye for exegetical detail and structural resonances, Abraham Kuruvilla leads us through a fresh approach to salvation and sanctification. In a culture in which everything revolves around the self, Kuruvilla, rightly, makes everything revolve around the glory of God. It made me helpfully re-examine the texts, on which I have often preached, on more than one occasion. All this makes this book both vital for preachers and a provocative challenge to our normal, even our normal church, agendas. It will make you think!'
Derek J. Tidball, formerly Principal, London School of Theology, London

'How we tell the story of our lives matters. Am I a character in a heroic adventure, a senseless tragedy, an absurdist farce, an animal in a documentary – a naked ape – with a natural history only? What *is* the meaning of life? Abe Kuruvilla's book is a timely reminder that the Bible tells a very different story, an *unnatural* history, a story of amazing grace. It's a divine comedy in which God gives us, through the Spirit, a share in the glory of Jesus Christ, the eternal radiance of the Father's glory: from glory to glory indeed!'
Kevin J. Vanhoozer, Research Professor of Systematic Theology, Trinity Evangelical Divinity School, Deerfield

'Here is a narrative that captures the struggle and delight of each believer. From deviant rebels trapped in the sordid ruin of our sin, to a community of God's beloved children rescued and raised to the cosmic heights of being united with Christ and heirs of the new creation, believers are empowered by the Holy Spirit to face the wicked traitor of the flesh and become like Jesus. Like a knowledgeable and passionate tour guide, Professor Kuruvilla directs our sights to the great landmarks of salvation history so that the real hero of the story, God, is glorified.'

David C. Wright, Dean of Students and Lecturer in Practical Ministry, Bible College of South Australia, Adelaide

FROM GLORY TO GLORY

FROM GLORY TO GLORY

An unnatural history of sanctification

Abraham Kuruvilla

APOLLOS (an imprint of Inter-Varsity Press)
SPCK Group, Studio 101, The Record Hall, 16–16A Baldwin's Gardens, London EC1N 7RJ, England
Email: ivp@ivpbooks.com
Website: www.ivpbooks.com

First published 2025

British Library Cataloguing-in-Publication Data
A catalogue record for this book is available from the British Library.

ISBN: 978–1–78974–450–7
eBook ISBN: 978–1–78974–451–4

Typeset by Fakenham Prepress Solutions, Fakenham, Norfolk NR21 8NL

Printed and bound in Great Britain by Clays Ltd, Elcograf S.p.A.

eBook by Fakenham Prepress Solutions, Fakenham, Norfolk NR21 8NL

Produced on paper from sustainable sources

Inter-Varsity Press publishes Christian books that are true to the Bible and that communicate the gospel, develop discipleship and strengthen the church for its mission in the world.

IVP originated within the Inter-Varsity Fellowship, now the Universities and Colleges Christian Fellowship, a student movement connecting Christian Unions in universities and colleges throughout Great Britain, and a member movement of the International Fellowship of Evangelical Students. Website: www.uccf.org.uk. That historic association is maintained, and all senior IVP staff and committee members subscribe to the UCCF Basis of Faith.

To
the people of God
kept in the love of God
being conformed into the image of the Son of God
by the power of the Spirit of God
for the glory of God!

Blessed be Yahweh God, God of Israel,
alone working wonders.
And blessed be His glorious name forever;
and may His glory fill all the earth.
Amen and amen!
(Ps. 72:18–19)

Contents

Introduction

But God, being rich in mercy,
because of His great love with which He loved us,
even while we were dead in transgressions,
co-enlivened [us with] Christ – by grace you have been saved –
and co-raised and co-seated [us] in the heavenlies in Christ Jesus.
(Eph. 2:4–6)[1]

'Natural history', relating to diseases, is a medical term denoting 'the uninterrupted progression in an individual of the development of disease' – those 'processes and outcomes from the moment of exposure to the disease and which lead to either resolution, disability, or death'.[2] The key element in the definition of natural history is that it paints 'the *uninterrupted* progression' of the disease from beginning to end; it assumes that there has been no external interference with this process, whether it be by diagnosis, management or treatment.

All humans have been afflicted with a lethal disease, sin against a holy God, and that by nature, thereby negating their ability to bring glory to God. Chapter 1 ('Sin: the disease') of *From Glory to Glory* details this deadly malaise of humanity. Created to redound to the glory of the Creator (Design),[3] the fall of man and woman (Deviance) infected the

1 All translations of Scripture in this work are my own. My renditions from the Hebrew and Greek attempt to be as literal and word-for-word as possible, not for the sake of slavish correspondence, but to aid the reader in catching a text's literary clues to its thrust: wordplays, unique word choices, chiasms, sequences, organisations, alliterations, puns, repetitions – the many filigrees of structure and nuances of language – most of which are hardly discernible in standard translations, unfortunately. Of necessity then, my translations will be somewhat wooden (and this also goes for the few translations of non-English extra-biblical texts herein), with the goal of attempting to retain the textual evidences to the thrusts of those texts, without plowing them under to subserve felicity of syntax and euphony of language. It is the inspiration of the text *qua* text that moves me in this direction: it must be privileged!

2 Bhopal, *Concepts of Epidemiology*, 184, 216; also see Porta, ed., *Dictionary of Epidemiology*, 193–4.

3 Psalm 19 will be scrutinised in detail here.

entire species, rendering them incapable of glorifying God.[4] And there is only one inexorable end for sinners: death, physical and eternal. In other words, the natural history of this disease is doom forever … if the affliction is allowed to run its course uninterrupted.

In the world of medicine, an uninterrupted course of disease (its natural history) is of course rarely, if ever, determinable in the modern day, for it would counter 'the ethical medical imperative to act to alleviate, contain, or treat the disease' that is at the core of the Hippocratic oath: *primum non nocere* ('first, do no harm').[5] Not treating a disease in order to study its natural history is, without a doubt, unethical and grounds for medical malpractice. But such immoral experiments have been undertaken in the history of medicine …

In 1972, Jean Heller of the Associated Press broke the heartbreaking story of how the United States Public Health Service (PHS) had, for forty years, been studying the effects of untreated syphilis, particularly tertiary syphilis, a constellation of the late manifestations of the disease,[6] upon African-American men in Macon County, Alabama, USA.[7] Situated in proximity to the county seat, Tuskegee, it came to be called the Tuskegee Study, exploring the natural history of syphilis in 399 subjects afflicted with the late, tertiary stage of the disease.[8]

In the fall of 1932, fliers began showing up around Tuskegee county: 'Free Blood Test; Free Treatment, By County Health Department and Government Doctors'. And, in all caps: 'YOU MAY FEEL WELL AND STILL HAVE BAD BLOOD. COME AND BRING ALL YOUR FAMILY.'[9] Only black men were picked for the study – an utterly unethical

---

4 Genesis 1–4 and the first part of Eph. 2:1–10 will be discussed in this regard.

5 The phrase is generally attributed to that Greek physician of the fifth century BCE. Indeed, 'the primary purpose of public health and medicine is to influence favourably the natural history of disease' (Bhopal, *Concepts of Epidemiology*, 216).

6 Syphilis is a sexually transmitted bacterial infection. Its signs and symptoms depend upon which of its stages the patient is going through. The early stages particularly affect the skin, a reason for my special interest in this malady – my occupation as a dermatologist in my other life. Its later phases, in addition to causing more skin issues, also affect bones, the liver and virtually any part of the body; its neuropsychiatric and cardiovascular manifestations are potentially fatal. Truly a bane!

7 Heller, 'Syphilis Victims', 1, 8. The exposé won Heller the Robert F. Kennedy Award for Excellence in Journalism in 1973 (as well as a number of other awards for her reportage).

8 And an additional 201 serving as controls; all 600 were black men. See Magner and Kim, *History of Medicine*, 138.

9 Brown, '"You've Got Bad Blood"'.

and unconscionably racist undertaking.[10] The PHS would periodically perform a number of blood tests on patients over the years and then conduct autopsies on those who died (with the offer of free burials thereafter). Astoundingly, none of the subjects were treated – not with old forms of treatment, not with new drugs.

Granted, at the beginning of the study the best forms of antisyphilitic therapy of the 1930s were all toxic and quite impotent against tertiary syphilis. Yet, none of these medications were provided for the hapless sufferers. But the most shocking aspect of withholding treatment was that, in the 1940s, a vastly more effective therapy – one with hardly any side effects – became available: penicillin. Of course, having decided at the outset not to treat subjects, 'investigators were not likely to experience a moral crisis when a new and improved form of treatment was developed' – and so penicillin was not made available to those unfortunates.[11] 'In an effort to determine from autopsies what effects syphilis has on the body, the Government from the moment the experiment began withheld the best available treatment for a particularly cruel disease. The immorality of the experiment was inherent in its premise.'[12] By the time the study formally ended in 1973, only 74 of the subjects were still living; 28 had died of syphilis, 100 had perished from complications related to the disease, 40 of the patients' spouses were infected, and 19 children developed congenital syphilis.[13]

But such a course is – praise God! – not the trajectory of humanity's fatal plague. In the economy of God, it was *not* going to be a *natural* history, but an *un*natural history, because somebody intervened – God himself (making it a *super*natural history). Chapter 2 ('Salvation: the cure') of the current work tells of the intervention of God to accomplish the remission of this deadly disease of sin. The redemption that took place because of the atoning work of God incarnate, Jesus Christ, in his life, death and resurrection, accomplished the liberation of humankind

10 Jones, *Bad Blood*, 1.

11 Jones, *Bad Blood*, 9.

12 Editors, 'Immoral Study', 48.

13 Magner and Kim, *History of Medicine*, 138. For other horrifying 'experiments' in the twentieth century seeking to study natural histories of diseases, see Magner and Kim, *History of Medicine*, 137–40.

(Deliverance), as he united believers to himself – baptised to him and bound to him. Thus was restored their capacity to bring glory to God by their new lives as they manifested good works of godly dispositions, deeds and discourses (Destiny).[14] The course of *natural* history was changed into that of an *un*natural history.

Thankfully, the natural history of the syphilitics who survived the Tuskegee Study also was disrupted by an intervention, howbeit late for most of the victims. In the latter half of the 1960s, Peter Buxtun, an interviewer working for the PHS, heard about the ignominious program and decided to look into it. His findings shocked him: it was obvious the subjects of the study had no idea what was going on when their blood was drawn, when spinal taps were conducted, and when they underwent physical examinations. The aghast whistleblower sent letters to the relevant authorities that were essentially dismissed; staff members of the PHS even attempted to intimidate him into silence. Months passed; nothing happened. Buxtun resigned from the PHS, but his letter-writing campaign continued. To no avail. The notorious study continued, too. Finally, pushed to the limit, in 1972, Buxtun recounted the saga to a friend of his at Associated Press. That agency undertook to investigate and assigned Jean Heller to the task. The rest is history.

Then came another intervention in the form of Senator Edward Kennedy, who convened a congressional hearing, labelling the debacle 'absolutely an outrageous and intolerable situation which this Government never should have been involved in'.[15] In 1973, a year after Heller had broken the story, lawyers for the victims filed a $1.8 billion class-action civil suit against the Department of Health, Education and Welfare, the PHS and the state of Alabama, among other entities. In 1974 the US government settled the case, agreeing to pay a total of approximately US$10 million (about US$65 million today) to the class of victims, survivors and their heirs.[16]

Things change when intervention occurs. And the 'normal' course of events, the natural history of humanity's death sentence, is re-directed

14 The primary text of Scripture considered here will be Romans 6, as well as the last part of Eph. 2:1–10.

15 Congress of the United States, *Quality of Health Care*, 3: 1042.

16 Too little, too late, but it was, at least, an admission of culpability. Jones, *Bad Blood*, 216–17.

when deity interjects himself to cause an *un*natural history of the sin syndrome afflicting humans, as he saves their lives for eternity. Chapter 3 ('Spirit: the healer') explains the ministry of the Third Person of the Godhead, 'the Lord and Giver of Life',[17] the work of the divine physician that enables and effectuates this consequential and momentous alteration of the course of the disease. Though believers have been united to Jesus Christ, they still bear the 'flesh', that immoral agent serving the evil authority of 'sin' (the personified entity controlling humanity, likely demonic). But these delivered ones are now also indwelt by the Holy Spirit, thus raising the spectre of a struggle that roils them – their still-present sinful tendency to follow the flesh vs their newly-granted inclination to submit to the Spirit (Discord). Attempting to subdue the flesh on their own contrivances and with their own exertions is an endeavour bound to fail: following the flesh produces sins (as opposed to following the Spirit and producing righteousness). But, in the grace of God, what they could not do themselves – obey God and his law, his 'righteous requirement' (Rom. 8:4) – the Holy Spirit does (Doctor), empowering the people of God to fulfil that 'righteous requirement' of the law, as he overcomes their weakness and incapacity, and enables them to 'overwhelmingly conquer' (8:37), thus pleasing their Father God as his adopted children.[18]

Hopefully, such shameful acts of vileness and violence, discrimination and disenfranchisement that characterised the Tuskegee Study will never happen again. But that does bring us back to the question: What exactly is a *natural* history if there is always going to be some sort of intervention? Even my discussion as a dermatologist with a patient regarding the ABCDEs of moles[19] is an intervention of preventative education and clinical counsel that, hopefully, subverts the otherwise uninterrupted progression of a mole to a deadly skin cancer. In the field of dermatology, advocacy for regular use of sunscreens, avoidance of direct sunlight between 10.00 a.m. and 3.00 p.m. and wearing of appropriate clothing

17 From the *Nicene Creed*, ca. 325 CE.

18 In this chapter, Romans 7–8 are tackled. As for the title of the second section of this chapter, 'Doctor', despite the obvious medical connotation, I primarily intend the sense of 'teacher' ('doctor' comes from the Latin, *docēre*, 'to teach').

19 Assessing the *a*symmetry, *b*orders, *c*olour, *d*iameter and *e*volution of suspicious lesions to preclude their progression to life-threatening melanomas.

have reduced the incidence of melanomas over the years. In the infamy of the Tuskegee Study, too, the intervention, though belated, resulted in definitive action after the abhorrent program was terminated.

On 12 July 1974, the National Research Act was promulgated by Congress and signed into law by President Richard Nixon – a direct consequence of the interventions of an indefatigable whistleblower, an intrepid journalist and an incensed senator. This Act included the creation of the National Commission for the Protection of Human Subjects of Biomedical and Behavioral Research with the explicitly stated aim: 'To amend the Public Health Service Act … to provide for the protection of human subjects involved in biomedical and behavioural research and for other purposes.'[20] The enacted law has undergone development over the decades, but its essence continues to direct and guide every operation of medical research in the US that deals with human subjects.

Yes, things should change with intervention that alters a natural history into an *un*natural one. And if that is essential following human interventions, how much more so after an intervention by deity? But how exactly should these now-saved believers' lives change to actualise and 'real-ise' the *un*natural history that they are part of? In other words, though we know that new lives are to be lived by the souls delivered by God, how are they to conduct their lives, declaring God's glory? Chapter 4 introduces the word of God as the agent that reveals how the people of God should live ('Scripture: the prescription') – i.e., what God's 'righteous requirement' is (Demand), for divine glory to be regained, so to speak. God's word, pericope by pericope,[21] outlines the responsibility of these in relationship with God to obey their Creator and glorify (Duty). Since the righteous requirement of God was perfectly fulfilled only by the incarnate God, Jesus Christ, the perfect Man, each pericope of Scripture is a depiction of a pixel of the image of Jesus Christ to which humans are to be aligned. After all, that is God's goal for his people – 'to be conformed to the image of His Son' (Rom. 8:29).[22] Thus is God glorified!

20 Congress of the United States, 'National Research Act (Public Law 93–348)', 342.

21 Or, portion by portion. I use 'pericope' to designate a size of text employed in preaching.

22 A variety of biblical texts from different genres will illustrate how God's 'righteous requirement' is present in every pericope of Scripture. The special case of the genre of law will be handled as an excursus. Also expounded in this chapter is the christiconic hermeneutic undergirding such an approach to biblical interpretation for application.

The *un*natural history of the human race and its sanctification are thereby unveiled in biblical theology: from the original *design* of humankind for God's glory, to *deviance* that wrecked humans' ability to glorify God, to divine *deliverance* that restored their *destiny* to glorify God by good works – even though, now, they continue to be wracked by the *discord* that accompanies salvation-in-progress – to the divine *doctor* guiding them in ongoing sanctification, by Scripture that outlines the *demand* of God and by empowering them to accomplish the specifics of their *duty* to bring glory to God: *From Glory to Glory!*

On 16 May 1997, at the White House, in the presence of a handful of survivors of the Tuskegee Study and their families, President Bill Clinton apologised on behalf of a regretful nation:

> Our nation failed to live up to its ideals, when our nation broke the trust with our people … The United States government did something that was wrong – deeply, profoundly, morally wrong. It was an outrage to our commitment to integrity and equality for all our citizens. To the survivors, to the wives and family members, the children and the grandchildren, I say what you know: No power on Earth can give you back the lives lost, the pain suffered, the years of internal torment and anguish. What was done cannot be undone. But we can end the silence. We can stop turning our heads away. We can look at you in the eye and finally say on behalf of the American people, what the United States government did was shameful, and I am sorry.[23]

A President's apology, a nation's remorse, law courts' reparations and legal prescriptions are all appropriate, of course, though utterly inadequate. But God's intervention[24] was not only a restoration of what had been (pre-fall and Edenic *posse non peccare* and *posse non mori:* 'possible not to sin' and 'possible not to die'), but a reorientation to what will be (post-resurrection and heavenly *non posse peccare* and *non posse mori:*

23 Clinton, 'Tuskegee Public Health Study Apology'.

24 Both Rom. 5:8 and Eph. 2:4 make the contrast between the natural and *un*natural histories of humankind's deadly affliction by beginning with 'But God …' Were it not for his drastic intervention …

'not possible to sin' and 'not possible to die').[25] God not only cured the disease, but also positively inculcated health in erstwhile sin-sufferers such that their latter saved state would be far better than their former pre-afflicted states, with a grander outcome transcending what once was. And thus, divine intervention rendered possible the movement *From Glory to* [even greater] *Glory*, for without this *un*natural sequence of events, there would have been attributes of God and aspects of his actions that humankind would never have known. A greater glorification of God, indeed, is being achieved and will become ultimate reality, soon and very soon! Because of deity's interjection of himself into the natural history of humanity's grave and eternally terminal disease, we know where it is all going and how it will all end – with the glory of God, the culmination of an *un*natural history! *Soli Deo gloria!*

There is no one like You among the gods, Lord,
and there is nothing like Your doings.
All nations whom You have made,
they will come and worship before Your face, Lord,
and they will glorify Your name.
For You are great and the One doing wonders;
You – You alone are God.
Teach me Your way, Yahweh;
I will walk in Your truth;
unite my heart to fear Your name.
I will give You thanks, Lord my God, with all my heart,
and I will glorify Your name forever.
(Ps. 86:8–12)

25 See Augustine, *Admonition and Grace*, 33; also Peter Lombard, *Four Books of Sentences*, Book II 19.110.3.

1
Sin
The disease

Be exalted above the heavens, God;
above all the earth, Your glory.
(Pss. 57:5, 11; 108:5)

Eastern Airlines flight 401 was bound for Miami from New York City, on 29 December 1972, with a full complement of holiday passengers. As the Lockheed Tri-Star approached Miami Airport for its landing, a light that was supposed to indicate that the landing gear had deployed failed to illuminate. The plane flew in large, looping circles over the swamps of the Everglades while the crew investigated.

Had the landing gear actually not deployed or was it just the light bulb that had gone out? First the flight engineer fiddled with the bulb. It wouldn't budge. Another crew member became curious and tried to help him out. And a third. (And even a fourth, an officially off-duty non-revenue passenger accompanying the crew.) Soon all eyes were on the bulb that refused to turn on. No one was monitoring the flight instruments. And no one noticed that the plane was losing altitude. In moments the aircraft, travelling at 227 mph, had flown right into the swamp, killing 98 of its 173 passengers. While an experienced and highly trained crew, whose combined career flying time added up to more than 50,000 hours, messed around with a paltry light bulb, precious lives and an aircraft were lost.

The National Transportation Safety Board attributed the crash to 'the failure of the flight crew to monitor the flight instruments during the final 4 minutes of flight, and [their failure] to detect an unexpected descent soon enough to prevent impact with the ground. Preoccupation with a malfunction of the nose landing gear position indicating system [the light bulb] distracted the crew's attention from the instruments and allowed the descent to go unnoticed.'[1] The crew had forgotten one of the most fundamental rules of aviation: fly the aircraft!

Design

There is a fundamental rule in life also, one that no human should forget, and the neglect of which is at the basis of the lethal disease afflicting every person on this planet. That rule tells humanity what it is here for, and inculcates godliness and spiritual health. Indeed, it answers what all of creation is here for. For the children of God this could be rephrased as questions that could be asked of the Creator: What is he all about? Why did he undertake creation and why the imprinting of his divine image on an entity at least partly constructed from dust? Why redemption and the choice of Israel and then of the rest of the people of God? Why all the other divine enterprises that promise to culminate in a new heaven and earth in eternity? These questions asked of the Creator are primary and foundational, for unless Christians (and all humans) figure out this critical aspect of God's grand Story, they can never find their own sub-stories, their places within the divine Story that this great God has called them to participate in. And the single answer, which comprises that rule believers should never forget, is the fount of the underlying rationale for God's activities, and the core of the Christian life.

Here it is, an answer that is straightforward, though not simple: 'All that is ever spoken of in the Scripture as an ultimate end of God's works, is included in that one phrase, "the glory of God."'[2] So the rule is: don't forget the glory of God. Indeed, it is all about the glory of God. For the glory of God is *the* goal of God and thus *the* goal of all creation, including humankind.

Isaiah 43:7 has God declaring that those 'whom I have made, whom I have even formed' were 'created for My glory'. Everything deity does is for the sake of his glory: 'For my sake – indeed, for my sake – I will act; for how can [My name] be profaned, and My glory I will not give to another'

1 National Transportation Safety Board, *File No. 1-0016*, 1.

2 Edwards, *Two Dissertations: Dissertation I*, 526. Edwards goes on to assert that the glory of God is the one 'great and last end of God's works' (*Two Dissertations: Dissertation I*, 530).

(Isa. 48:11; also 42:8). The NT echoes these OT sentiments: '[God] chose us in Him before the foundation of the world … he predestined us for adoption as sons, through Jesus Christ … for the praise of the glory of His grace' (Eph. 1:4–6), as he consummates all things 'in Christ' (1:10) … 'for the praise of His glory' (1:12).[3] And on that final day, 'at the name of Jesus every knee will bow – in the heavens and on the earth and [in] the underworld – and every tongue will confess that Jesus Christ is Lord to the glory of God the Father' (Phil. 2:10–11).[4] This is the end, the goal, the terminus, the omega of all creation: the glory of God. *Don't forget the glory of God!*

But what exactly is 'glory' (Hebrew: *kavod*)? The related adjective, *kaved,* means 'heavy' (1 Sam. 4:18; Isa. 32:2; it also designates what was thought to be the heaviest organ in the body, namely the liver, Exod. 29:13[5]). Figuratively, it indicated 'heaviness' of eyes or heart (Gen. 48:10; Exod. 9:7; and using the root *kvd* as a verb, 'to make heavy': 1 Kgs. 12:10, 14; Lam. 3:7); or 'wealth' (Gen. 31:1) – financial 'weight' so to speak; or 'greatness' (as of sin, Gen. 18:20; or of famine, 43:1; et cetera). Theologically then, when applied to deity, the noun *kavod* indicates God's substantiality and significance, his greatness and grandeur, i.e., his glory (Exod. 24:16–17; Ps. 19:1).[6]

Not only is glory an *intrinsic* attribute of God (the noun), the 'God of glory' (i.e., God who is glorious[7]), there is also glory resulting from an *extrinsic* attribution to him (the verb), the 'God who is glorified' – an act performed by agents other than God himself, as they glorify deity. The first is essential to God (part of the essence of the Godhead), the other is reverential towards him (an act of reverence on the part of non-God agents). The former is God's; the latter is given to God. To use Edwards' terms, God's intrinsic glory 'emanates' from him, and God's extrinsic

3 We will examine these verses from Ephesians more closely in Chapter 2.

4 Since the Second Person of the Trinity is the 'radiance of His [God's] glory and the representation of His subsistence' (Heb. 1:3), possessing 'glory as of the only begotten of the Father', a glory that was manifest to those who saw him (John 1:14), the exaltation of Jesus Christ is also the glorification of God. Also see 2 Cor. 4:4, 6; Rom. 16:27.

5 It is not. The skin is. Or blood, if you consider a fluid an 'organ'. At any rate, the noun, by extension, can also therefore mean 'dense' (Exod. 19:16), 'severe' (Gen. 12:10), and even 'large' (Gen. 50:9; 1 Kgs. 10:2).

6 In fact, 2 Cor. 4:17 employs a wordplay combining the notions of heaviness and glory.

7 Also see Exod. 16:7, 10; 24:17; 33:18; Lev. 9:6, 23; Num. 14:10; 16:19; Deut. 5:24; Pss. 24:7–10; 29:3; Isa. 40:5; Ezek. 3:23; 10:4, 18–19; 11:22–23; 43:4–5; 44:5. Likewise in the NT, employing the Greek *doxa:* Matt. 24:30; Luke. 2:9; 9:31–32; John 1:14; 2:11; 11:40; Acts 7:2, 55; Eph. 1:17; Titus 2:13; Jas. 2:1. So much so, in 2 Pet. 1:17 'glory' is a designation for deity.

glorification 'remanates' to him. 'The refulgence shines upon and into the creature, and is reflected back to the luminary. The beams of glory come from God, and are something of God, and are refunded back again to their original. So that the whole is *of God*, and *in* God, and *to* God; and God is the beginning, middle and end in this affair.'[8] This second aspect of God's glory, his glorification (the remanation), is indicated by the verbal root *kvd*, 'to glorify'[9] (and by the corresponding Greek verb *doxazō*, 'glorify'[10]). His own people are to glorify him (Ps. 22:23), but so also are 'all the nations' (86:9), and this from generation to generation (145:4–12), a vision transcending both time and space and encompassing every tribe and tongue! Indeed, *all* of creation was intended to glorify God, even animals (Isa. 43:20), and even anti-God entities who, in God's sovereignty, will 'glorify' him (Exod. 14:4, 17, 18; Ezek. 28:22; also see Phil. 2:10–11).[11]

When all is said and done, the ultimate agent of God's glorification is the sovereign God himself, as he declares his own intent to 'glorify' himself (Ps. 115:1; Isa. 60:7; Ezek. 39:13). But this, of course, is not symptomatic of any narcissistic tendency on the part of a glory-seeking deity; rather it is a function of God's intrinsic divine disposition to manifest his glory in his being and in his doing. That is who God is, and this is what God does. Edwards is right as he asserts:

> God in seeking his glory, therein seeks the good of his creatures: because the emanation of his glory (which he seeks and delights in, as he delights in himself and his own eternal glory) implies the communicated excellency and happiness of his creature ... Because their good, which he seeks, is so much in union and communion with

8 Edwards, *Two Dissertations: Dissertation I*, 531 (italics original).

9 As in 1 Sam. 2:30; Isa. 43:23; Pss. 22:23; 50:15, 23; 86:9, 12; et cetera. Similarly, but employing an auxiliary verb plus the noun, the concept of glorification is found in 1 Chr. 16:24, 28–29; Pss. 19:1; 29:1–2; 96:7–8; 145:12; Isa. 42:12; et cetera (the auxiliary verbs used include 'tell of', 'ascribe', 'make known', 'give', et cetera; they imply the manner in which divine glory is attributed).

10 As in Matt. 5:16; John 8:54; 21:19; Rom. 15:6, 9; 1 Cor. 6:20; 2 Cor. 9:13; 1 Pet. 2:12; 4:16; Rev. 15:4; et cetera.

11 Even the depredations in this life glorify God in some inscrutable way (John 11:4) and, indeed, the death of Jesus Christ (Acts 3:13–15). This extrinsic attribution of glory to deity by non-God entities is not to say these agents of glorification *make* God glorious – nothing and nobody can: Job 35:7; Acts 17:25. They only (extrinsically) acknowledge and announce the glory of God, glory that he (intrinsically) possesses.

> himself. God is their good. Their excellency and happiness is nothing but the emanation and expression of God's glory: God in seeking their glory and happiness, seeks himself: and in seeking himself, i.e. himself diffused and expressed ... he seeks their glory and happiness.[12]

God's delight in his creatures seeks their greatest good (their optimal health, so to speak), and that greatest good (and optimal health) is only accomplished as those beings attribute glory to him in all they are and in all they do. In pursuing this supreme end, God is zealous for his own glory, without which glory ('emanated' from him and 'remanated' to him) creation would not accomplish its intended end. 'I am Yahweh, that is My name! And My glory to another I will not give, or My praise to idols' (Isa. 42:8; also 48:11).

In sum, the glory of God is the Story of God, his ultimate objective. Glory is God's demand; and glorifying God is humanity's mission.[13] How then is mankind to fulfil its mission to glorify God? The way human sub-stories are interwoven with the divine Story is by humanity's very existence (all it is and all it does) being dedicated to the glory of God, as he intended from the beginning. 'For from Him, and through Him, and to Him are all things. To Him be glory forever! Amen!' (Rom. 11:36). In the *Larger Catechism* created by the Westminster Assembly in the seventeenth century, the first question and its answer relate to the glory of God, and humankind's ultimate purpose:

> *Q.* What is the chief and highest end of man[kind]?
> *A.* Man[kind]'s chief and highest end is to glorify God, and fully to enjoy him forever.[14]

This is the 'chief and highest end' of humankind for, on planet earth, it is these denizens thereof who alone are created to glorify God intentionally, vocally and actively – they were designed for this 'chief and highest end'.

---

12 Edwards, *Two Dissertations: Dissertation I*, 459.

13 And, indeed, the mission of all creation, human and otherwise, living and otherwise, seen and otherwise, is this second aspect of God's glory, the glory that is attributed, 'remanated', to him, an extrinsic reflection of his intrinsic glory. This glorification of God – its loss and its regain, *From Glory to Glory* – is the focus of this work.

14 Westminster Assembly, *Larger Catechism*, 3.

So the question becomes: If this is what mankind is to be all about, then *how* is it to glorify God? Both the Old and New Testaments offer a variety of specifics on how God's people go about this glorification of God. Here are a few examples:

God is glorified with one's worship:

> And the shepherds returned glorifying and praising God for all what they heard and saw.
> (Luke 2:20)

With one's love:

> … know the love of Christ surpassing knowledge, so that you may be filled to all the fullness of God … to Him [be] the glory in the church and in Christ Jesus to all generations, forever and ever. Amen!
> (Eph. 3:19, 21)

With one's resources:

> Glorify Yahweh from your wealth,
> and from the first of all your produce.
> (Prov. 3:9)

With one's aid to the needy:

> The one oppressing the helpless reviles his Maker,
> but he glorifies Him, the one being gracious to the poor.
> (Prov. 14:31)

With one's righteousness:

> … be sincere and blameless unto the day of Christ, having been filled with the fruit of righteousness that is through Jesus Christ, to the glory and praise of God.
> (Phil. 1:10–11)

With one's good works:

> [May God] fulfil in power all [your] desire for goodness and the work of faith, so that the name of our Lord Jesus being glorified in you, and you in Him, according to the grace of our God and the Lord Jesus Christ.
> (2 Thess. 1:11–12)

With one's body:

> ... glorify God in your body.
> (1 Cor. 6:20)

All of this gives the impression (and rightly) that the entirety of one's life – disposition, discourses and deeds, (thinking, saying and doing): everything – ought to glorify God.

> So whether you eat, whether you drink, or whatever you do, do all things for the glory of God.
> (1 Cor. 10:31)

> Whoever speaks, [let it be] as [one speaking] the words of God ... so that in everything God may be glorified through Jesus Christ, to whom be glory and power forever and ever. Amen!
> (1 Pet. 4:11)

Sun and servant (Ps. 19:1–14)

Psalm 19 gives us a more specific answer to what it means to glorify God and how that may be accomplished. Its exhortation will encompass and bring together the different threads noted above. Let's take a dive into that magnificent song.[15]

> The heavens declare the glory of God;
> and the work of His hands is announced by the sky.
> (Ps. 19:1)

15 See Kuruvilla, *Psalms 1–44*, 142–9.

At the outset, the psalmist is struck by the fact that the creative products of God's work in the heavens announce his greatness, his grandeur, his glory.[16]

A children's book captures the immensity of the heavens and the universe well.[17] The largest animal on earth is the blue whale. Just the flippers on its tail are bigger than most animals on earth. But a blue whale isn't anywhere near as big as a mountain. If you put 100 blue whales in a huge jar, you could put millions of whale jars inside a hollowed-out Mount Everest.

But Mount Everest isn't anywhere near as big as the earth. If you stacked 100 Mount Everests on top of one another, it would all be just a whisker on the face of the earth. And the earth isn't anywhere near as big as the sun. You could fit more than a million earths inside the sun. But the sun, which is only a medium-size star, isn't anywhere near as big as a red supergiant star called Antares. Fifty million suns could fit inside of Antares.

But Antares isn't anywhere near as big as the Milky Way galaxy. Billions of stars, as well as countless comets and asteroids, make up the Milky Way galaxy. This, humanity's home-galaxy, is 100,000 light-years in diameter – that is about 600,000 trillion miles (the number 6 followed by seventeen zeroes). But the Milky Way galaxy isn't anywhere near as big as the universe. There are about 200 billion other galaxies in the universe, each with an average of 100 million stars.

Can you imagine the vastness of the heavens? Then can you imagine the greatness of a God who created it all?

Yes, indeed, 'the heavens declare the glory of God!' These cosmic elements are broadcasting the grandeur and majesty of this great deity:

---

16 Psalm 19:1–6 talks about creation and 19:7–11 talks about the law of God. It appears that they are disparate topics, but they are not. There are verbal and conceptual links between the two sections: 'speech' (19:2, 3, and 19:14), 'hidden' (19:6 and 19:12) and the notion of joy (19:5 and 19:8). And common throughout the psalm is the motif of speech, either explicit or implicit: 'declare', 'announced' (19:1), 'speech' (19:2, 3, 14), 'proclaims knowledge' (19:2), 'words', 'voice' (19:3), 'sound' and 'utterances' (19:4), as well, the six synonyms for divine speech ('law', 'testimony', 'precepts', 'commandment', 'fear' and 'judgements'; 19:7–9). See below for the clinching connection between the two sections that reveals what the psalmist is *doing* with what he is saying.

17 Wells, *Is a Blue Whale the Biggest Thing There Is?*, 1–30.

> Day after day it [i.e., the heavens and the skies] pours forth speech,
> and night after night it proclaims knowledge.
> There is no speech, and there are no words;
> their voice is not heard;
> [but] through all the earth their sound has gone out,
> and to the end of the world their utterances [go out].
> (Ps. 19:2–4)

The entirety of the cosmos is declaring God's glory: all of the heavens and all of the skies, all of astronomy and all of astrodynamics – they all assert his substantiality and his supremacy. They glorify God, acknowledging and attributing to him glory, reflecting and reverencing his glory. Notice that there are six pronouncements of divine glory in 19:1–2 and 19:4: 1) 'heavens declare'; 2) 'announced by the sky'; 3) 'pours forth speech'; 4) 'proclaims knowledge'; 5) 'their sound has gone out'; and 6) 'their utterances [go out]'.[18]

But what is striking is that these proclamations of the glory of God have 'no speech', they have 'no words', and of these agents making these announcements it is stated that 'their voice is not heard' (19:3) – a surprising contradiction, coming right after 19:2 that affirmed that 'day after day it [the sky] pours forth *speech*'. But the thrust of the psalmist is clear: these stunning revelations of nature 'speak' without needing to do so. Notice that both time ('day after day' and 'night after night') and space ('through all the earth' and 'to the end of the world') are encompassed in those declarations described in 19:2 and 19:4. These 'speeches' without speaking, these voices without sounding, and these words without uttering go out unremittingly and unceasingly throughout the entirety of the cosmos as vivid and forceful, albeit silent, testimonies – in tremendous orderliness and conformity to divine design that has (so far) persisted since creation. Amazing! All of these eloquent universal witnesses are glorifying God … without a word!

So how *do* they declare the glory of God? How is God glorified, speechlessly, soundlessly, wordlessly and noiselessly by these astronomical elements? There must be more to glorification than just the audible

18 The significance of this number will be evident below.

declaration thereof. What is this glorification and how does it occur? We'll get to the answer as we arrive at the end of the psalm, but in this first part of the song, the poet focuses next on one particular heavenly entity, the sun, as the exemplar and the most impressive proclaimer (at least to us earthlings) of the glory of God.

> For the sun, He has placed a tent in them,
>   and it is like a bridegroom going out of his chamber.
> (Ps. 19:4–5a)

God has placed in the heavens a resting place, a 'tent', for the sun, which then performs its routine, rising in the morning – a smiling bridegroom coming out of the newlyweds' bridal chamber, its God-established bivouac, the morning after the wedding night. The sun, the psalmist affirms, appears to be one happy camper engaged in this endeavour.

> It exults like a warrior to run his course;
>   its going out is from [one] end of the heavens,
>   and its circuit to the [other] ends of them,
>   and there is nothing hidden from its heat.
> (Ps. 19:5b–6)

That the activity of the sun is connected to what preceded in the first few verses of the psalm is clear: 'go out' (Hebrew: *yts*'), used in 19:4a of the 'sound' and 'utterances' of the heavens and skies, is echoed in the description of the sun as 'going out' (again *yts*') in 19:5, and once more in 19:6, 'going out' (also from *yts*'). And '*end* of the world' in 19:4 is reflected in '*end* of the heavens' and '*ends* of them' in 19:6. In other words, sunrise, sunset, sunrise, sunset, sunrise, sunset, sunrise, sunset – the sun is doing its thing: happy, exultant, glorifying God, declaring him, proclaiming him, revering him. How, you ask? Silently, of course but, as the psalmist takes pains to detail, the sun achieves its purpose by obeying God, doing what it was intended to do by its Creator, 'running its course' as appointed to it by the God of the heavens.

Well, that's all well and good for the sun and stars and stuff. What does all this have to do with humans (and with the rest of the psalm)? With a rather perplexing turn, Psalm 19 now makes a detour in the remaining verses to talk about the word of God, seemingly disparate from all that has preceded. In fact, one can see that even God is described differently in this last half of the song: seven times he is 'Yahweh' (19:7–9, 14), the covenantal and personal God of his people. But in the first half of the song he was only called 'God' (19:1), the rather impersonal Creator and sustainer of all things. That is to say, in the second section of our psalm, the astronomical distance between deity and humanity has been bridged by a transcendent 'God' who has now become the immanent 'Yahweh', the God of his people, their personal God, their covenantal God.[19] And hereon, it is exclusively 'Yahweh' for the remainder of the psalm. Why this shift? Because the rest of the psalm, now with 'Yahweh' as the protagonist, not 'God', is going to deal with matters close to humanity, matters relating to God's people, matters concerning their lives, specifically how humanity may glorify God.

We saw earlier that in the first section of this psalm there were six pronouncements of divine glory – six announcements (without words and in utter silence) of God's glory. And what do we have in this second section? Another six items in 19:7–9: six descriptors of God's word, two in each verse: 'law' and 'testimony' in 19:7; 'precepts' and 'commandment' in 19:8; and 'fear' and 'judgements' in 19:9.[20] But though there are only six synonyms for God's word, there are fourteen (7 × 2) descriptive aspects of the Torah in 19:7–10: 'blameless', 'restoring', 'reliable', 'making wise' (19:7), 'right', 'rejoicing the heart', 'pure', 'enlightening the eyes' (19:8), 'clean', 'enduring for always', 'true', 'righteous altogether' (19:9), 'more desirable than gold' and 'sweeter than honey' (19:10).

> The law of Yahweh is *blameless*, *restoring* the soul;
> the testimony of Yahweh is *reliable*, *making wise* the simple.
> The precepts of Yahweh are *right*, *rejoicing* the heart;
> the commandment of Yahweh is *pure*, *enlightening* the eyes.
> The fear of Yahweh is *clean*, *enduring* for always;
> the judgements of Yahweh are *true*, *righteous altogether*.

19 The nomen 'Yahweh' is Trinitarian in connotation, and includes the Father, the Son and the Spirit.

20 'Fear' is likely a poetic shorthand referring to God's word, as do the other five descriptors: i.e., '*God's word*, that inculcates fear, is clean.'

More desirable than gold, even than much fine gold;
and *sweeter than honey*, even the flow of the honeycomb.
(Ps. 19:7–10)

Elsewhere in the OT, those descriptive words used in Psalm 19 of Scripture – 'blameless', 'reliable', 'right', 'pure', 'clean', 'fear[-manifesting]' and 'true' – describe people as, for instance, in Psalms 7:10; 11:2; 15:2; 18:20, 23, 24; 31:19; 51:10; 101:6. But here they describe God's speech, God's word. Therefore, these adjectives must indicate that the blameless, reliable, right, pure, clean, fear-of-Yahweh-teaching and true word of God produces *people* who are blameless, reliable, right, pure, clean, Yahweh-fearing and true.[21]

So where is all this going? Why the shift in topic now to Scripture, seemingly disconnected from the astronomy of the first six verses? Why the altered labelling of deity? What is the psalmist up to, and what is he *doing* with what he is saying?

Notice that the six lines of 19:7–9 are set in two parallel triads, with the only plurals therein referring to divine revelation in the third and sixth lines (in 19:8a – 'precepts'; and in 19:9b – 'judgements'; see Figure 1.1). It is intriguing that this might be a deliberate allusion to the six days of creation which is itself divided into two triads. The first triad in Genesis 1:3–13 comprises the first three days and the creation of compartments, so to speak, with the third day having *two* creative acts, unlike the first two. Significantly, the third day also has God's speech mentioned *twice* (along with the blessing, 'it was good', also twice). And, likewise, the second triad in Genesis 1:14–31 comprises the next three days and the creation of elements to fill those compartments, with the sixth day also having *two* created acts, and here again, God's speech is mentioned *twice* (and the blessing, 'it was good', also twice). In addition, the sun and moon were created on the fourth day; correspondingly, perhaps, the fourth line of our psalm, Psalm 19:8b, mentions 'enlightenment'.[22]

21 Labuschagne points out that this multiple of seven (here: 7 × 2) corresponds to the seven cosmic elements and phenomena named in 19:1–6: 'heavens', 'sky' (19:1), 'day', 'night' (19:2), 'earth', 'the end of the world' and 'sun' (19:4). Strikingly, the psalm also has seven instances of 'Yahweh' (Labuschagne, 'Significant Compositional Techniques', 593).

22 See Denninger, 'Creator's Fiat', 160–2; and Kuruvilla, *Genesis*, 11.

Words of Deity (Ps. 19:7–9)	Acts of Creator (Gen. 1:3–31)
FIRST TRIAD	
Singular: 'law' (Ps. 19:7a)	*One*: light–darkness (Gen. 1:3–5)
Singular: 'testimony' (Ps. 19:7b)	*One*: waters–heaven (Gen. 1:6–8)
Plural: 'precepts' (Ps. 19:8a)	***Two***: dry land, plants (Gen. 1:9–13) 'and God said' (×2; Gen. 1:9, 11) 'it was good' (×2; Gen. 1:10, 12)
SECOND TRIAD	
Singular: 'commandment' (Ps. 19:8b) ['enlightening the eyes']	*One*: sun–moon (Gen. 1:14–19) [elements dealing with light]
Singular: 'fear' (Ps. 19:9a)	*One*: fish–birds (Gen. 1:20–23)
Plural: 'judgements' (Ps. 19:9b)	***Two***: land creatures, humans (Gen. 1:24–31) 'and God said' (×2; Gen. 1:24, 26) 'it was good' (×2; Gen. 1:25, 31)

Figure 1.1

This correspondence between the speech-acts and creation-acts of God underscores the tremendous significance of the former in this psalm: if creation is important, well, so are the utterances of God – they must be heeded, and heeded carefully! Why?

And then, in 19:11, God is directly addressed for the first time in the psalm:

> Also, *Your* servant is warned by them;
> in keeping them is much reward.
> (Ps. 19:11)

In this verse (and in 19:10) we find out the value of God's word and the necessity of heeding it. The speech of God tells his people how to live, and if they live the way recommended, they will be rewarded – i.e., God is pleased by their abiding by his utterances. Yes, there is 'much reward' in keeping God's demand (19:11). In fact, Jesus himself declared as much in Luke 11:28: 'Blessed are those who hear the word of God and keep it.' Blessings here and now, not to mention eternal rewards in the future for those who abide by God's will. In sum, the words of deity correct and guide his people along the path God wants them to walk, as they do what they were intended to do by their Creator.

Who can discern errors?
  acquit me of those that are hidden.
Also from presumptuous [sins] withhold Your servant;
  let them not rule over me;
then I will be blameless,
  and I shall be acquitted of much rebellion.
(Ps. 19:12–13)

All that to say, the speech of God in Scripture points out what sin is, describes what righteousness is and directs one on how to be righteous, how to be blameless in God's eyes. That is, Scripture delineates God's demands, his will, his gracious direction for the lives of his people, how they ought to live in his ideal world. Such direction is essential because sinful (and sick[23]) humanity is prone to wander. This is true of all God's people, even the redeemed. Saved by the grace of God in Christ they may be, but they still tend to go astray, and are inclined to fall into sin.[24] Only the word of God (by the grace of God and by the Spirit of God) can bind wandering hearts to God, instructing the children of God of the divine order they are to adhere to.

Now back to the big picture to bring it all together in this psalm. Why did Psalm 19 have that first section about the cosmic elements, exemplified by the sun as the paradigm God-glorifier? How does that connect with the second half that deals with God's word and its guidance of humans to keep them from sin? Take a look again at 19:4: 'For the sun, He has placed a tent *in them*.' For the sun to move around, God placed a tent, a path, an orbit, 'in them', i.e., in the heavens/skies. 'In them' translates the single Hebrew word *bahem*. This orbit, this tent – the operating guidelines for the sun as laid out by its Creator – 'in them', *bahem*, and by them, the sun is guided into obedience to the will of God. 'In them', *bahem*, the sun hearkens to the dictates of God and manifests its submission to divine will.

Now look at 19:11: 'Also, Your servant is warned *by them*.' God's people, his followers, are warned and guided by the Scriptures, the speech of

23 The result of the fall, for which see below.

24 The role of the irredeemable 'flesh' that is part of humanity, that prompts and provokes it to sin, will be considered later in this chapter (and continued in Chapter 3).

God. And – surprise, surprise! – 'by them' here in 19:11 translates the same Hebrew word, *bahem*, 'in them', as in 19:4. Do you catch what the psalmist is *doing*? Just as the sun, God's star, has a guide, just as it has its directions, its prescription set for it by its Creator on how to behave and how to orbit within the heavens – 'in them' (*bahem*; 19:4) – so also God's people have a guide, their directions, their prescription set for them by their Creator: the word of God. And they are warned, guided, directed and instructed 'by them' (*bahem*; 19:11). The sun has a guide for its path set by God. God's servants have a guide for their path, the Scriptures of God. In other words, the word of God provides his people with the planned orbit they are to move on. And that's how God is glorified by humans, just as he is glorified by the heavens!

In the heavens, the sun, a created impersonal element, faithfully and consistently follows its divinely appointed course, 'in them [*bahem*]', day in and day out, for days, months, years, centuries and millennia. And this faithful celestial follower, the sun, is being paralleled in a human world with God's people, created personal beings, also likewise instructed by God, in the Scriptures – 'by them [*bahem*]'. So in Psalm 19 we have two servants: the sun, an astronomical servant, faithfully following the path set by God 'in them [*bahem*]'; and human servants of God, supposed to follow the path set by the speech of God, the Scriptures – 'by them [*bahem*]'.

The sun follows God and rejoices: 'It *exults* like a warrior to run his course' (19:5). And just as the sun does, God's people, too, find true happiness and rejoicing only – *only!* – by following the path God has set for them in his Scriptures: 'The precepts of Yahweh are right, *rejoicing* the heart' (19:8). To reiterate, we see two servants in this psalm: the sun following God rejoicing; and the people of God, *if* they follow God's scriptural guidance, also finding true happiness because, by abiding by the will of God, *they are glorifying God!*

> Thus 'tis easy to conceive how God should seek the good of the creature, consisting in the creature's knowledge and holiness, and even his happiness, from a supreme regard to himself; as his happiness arises from that which is an image and participation of God's own beauty; and consists in the creature's exercising a

> supreme regard to God and complacence in him; in beholding God's glory, in esteeming and loving it, and rejoicing in it, and in his exercising and testifying love and supreme respect to God: which is the same thing with the creature's exalting God as his chief good, and making him his supreme end.[25]

Cosmic order and moral order thus come together in Psalm 19, stemming from the same divine source who is prescribing, guiding, instructing and appointing elements of creation, both heavenly planets and human beings, to follow divine requirement, respect divine intent and keep divine will, thus maintaining and sustaining spiritual health and godliness. And thus is God glorified!

We need to learn from the heavenly entities – especially the sun – that obey God. Watch these astronomical elements marching across the sky all day and all night. I doubt if there is anything more impressive. I mentioned that the average galaxy has 100 million stars. It is estimated that there are 200 billion galaxies in the universe. That yields a mind-boggling total of 20,000 trillion stars in the universe – that is, the number 2 followed by 16 zeroes. Despite their incredible numbers, there is no sign of unruliness or disobedience from even a single member of that cosmic cohort. At least from what humans can perceive, they have all remained in exactly the same formation from dusk to dawn for thousands of years.

You would think that floating individually in the capacious expanse of the sky, these high and mighty celestial warriors and gladiators would show some individual initiative or strike out on their own to prove their independence.

> Hey, I'm the sun, I'm the famous yellow dwarf star that gives energy to billions of earthlings. I'm something else. I float like a butterfly, I sting like a bee. Catch me if you can. So, starting next week, I'm gonna do my own thing. Enough of this God-stuff that I've been doing for ages. Boooorrrriing! Well, I'm done with all that. Now for some fun. Starting tomorrow – earthlings get ready!

---

25 Edwards, *Two Dissertations: Dissertation I*, 533.

– I'm gonna rise in the west and set in the east. And that's only till I tire of that route. I'll change things up again when I've had enough of that.

We see nothing at all of that independent stuff. The march of the sun and the parade of the stars continues, in total, utter, absolute obedience to their Creator and the path he has set for them, day after day, month after month, year after year, century after century, millennium after millennium … Round and round, on and on, to and fro they go, with no deviation, no alteration, no detour, no retreat, no backtracking, no indiscipline, no disobedience. That is how the heavens declare the glory of God – by abiding by the will of God. That is how these astronomical entities glorify God – by adhering to his guidelines for them. That is what impressed the psalmist, and that is what should impress all mankind. Every one of those celestial beings, and especially the sun, the parade example, totally, utterly and absolutely defers to God's design and his orders, without question, doubt or second thought. That is what God's astronomical servants do, and that is what God's human servants should do, too, this psalm recommends. For if the sun and moon and stars are faithfully obeying God, and thereby glorifying him as his servants, why not humans? If they do so, 'then [they] will be *blameless*' (19:13), as are those astronomical, non-human servants of God. And that blamelessness comes only as God's human servants are guided by the 'blameless' speech of God, his word, Scripture, for 'the law of Yahweh is *blameless*' (19:7). This is the psalmist's prayer for himself, a devout desire to be pleasing to his God:

May they be acceptable – the speech of my mouth
  and the meditation of my heart – before Your presence,
  Yahweh, my rock and my redeemer.
(Ps. 19:14)

Indeed, that ought to be the prayer of God's people as well: *May we be as obedient to you, God, and to your speech, the Scriptures, as are the sun and moon and those 20,000 trillion stars to their marching orders from you.* That's how God is glorified!

> As therefore God values himself, as he delights in his own knowledge; ... as he delights in his own light, he must delight in every beam of that light: and as he highly values his own excellency, he must be well pleased in having it manifested, and so glorified ... The creature partakes of God's own moral excellency, which is properly the beauty of the divine nature. And as God delights in his own beauty, he must necessarily delight in the creature's holiness; which is a conformity to, and participation of it [divine beauty], as truly as the brightness of a jewel, held in the sun's beams, is a participation, or derivation of the sun's brightness, though immensely less in degree. And then it must be considered wherein this holiness in the creature consists ... all which things are nothing else but the heart's exalting, magnifying, or glorifying God; which ... God necessarily approves of, and is pleased with, as he loves himself and values the glory of his own nature.[26]

Obedience to God, abiding by his will as found in Scripture, is what glorifies God and 'remanates' to him the glory due him. And, in fact, this was what humanity was designed for, to glorify God – their normal, healthy lifestyle.[27] We shall see this again in the creation account.

Divine glory and human agency (Gen. 1–2; Ps. 8:1–9)

The longest description of a day of creation is that of Day 6 (Gen. 1:24–31), in which creation reaches its zenith: humans are formed in the image of God. A number of distinctions are found between God's previous creations and this one. Unlike his operations of days past that he saw as being 'good' (1:4, 10, 12, 18, 21), here for activities on the sixth day God affirms emphatically: 'Behold, it was very good' (1:31) – whole, sound and healthy, conforming totally to divine will. On this day, moreover, there are no less than four divine utterances ('and God said', 1:24, 26, 28, 29); the other days had only one or two such utterances each (1:3, 6, 9, 11, 20). In all his other enterprises in Genesis 1, divine speeches introduced the newly created entity referred to; on the sixth day, however,

26 Edwards, *Two Dissertations: Dissertation I*, 441–2.

27 As opposed to the abnormal, diseased way of life post-fall (for which see below).

his intention and purpose for his final creation are stated in a first-person announcement (1:26) *before* he proceeds to create (1:27). This final event of Day 6 was the only one to have such a prelude, implying that it was an occasion of seriousness and moment, one that called for God's direct and immediate involvement. Three times the first-person plural is employed: 'let *us* make', 'in *our* image', and 'according to *our* likeness' (1:26). Also, it is implied that humanity, directly dependent upon God, is not dependent on its habitat for its source of life or its identity, as are vegetation, sea creatures and land animals, for the earlier creation commands were: 'let the earth sprout …'; 'let the waters teem …'; and 'let the earth bring forth …' (1:11, 20, 24). Humans alone are in an exalted position, created directly by God without mediation by other agents: 'let *us* make'. The text emphasises this in yet another way: while the Hebrew *bara'*, 'to create', had already shown up twice (in 1:1 and 1:21), in 1:27 with the creation of mankind it is used three times. And, after creating humans, God for the first time speaks *to* someone – he addresses man and woman with a blessing (1:28): the first time in Scripture that God's communication occurs to those capable of receiving it.[28] Something momentous has happened on Day 6: the image of God has been placed upon a species of God's created beings with whom he can communicate.[29]

> God created man in His image; in his image, God – He created him:
> male and female He created them.
> (Gen. 1:27)

The significance of the *imago Dei* in which humans were made has been the source of much debate. From the prepositions employed with 'likeness' and 'image' ('*according to* his likeness' and '*in* his image'; 1:26–27), to the actual meaning of these two terms, scholarly opinion scatters itself all across the spectrum.

---

28 The blessing of the sea creatures ('God blessed them, saying …'; 1:22), no doubt also involved divine speech, but it was not explicitly said to be directed *to* those beings, as was his blessing of man ('and he said *to them*'; 1:28). Perhaps not surprisingly, then, the first described act of humans in the garden is also vocal: the man 'calls' (2:19), following which he proceeds to 'say' (2:23).

29 The emphatic description of human creation in 1:27 ('… God – He created him …') further underscores the significance of this event.

The Hebrew preposition *b* before *tselem*, 'image', in 1:26–27, is best taken to mean 'as'. Thus, the creation of mankind is '*as* God's image', quite congruent with '*according to* [Hebrew preposition *k*] his likeness', as well.[30] In that case, a human does not *possess* the image of God, neither is one made *in* the image of God; rather the person *is* the image of God – 'the visible corporeal representative of the invisible, bodiless God'. A human being is thus the representation of God 'who is imaged in a place where he is not'.[31] And, it must be noted, this human representation of the divine is the human being in entirety – the integrated constituents thereof, both material and immaterial, become the *imago Dei*.[32] Thus, while Genesis 1 powerfully establishes the transcendence of God outside and above the created order, in the doctrine of the *imago Dei* we find the immanence of God in and with the world through his image-bearers, humans. The role of humanity was to represent God to every other part of God's creation, to make a transcendent God immanent, visible and tangible, if you will, to the world. 'Humankind is made to be a sign of God, to represent the creator who is not directly perceptible in the created world … As words are composed in a text to be the icons of the newly presented meanings, human beings are created in the world to be icons of God.'[33] This representation of the divine regent no doubt involves the 'remanation' of his glory by these beings themselves invested with the glory of the divine, image-bearers as they are.[34]

Psalm 8 echoes this notion of God's image in humankind and brings to the fore the awesomeness and wondrousness of this divine condescension: 'What is a human that You are mindful of him, and a mortal

30 This is to see the preposition *b* (i.e., *beth*) functioning as what is called a *beth essentiae*, a predicate marker. Exodus 6:3 has a similar construction: *bʾel shadday*, '*as* El Shaddai'. See Boulet, 'Biblical Hebrew *Beth Essentiae*', 1–27; Clines, 'Image of God', 75–80; and Walton, *Genesis 1*, 77–85. The prepositions *b* ('in') and *k* ('according to'), used with 'image' and 'likeness', respectively (1:26–27), appear to be interchangeable: 1:26 has '*in* His image' and '*according to* His likeness', but 5:1, 3 inverts the prepositions with '*in* the likeness of God' and '*according to* his [Adam's] image'. Besides, the LXX makes no distinction between the prepositions in 1:26–27 and 5:1, 3: they are all translated as the Greek *kata*, 'according to'. And in 1:26, 27 the LXX uses *eikōn* for the Hebrew *tselem*, 'image', but in 5:1 *eikōn* translates the Hebrew *dmut*, 'likeness', again suggesting the synonymity of those original Hebrew terms.

31 Clines, 'Image of God', 87, 101.

32 How exactly this correspondence of image works out in human anthropology, constitution and physiology is a matter of speculation that need not concern us here.

33 Wolde, 'Text as an Eloquent Guide', 151.

34 See Ps. 8:5, below.

A	*'Yahweh, our Lord,* *how majestic is Your name in all the earth!* **[8:1a]**	**Praise**
B	… Your splendour upon the *heavens* … **[8:1b–2a]**	**Deity's Rule**
C	You have established [Your] strength … **[8:2bc]**	
D	When I see Your heavens, the *works of Your fingers* … **[8:3]**	
E	what is a *human* that You are mindful of him, and a *mortal* that You care for him? **[8:4]**	**Humanity's Meekness**
E'	But You make him lower than *God* by a little, and with glory and splendour You crown him! **[8:5]**	**Humanity's Greatness**
D'	You make him rule over the *works of Your hands* … **[8:6]**	**Humanity's Rule**
C'	sheep and oxen – all – and also beasts of the field **[8:7]**	
B'	birds of the *heavens*, and fish of the sea … **[8:8]**	
A'	*Yahweh, our Lord,* *how majestic is Your name in all the earth!'* **[8:9]**	**Praise**

Figure 1.2

that You care for him!' (8:4). (See Figure 1.2 for a depiction of how the text of the Psalm is carefully structured.[35])

It begins and ends with an identical statement of praise of a great deity (*A, A'*; 8:1a, 9). Deity's rule (*B, C, D*) is described in 8:1b–3: his 'splendour' (8:1b), his 'strength' (8:2) and especially the cosmic products of his creative activity (8:3). That leads the psalmist to wonder about the meekness of humanity (*E;* 8:4), because this great God has crowned this lowly and minute species with *glory* (and with the same 'splendour' that he himself has, *E'*; 8:5; see 8:1b). This is certainly equivalent to the investiture of humans with the divine image at their creation. And the sharing of divine attributes with insignificant humanity is by design: they are to reflect his 'glory and splendour'.[36] This is what they were created for

35 The italics in the figure indicate the parallel or contrasting elements in the corresponding sections of the chiasm. For more details on this psalm, see Kuruvilla, *Psalm 1–44*, 77–81.

36 It is very likely that 'splendour' is the radiation and effulgence of divine 'glory': the two coalesce in several texts in the OT (1 Chr. 16:27–28; Pss. 29:1–3, 4–5, 9; 96:3, 6–8; 104:1, 31;

and this is why they bear the divine image – to 'remanate' God's glory. But how? How is humanity bearing the image and likeness of God to glorify him? What is it about their role that enables them to manifest divine glory and splendour? And in Psalm 8, adding another layer to the glorification of God that we saw in Psalm 19, the poet answers: 'You make him rule over the works of Your hands' (*D′*; 8:5). It is this rulership that humanity has been deputised with that facilitates their glorifying God, their living by the speech of God, a life of normality as designed by God, whole, sound and healthy. It is, in sum, a reflection of humankind's obedience to the dictates of God regarding how it is to function in the divine economy.[37]

This notion of human vice-regency on earth (their surrogacy for the rulership of the Creator, God) was clearly communicated in the creation account of Genesis 1. Right after the initial use of *tselem* in 1:26, its implications are spelled out in the same verse: 'and let them rule'. Thus, the 'image of God' in Genesis 1 is 'a royal designation, the precondition or requisite for rule', the mandate to humanity reiterated in the imperative of 1:28: 'rule over …' As image-bearers and likeness-carriers of the sovereign and glorious God of the universe who rules over all by virtue of his creatorship, humanity rules for God as God's '*locum tenens* vizier'.[38] Psalm 8 appropriately links all of humanity with this deputised dominion and confers upon all individuals the status of (surrogate) rulership. This identity of image/likeness between God and humans is, therefore, at least a correspondence of the two parties' role and character – the royal office of humans as God's representatives and agents, authorised to actualise and manifest the rule of God over his creation, thus reflecting his glory. 'Just as powerful kings [in the ancient Near East], to indicate their claim to dominion, erect an image of themselves in the provinces of their empire where they do not personally appear, so man is placed

---

145:5, 11–12; and for the divine donation of these attributes to humans, see also Pss. 21:6; 45:3, 13; 149:5, 9).

37 Functioning as God intended his creation to function brings him glory, whether as the astronomical servant or as the human servant. In the case of the latter, this obedience is manifest in representative rulership as the Genesis 1 account of the creation of humans avers.

38 Clines, 'Image of God', 98. This is also substantiated by the use of the verb *nwch*, 'to place', for Adam's positioning in Eden (2:15); the same word describes deity's own seventh-day 'rest' in the Decalogue (Exod. 2:11): yes, humans (are to) image deity, functionally and in character.

upon earth in God's image as God's sovereign emblem.'[39] And it is by doing so that the glory of God is manifested in his creation by his human representatives.

In light of the divine transcendence and sovereignty constantly emphasised in Genesis 1:1–2:3,[40] it is quite remarkable that God allocates such representative status to one of his created beings, not adventitiously or accidentally, but in a divinely intentioned creative undertaking. And totally unique: nobody else (and nothing else in the cosmos, as far as we are told in Scripture) bears divine likeness. What a wonder – an amazement that the psalmist expressed poetically in Psalm 8:4: 'What is a human …?'[41] Being 'mindful' of his creation is one thing, and so is God's 'care' for it, but to 'crown him' with the divine attributes of glory/splendour, 'making him lower than God by a little'? Incredible!

And the psalm reiterates the purpose for this 'crowning' – appropriate for regents: 'You make him rule over the works of Your hands' – beasts,

39 Rad, *Genesis*, 58. Also see Wenham, *Genesis 1–15*, 31–32; and Brueggemann, *Genesis*, 32.

40 The creation activities of Day 4 (1:14–19) will suffice as an example of the depiction of God's absolute sovereignty in this originary account. The description of this day is unusually long, because of an extended and repeated concern with the functions of the sun and moon. Such concern probably arose because of the dominance of these two entities (and that of stars) in the pantheon of Israel's neighbours, and their purported sway over human destiny. For the biblical author, however, these are only creatures in the hands of their Creator – he makes them, he places them, he regulates them (1:16, 17), as creatures with a finite beginning to their existence and a defined function for their *raison d'être*. These luminaries were created to function under God, for God, according to God. Strikingly, 'light' created on Day 1 was turned over to the sun and moon that they may regulate day and night; i.e., these celestial bodies were reduced to mere managers of light ('to govern', 1:16) and intrinsically impotent cosmic clocks over time, serving the interests of humans. The seeming bureaucratic functions of the luminaries, 'to separate' (1:14a, 18b), 'to govern' (1:16, 18a) and 'to give light' (1:15, 17), are each mentioned more than once, underscoring their totally subservient status. 'The utter creatureliness of the heavenly bodies has never before been expressed in such revolutionary terms' (Westermann, *Creation*, 44). And, remarkably, these middle-level bosses are anonymous: the common labels 'sun [*shemesh*]' and 'moon [*yareach*]' are not used at all in the Genesis account, perhaps a conscious avoidance of names that were also given to the respective deities by Israel's neighbours: the Ugaritic sun and moon gods, Shamash and Yarich, respectively (echoed in the names of Canaanite cities, Beth-shemesh [= temple of the sun] and Jericho [*yricho*]). Incidentally, the mention of 'stars' in 1:16 occurs almost as an afterthought, clearly denying any metaphysical role for these astronomical actors. And that is all that is said about stars in this primary chapter of the Torah, an unusual de-emphasis of entities that were being worshipped in Israel's contemporary culture. Indeed, any shift from focus upon the sovereignty of Yahweh on the part of his people came with the severest penalty: stoning to death was the sentence attached to the worship of 'other gods … or the sun, or the moon, or any of the host of the heavens' (Deut. 17:2–5; also see 4:15–20). All that to say: God, and God alone, is sovereign!

41 Needless to say, the image is not effaced after the fall, it is only defaced. It is mentioned post-fall in Gen. 9:6, and the same commandment of 1:28 is reissued in 9:1, 7. Also see 1 Cor. 11:7; Jas. 3:9; et cetera.

all birds, all fish, all things in the waters (*D′, C′, B′;* 8:6–8; see above). Thus, everything – 'all things bright and beautiful, all creatures great and small, all things wise and wonderful'[42] – made by the Lord God and falling under divine (direct and sovereign) dominion, is also within human (indirect and delegated) dominion. The fact that humanity's meekness and humanity's greatness form the centre of Psalm 8 is telling. Remarkably, the only verb in all of Psalm 8 that has the psalmist (or even any human) for a subject is 'see' in 8:3a. That is all humankind does, apparently – gaze in awed wonder! And so the same exclamatory query raised earlier of God, 'how …' (Hebrew: *mah*; 8:1, 9), is now raised again of humanity: 'what …?' (also *mah*; 8:4a): humanity now shares the glory of deity![43] No wonder the psalmist was astounded! Great is mankind's responsibility to God, under God – to glorify God as they represent him to his world.

In sum, deity's rule is precisely paralleled by humanity's rule (*B, C, D* and *D′, C′, B′;* 8:1b–3 and 8:6–8; see Figure 1.2). And that is how they fulfil their divinely ordained mission as God's ruling representatives, to 'remanate' his glory in all they are and in all they do. Genesis 1 exhorts all of God's people, without exception or distinction, to acknowledge their royal vocation as God's representatives within his creation, so that God may be glorified.[44] That this glorification of deity is the especial role of the people of God is explicitly stated by Yahweh, the Creator, himself, in Isaiah 43:6–7:

> 'Bring My sons from afar
>   and My daughters from the ends of the earth,
> everyone who is called by My name,
>   and *whom I have created for My glory,*
>   whom I have formed, even whom I have made.'
> (Isa. 43:6–7)

42 The title and first line of a hymn by Cecil Frances Alexander (1848).

43 'What is a human that You are mindful of him' and '[what is] a mortal that You care for him' (8:4) are not questions to be answered, but exclamations and proclamations of wonder!

44 The ultimate consummation of the image of God was accomplished in Christ, the perfection of the divine image (Heb. 1:3), an image mankind will share in full at the eschaton (1 John 3:2).

But tragically, that glorification did not happen with human beings. In fact, God's purpose for mankind was not realised even with the first pair of these created species. Instead, evil devastation was wrought upon God's good creation.

Deviance

The design of God was foiled by Satan and sinful humans who manifested their willful deviance from divine design, falling into the sickness that has affected the entire race. This is described in Genesis 2–3, immediately following the creation and design account of Genesis 1.

The fall (Gen. 2–3)

Genesis 2:5–3:24 is carefully constructed as a chiasm with several literary and linguistic parallels, as well as a neat arrangement of narrative and dialogue (see Figure 1.3).[45] The account begins with the introduction of mankind into the Garden (*A*) and ends with its expulsion therefrom (*A'*); the infamy of sin is right at the centre (*D*).[46]

Genesis 3:6b is the midpoint of the account with: 'and she ate … and he ate'. And in that central scene (*D*, 3:6–7), the two humans are alone – there is no God, there is no snake. Man and woman eat, and the rest is sordid history. In effect, Genesis 2:5–3:24 informs readers of what happened to God's creation that he had declared 'good' and 'very good' (1:4, 10, 12, 18, 21, 25, 31): evil was introduced into wholesomeness, making it entirely insalubrious. The devastation of this event is depicted in the stark contrasts between the creation of the 'good' by God: design (Gen. 1:1–2:3) and the overturning of the 'good' by Satan and humans: deviance (Gen. 2:4–3:24; see Figure 1.4).[47]

How did this disaster occur? Let's retrace the events described in Genesis 2–3.

The cosmos was created to be, effectively, the Temple of God, with

45 Much of this material is adapted from Kuruvilla, *Genesis*, 52–74.

46 From Ouro, 'Garden of Eden', 224–42; Wenham, *Genesis 1–15*, 50–1; Cotter, *Genesis*, 28; and Walsh, 'Genesis 2:4b–3:24', 161.

47 Ouro, 'Linguistic and Thematic Parallels', 44–54.

Narrative Introduction / Transition (2:4)

A **Introduction of mankind into the Garden** (2:5–17)
Narrative – God: sole actor; man: present, but passive
'work' (2:5, 15); 'ground' (2:5, 7); 'garden', 'Eden', 'east' (2:8)
'tree of life' (2:9); 'knowledge of good and evil' (2:9); 'keep [*shmr*]' (2:15)

B **Organisation of human life** (2:18–25)
Narrative – God: main actor; man: minor role; woman, animals: passive
man 'calls' woman (2:23)
harmonious relationships among man, woman, animals
'wife', 'mother' (2:24); unclothed (2:25)

C **Temptation** (3:1–5)
Dialogue – Serpent and woman; serpent dominating
'eat' and 'tree' (3:1, 2)
three utterances (3:1, 2–3, 4–5)

D **Disobedience** (3:6–7)
Narrative – man, woman: sole actors

C' **Judgement** (3:8–13)
Dialogue – God, man and woman; God dominating
'eat' and 'tree' (3:11)
three questions + answers (3:9–10, 11–12, 13)

B' **Reorganisation of human life** (3:14–21)
Narrative – God: main actor; man: minor role; woman, serpent: passive
man 'calls' woman (3:20)
disharmonious relationships among man, woman, animals
'wife', 'mother' (3:20); clothed (3:21)

A' **Expulsion of mankind from the Garden** (3:22–24)
Narrative – God: sole actor; man: present, but passive
'work' (3:23); 'ground' (3:23); 'garden', 'Eden', 'east' (3:24)
'tree of life' (3:24); 'know good and evil' (3:22); 'guard [*shmr*]' (3:24)

Narrative Conclusion / Transition (4:1)

Figure 1.3

deity taking residence there and resting/reigning.[48] But within this cosmos-Temple, there was a special locus, the Garden of Eden. In Genesis 2 this station is a 'localised place that is spatially separated from its outside world', with the presence of God within it, humans settled in it (2:8, 15) and cherubim guarding it (3:24) – all demarcating this

48 For which see Kuruvilla, *Genesis*, 39–49, 58–60, as well as for parallels between the creation story of Gen. 1:1–2:3 and the accounts of the tabernacle/temple. Also see, among others, Walton, *Genesis 1*, 100–21, 178–92; Levenson, 'Temple', 275–98; Levenson, *Sinai and Zion*, 89–142; and Beale, *Union with the Resurrected Christ*, 24–33.

Genesis 1:1–2:3 (Design)	Genesis 2:4–3:24 (Deviance)
God's speech obeyed by creation (1:3, 6, 7, 9, 11, 14, 15, 20, 24, 26, 30)	God's speech disobeyed by humans (3:1–7)
Food permitted, including fruit of trees (1:29–30)	Food prohibited, fruit of a tree (2:16–17)
God blesses (1:22, 28; 2:3)	God curses (3:14, 17)
Animals: 'good' (1:25)	One animal: 'more crafty'/'cursed' than others (3:1, 14)
Dry land (feminine singular): 'good' (1:10)	Ground (feminine singular): 'cursed' (3:17)
Earth's products: 'good' (1:12)	Ground's products: cursed (3:18)
God's blessing: 'multiply' species (1:28)	God's curse: 'multiply' sorrow (3:16)

Figure 1.4

horticultural quarter as a divine sanctuary within the cosmic Temple, akin to the Holy of Holies within other comparable sanctuaries constructed subsequent to the fall.[49] Moreover, Ezekiel 28:13–14 identifies the Eden as the archetypal holy mountain of God.[50] Mankind is thus placed in the very 'sanctuary', the Holy of Holies of the cosmos-Temple, the place of God's dwelling, in his presence. Again, this special privilege afforded to humankind reinforced its intimacy with the Creator, with whom man and woman were designed to abide in close relationship.

Genesis to Revelation thus outlines a trajectory of human history that begins in a verdant garden containing the tree of life (Gen. 2:8–17) and ends in a magnificent city that also contains a tree of life (Rev. 22:1–2). The garden at the commencement of the story served as the place where humans engaged in *'avad* ('cultivation', Gen. 2:5, 15). The verb is

49 Dumbrell, 'Gen 2:1–17', 56. For the other sanctuaries in Scripture, see Exod. 25:18–22; 26:31; 1 Kgs. 6:23–29; Ezek. 40–43 (as well, Rev 21:22). Cherubim signify the presence of God: Exod. 19:18; 1 Kgs. 6:23–35; 2 Kgs. 19:15; Pss. 18:10; 104:4; Ezek. 41:18–25; et cetera. The Hebrew verb *shkn*, describing the 'stationing' of the cherubim in the Garden (Gen. 3:24), is also used of God's 'dwelling' in his sanctuaries (Exod. 24:16; 25:8; 29:45, 46; 1 Kgs. 6:13; Ezek. 43:7, 9; et cetera) – in fact, the noun *mishkan*, 'tabernacle', is derived from this verb.

50 The paradisaical garden and the temple mount are also equated in Ps. 36:7–9, where the temple is a place of refuge, and where God shares his victuals with his people; besides, with this sanctuary, too, there is a river and a fountain of life wherein is found 'Your luxuries' (Hebrew: *'adaneka,* the plural and suffixed construct of *'eden*, 'Eden'; 36:9) that saturate God's people. Divine presence is also linked with life-giving waters in Ezek. 47:1–12; Ps. 46:4; Jer. 17:12–13; Zech. 14:8; Rev. 22:1–2.

commonly used of agricultural tasks;[51] it later acquired strong liturgical connotations and came to be used regularly for the service of God and his worship.[52] Likewise, *shamar*, 'to keep/guard/watch' (2:15), is employed in a non-sacral sense (in 3:24; 4:9; et cetera), as well as for the fulfilling of covenantal responsibilities towards God.[53] But this verb, too, connotes priestly duties with regard to the sanctuary.[54] All of this hints at the kind of activity humans had symbolically been engaged in, in that primeval agricultural paradise that served as the Temple and its special sanctuary, the Garden of Eden: the worship by humans of a transcendent God in his Temple, in his perfectly ordered creation, as they fulfilled his design and their divinely bestowed duty as the vice-regents of God, imaging him in all of creation, and thereby glorifying him. But this responsibility was abdicated, in a horrific act of human deviance, as the first pair of humans disobeyed divine demand and directive.[55]

While there is no explicit assertion in Genesis 3 that the serpent was operating from ulterior motives, there are plenty of implicit pointers to the whole affair being evil, particularly in the description of the serpent's activities: questioning (3:1); conversion of God's 'commanding' (2:16) to God's 'saying' (3:3); exclusive use of 'God' in a section otherwise punctuated by 'Yahweh God';[56] negation of God's liberality, making deity's generous command (2:16) an absolute prohibition (3:1); outright repudiation of God's warning ('you will surely die', 2:17, vs the serpent's 'no – you will surely [not] die', 3:4); attribution of a base motive for God's prohibition (3:5); and alteration of God's statement of negative consequences (2:17) to positive outcomes (3:5). Add to this the woman's

---

51 See Gen. 3:23; 4:2, 12; 9:25, 26, 27; et cetera.

52 See Exod. 3:12; Num. 3:7–8; 4:23, 24, 26; 8:25–26; 18:5–6; Deut. 4:19; et cetera. The noun form of the verb, *'avodah*, 'service', also describes Levitical duties in the tabernacle and Temple (Exod. 38:21; Num. 3:10; 18:6; 1 Chr. 24:3, 19; 2 Chr. 8:14).

53 See Gen. 17:9–10; 18:19; 26:5; Lev. 18:5; Deut. 4:6; 7:12; 29:9.

54 See Num. 1:53; 3:7, 8, 10, 28, 32, 38; 28:2; et cetera.

55 The story is familiar, so for want of space, I'll restrict myself to commenting on the nefarious nature of the deviance that transpired. For more details, see Kuruvilla, *Genesis*, 52–74.

56 The coupled name 'Yahweh God' is used nineteen times in Genesis 2:4–3:24 (and elsewhere in the Pentateuch only in Exod. 9:30) but, unsurprisingly, the personal and ethical name of deity is absent when disobedience is contemplated and accomplished in Gen. 3:1b–7 (3:1a refers to 'Yahweh God' as the Creator). See Mathews, *Genesis 1–11:26*, 192–3; Cassuto, *A Commentary on the Book of Genesis*, 87. The sinners have moved away from a personal, dependent relationship with their Creator.

acquiescence to the serpent's employment of 'God' (3:3), and her own tweak of divine demand, from 'commanding' to 'saying' (3:3), along with other alterations of God's prescription and proscription (see 3:2–3 vs 2:16–17), et cetera. And, at the very least, the beast appears to be a being (or possessed by one) that has intellect (it is crafty, it reasons, it speaks and it deceives) and that is obviously anti-God.[57] 'The tempter thus initiates a new cult that has the serpent as a competing lawmaker and so ultimately a rival god.'[58] The long and short of it is that the human pair in the Garden succumb to temptation and they disobey God!

After the deviant act perpetrated by Adam and Eve, 3:8 describes them 'hearing' (from *shm*', which also means 'to obey') the voice of Yahweh. When questioned, Adam responds in 3:10: 'Your voice I heard [*shm*'] in the garden, and I was afraid.' The irony is palpable: mankind had *not* heard/obeyed what it should have, and humans had *not* feared the way they should have. Instead, lacking the fear of God, they refuse to hear the voice of God. And, Yahweh accuses, Adam had instead 'heard [*shm*'] the voice of the woman' (3:17). One remembers that all this happened after the powerful voice of God had created the entire cosmos with no opposition whatsoever to his utterances! Resounding throughout the creation account of Genesis 1 were 'and God said' (1:3, 6, 9, 11, 14, 20, 24) and 'and it was … [*wayhi*]' (1:3, 5, 7, 8, 9, 11, 15, 19, 23, 24, 30, 31). Everything happened just as God's voice commanded … until humans entered the scene! Here, in Genesis 3, God's speaking fails to accomplish what he had commanded: humans negate God's voice, disregard it and render it fruitless.

It is notable that in the accusatory and judgemental phase of the narrative, the tree of interest mentioned by Yahweh is not designated the 'tree of the knowledge of good and evil' as it was when the prohibition was first uttered (2:17); instead, now God labels it 'the tree *of which I commanded you not to eat*' – a description that is repeated (3:11, 17). The focus is, obviously, not upon the specific tree at this point, but upon the

57 For the strong indication that the 'serpent' is a wicked entity, even demonic in intent and behaviour (without necessarily seeking recourse to Rom. 16:20; Rev. 12:9, 14, 15; 20:2; or Wis. 2:23–24), see Kuruvilla, *Genesis*, 64–5. The speech by an animal is clearly being considered supernatural in this account of the fall. The only other utterance by an animal in the OT is explicitly noted to be so – Balaam's donkey, in Num. 22:28.

58 Emmrich, 'Temptation Narrative', 16.

command of God, the voice of God, the demand of God, that had been summarily dismissed. For humans had decided that *they* would be the arbiters of what to eat and what not to, what to do and what not to, what to abide by and what not to. God's words were not going to preclude them from making a decision of their own, even if it were contrary to divine design. This was deliberate disobedience and deviance, rebellion against deity, as the sinful pair arrogated to themselves the responsibility for deciding on future actions, rather than depending upon God and his word.

Humans were created to depend on God, completely, totally, utterly. They were carefully formed from the ground by God; they were animated by the breath of God; their sustenance was provided by God; companionship and community was formed for them by God; the garden was created for them by God; their enjoyment was guaranteed by God; and, importantly for this account of their fall, their limits in the universe were ordained by the speech of God: *he* would tell them how to live and how to act. The creatureliness of mankind would allow for no other state than one of dependence upon its Creator. But now, gone was the obligation to depend upon God for direction and guidelines for wholeness, soundness and health: humans take on divine prerogatives and perform the greatest act of deviance ever – they sin, afflicting themselves and their descendants with a lethal illness. This is a story of humanity wanting to usurp the exclusive rights of deity, and falling into the trap of the temptation that seduced them: 'In the day you eat from it [the tree of the knowledge of good and evil], then your eyes will be opened, and you will be like God, knowing good and evil' (3:5). Like God, indeed! 'Deification is a fantasy difficult to repress and a temptation hard to reject … Whenever one makes his own will crucial and God's revealed will irrelevant, whenever autonomy displaces submission and obedience in a person, that finite individual attempts to rise above the limitations imposed on him by his creator.'[59]

But, rather than becoming godlike and 'knowing' good and evil after eating the fruit, all man and woman end up 'knowing' is that they were naked – hardly what they had bargained for! The actual consequences of their sin, displayed in the parallels and contrasts between 3:5 and

59 Hamilton, *Book of Genesis: Chapters 1–17*, 190.

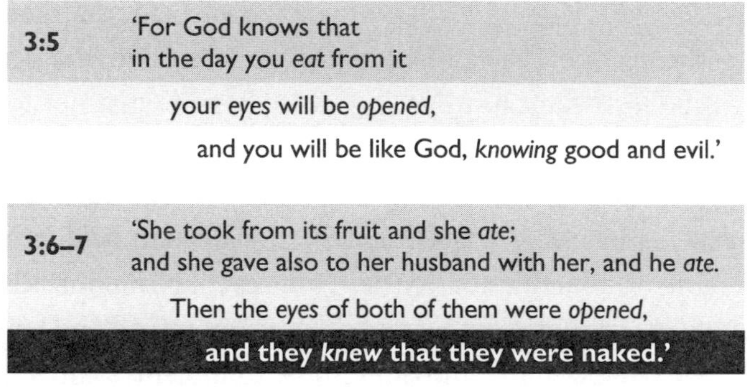
3:5	'For God knows that in the day you *eat* from it
	your eyes will be *opened*,
	and you will be like God, *knowing* good and evil.'
3:6–7	'She took from its fruit and she *ate*; and she gave also to her husband with her, and he *ate*.
	Then the eyes of both of them were *opened*,
	and they *knew* that they were naked.'

Figure 1.5

3:6–7 (see Figure 1.5), 'are so comic as to be hilarious, were it not for the seriousness of the subject'.[60]

The nakedness that did not engender shame prior to sin (2:25) becomes, post-fall, a source of shame between the two humans that necessitates covering (3:7). And to underscore that the unity between the humans that had been established at their creation (the 'one-fleshedness' of 2:23–24) had been lost, in 3:9–13 the plural forms of pronouns and verbs indicating the couple jointly completely disappear: it is only 'he' and 'she' – everyone singularly for himself and herself. Their eating in 3:7 is their last act together in the narrative. From now on, they are addressed separately by God (with the singular pronoun 'you': 3:9, 11, 13), and they accordingly respond separately and individually to God. In fact, man expressly confesses his own actions: '*I* ate' (3:12), '*I* heard', '*I* was afraid', '*I* was naked', '*I* hid' (3:10) – all in the first-person singular.

Besides, this nakedness provokes not only shame between themselves, but also fear of God (Adam: 'I was afraid, for I was naked, so I hid myself'; 3:10); there had been no such fear prior to the disobedience, even though they had been naked then (2:25). These humans wanted to be 'like God' (3:5); now they do not even want to be in his presence (3:8–10). And during the inquiry conducted by God, man proceeds to blame 'the woman' (3:12), the one he had earlier waxed poetic about (2:23). Until this point in the narrative, whenever she had been mentioned in relationship to him, it had always been as 'his woman' (i.e.,

60 Wenham, *Genesis 1–15*, 75. The italics in the figure indicate compared elements; notice the stark contrast between what is in the unshaded box and what is in the black box.

his wife; 2:24, 25; 3:8). Here it is '*the* woman' who is being pointed at with an emphatic 'she' (3:12): 'the woman, whom You gave me, she – she gave me ...' So it's all God's fault now![61]

Relationships between humans and between humans and God had now been disrupted permanently by this disobedience. Sin had broken everyone apart. Alienation was complete. The disease had entrenched itself. Preferring independence to dependence, opting for autonomy rather than trust, humans find only separation from God, and pain and death – life *un*abundant, unwhole, unsound, unhealthy. Deviance, indeed! And the ramifications for this failure to glorify God by obedience are severe.

There are three explicit divine blessings on the 'day' of creation (1:22, 28; 2:3, of sea creatures and birds, of man and of the seventh day, respectively), but after the fall there are three divine curses uttered (3:14, 17; 4:11, of the serpent, of the ground and of Cain, respectively). Literarily, the cursing may be viewed as the undoing of the blessing of creation. The consequences of that unravelling are pronounced by Yahweh as a series of sentences upon the protagonists – primarily, for our interest, the penalty upon humanity: death (the culmination of the natural history of the disease of sin).

God's command to the humans in the Garden included a warning: 'From any tree of the Garden you may surely eat, but from the tree of the knowledge of good and evil – you will not eat from it, for in the day you eat from it, you will surely die' (2:16–17). As was noted, the serpent tempting the woman provided a direct contradiction: 'No – you will surely [not] die' (3:4).[62] Was the snake right? After all, nothing happened when the two perpetrated the deviant act of sin. In fact, Adam actually goes on to live for a total of 930 years, 800 of them after the post-fall birth of Seth (5:4–5). But the fact is that the process of death had begun 'in the day' of disobedience (2:17); the clock of demise marking the natural history of the affliction of sin had begun to tick.[63] In other

61 'God has moved from beneficent provider to cruel oppressor' (Hamilton, *Book of Genesis: Chapters 1–17*, 189).

62 The structure of the beast's utterance, with the negation opening the sentence, is very emphatic.

63 Death as penalty for sin is oft noted in the Bible: Gen. 2:16–17; 3:3–4; Lev. 18:5; Deut. 30:19; Rom. 1:32; 5:12–14, 18–21; 6:23; 7:9–11; 8:2, 13; 1 Cor. 15:56; Col. 2:13; Rev. 3:11.

words, the threatened death in Genesis 2:17 had begun to be fulfilled in the expulsion of 3:24, as the humans were driven away from God the source of life, away from the tree of life, away from deathlessness. Now the only way expelled mankind could live was in the thrall of sin, the only subjection they would know would be to the dominion of sin, and the only sphere in which they would exist would be in the realm of sin. Deviant and diseased through and through. Though 'death' is not explicitly mentioned in the sentencing phase, it is clearly implied: humans formed from the dust (2:7) would return to dust *sans* the life God had breathed into them (3:19). The God-complex of sinful humanity is struck a severe blow – a reality check emphasised in the neat structuring of 3:19b (see Figure 1.6).[64]

A	"'... you *return*		
	B	to the ground,	
		C	*for* from it you were taken;
		C'	*for* dust you are
	B'	and to dust	
A'	you will *return*.'"		

Figure 1.6

The narrator can avoid explicit mention of death because it would be evident to readers that only life within the Garden and in the presence of God was true life, life abundant, life indeed – life lived *God's* way, whole, sound and healthy. And lest humans 'stretch out' (Hebrew: *shlch*) their hands (to eat of the tree of life; 3:22), God 'sends' (also *shlch*) them out of the Garden (3:23). And thus the doom of the first humans and all of their descendants were sealed – the natural history of the malevolent malady would terminate in death, for one and for all.[65]

Elements of the story clearly indicate that the drastic effects of the fall are ongoing; even the crawling of snakes that persists to this day points

64 Mathews, *Genesis 1–11:26*, 253.

65 In light of the significant cultic parallels that construe the Garden of Eden as a sanctuary (as we have seen), the subsequent expulsion from the Garden (2:17; 3:24) is congruent with exclusion of the unclean from the camp of Israel: 'Whether male or female you will send [*shlch*]; outside the camp you shall send [*shlch*] them, so they will not defile [by uncleanness] the camps, where I am dwelling amid them' (Num. 5:3; also Lev. 13:45–46; et cetera). This expulsion away from the presence of God was a discharge into the sphere of death, alienated from the source, centre and fullness of life.

to the continuing ramifications of sin, not to mention the turmoil of childbirth, the toil of human labour, the ever-present spectre of death and the irreversible banishment from the bliss of the Garden (3:14–19) – the inheritance and lot of mankind from their progenitors, Adam and Eve: a genetic affliction.[66] Of course, the original situation of that first pair within the Garden, and their removal without it, is not the direct experience of any of their descendants; instead, all the latter begin life outside the Garden, outside the presence of God – essentially dead (see below). Therefore, the condition of sinfulness remains the same for every human post-fall, as the very next chapter in Scripture, Genesis 4, details graphically.[67] God's 'good/very good' creation was now corrupted and remains so even now, a congenital, debilitating and terminal bane. Tragically, the *imago Dei* had become the *imago Adam*: deviance had led to death, in ways more than one.

Walking in sin (Eph. 2:1–3)

But exactly how bad off did humans become because of the fall? For that we turn to Ephesians 2, which begins …

> And while you were dead in your transgressions and sins …
> (Eph. 2:1)

66 The OT is quite clear about the universality of sin and the 'experience of brokenness at every level of existence' (Fretheim, 'Is Genesis 3 a Fall Story?', 145): see 1 Kgs. 8:46; Pss. 14:1–3; 51; 53; et cetera. Also see Wis. 2:23–24; Sir. 25:24; 2 Esd. 3:4–11, 21–22; et cetera, for other early Jewish appropriations of the concept of an Adamic fall.

67 For which see Kuruvilla, *Genesis*, 75–90. But briefly, let us note that there are remarkable similarities between the accounts of Genesis 2:3–3:24 and 4:1–26 that tell us that the plague of sin had become generational: principal characters – two in each case – introduced by function (2:5, 15, 18; 4:2; et cetera); prohibition and warning before disobedience (2:17; 4:7); central scene of sin (3:6–7; 4:8); divine questioning (3:9–13; 4:9–10); judgement (3:14–19; 4:11–12); post-sin, Adam and Eve are clothed by God (3:21), and Cain is marked by him (4:15b); the transgressors are 'driven' (3:24; 4:16) from the presence of God; and they move east of Eden (3:24; 4:16). The primary protagonists of the two narratives, Adam and Cain, have the same occupation – 'cultivation' of the ground (*'avad* is employed in 2:5, 15; 3:23; 4:2, 12), their sins are linked with 'fruit' (3:1–6; 4:3), their alienation from God results from their 'knowing' (3:5, 7–13, 22; 4:9), and their examination and sentencing follow a similar pattern. But unlike the fall story that began with intimacy between God and humanity and ended with alienation, the Cain-and-Abel narrative begins with alienation (God not accepting Cain's sacrifice; 4:4–5). Besides, Cain is not just a chip off the old block; his fratricidal deviance is greater in magnitude than those of his parents. Yes, the dire sickness of the fall has become unremitting across generations; in fact, it has only worsened in intensity and become further entrenched within creation.

The state of unsaved humanity is described here as 'dead'. Medically, death is defined as the complete functional destruction of the brain that cuts the person off from all personal life and consciousness, not temporarily but permanently: brain death – the complete and irreversible absence of all brain function.[68] What is most characteristic of human life – personal interaction – is now impossible. No matter how the body's continued functioning is maintained with the best medical technology available, employing tubes galore, machines complex, and software intricate – however heroic medical efforts have been, at some point healthcare personnel have to confess that they have 'lost' the patient – he or she is 'gone'. That individual is no longer able to interact with anything or anyone: death causes a loss of response of the person with the environment and with people. And such a lack of response forms the basis of the diagnosis of irreversible loss of brain function.

There are essentially two parts to the medical assessment of brain death in a person: the subject has to be in a coma and there has to be an absence of brainstem reflexes.[69] The former is manifested by *a lack of response* to noxious, painful stimuli: pressure on the brow, nailbed, temporomandibular joints or sternum does not evoke grimacing or eye opening. The latter is manifested by the absences of certain reflexes: pupillary response to light (constriction), corneal response to touch (blinking), gag reflex to touching the soft palate, coughing in response to tracheal suctioning, et cetera – all again underscoring *a lack of response* to external incentives. These failures to respond to pain or to generate a reflex when provoked by an appropriate stimulus constitute brain death.[70] In sum, physical death is nothing but a lack of response to the outside.

One can helpfully annex this notion of physical death to comprehend spiritual death, that which was the fate of every human being after the fall, afflicted by sin. So to be dead spiritually is to have no response to

---

68 The Uniform Law Commission promulgated the 'Uniform Determination of Death Act', adopted by most states in the USA since the 1980s. It affirms that death can be declared if someone has experienced 'irreversible cessation of all functions of the entire brain'.

69 The brainstem is the stalk-like portion that connects the bulk of the brain (cerebrum) with the spinal cord. Though it constitutes less than five percent of the totality of the brain, it plays a critical role in maintaining the baseline functions of the body.

70 See Wijdicks, 'The Diagnosis of Brain Death', 1215–21.

God[71] – utterly unrelated to him and unable to respond to his loving rule as one of his subjects by bearing his image, being his ruling representative on earth and thus glorifying him (as was God's design for humanity at creation). This is a function of bearing the *imago Adam*: separated from God (like Adam), unresponsive to God (like Adam), with no relationship to God (like Adam) – 'having no hope, and godless in the world' (Eph. 2:12).[72]

> ... in which [transgressions and sins] you formerly walked according to the course of this world, according to the ruler of the authority of the air, [the ruler] of the spirit that is now working in the sons [and daughters] of disobedience.
> (Eph. 2:2)

Indeed, since the fall, unsaved humans live 'in' the domain of sin, 'walking' in that sphere of life, governed by the way the world runs, superintended by the 'ruler of the authority of the air', Satan, and manoeuvred by this ruler 'of the spirit [a satanic adjutant?] that is working in the sons [and daughters] of disobedience'. So powerful and effective are all these malign influences that their human victims are referred to as 'sons [and daughters] of disobedience', people characterised by disobedient lives, 'rebels against the authority of God who prefer to answer the promptings of the archenemy'.[73]

Clearly, then, the continuing malady of sin, the deviance of humans, is a manifestation of being 'dead' to God. By that token, being 'alive' to God requires one to be holy, for sin is the violation of the standard of God's won purity and the failure of humans to glorify deity by reflecting ('remanating') his transcendent holiness. Instead, sinners followed Satan (and his anti-God cohort), reflecting him – his rebellion and disobedience

---

71 Involving alienation from God and from the presence of God, as we have already seen.

72 And, as we saw earlier, this bearing of the *imago Adam* also had dreadful consequences for interpersonal relationships among humans, as well as for the relationship of humans to the rest of God's creation.

73 O'Brien, *Letter to the Ephesians*, 161. This labelling of a person as a 'son of *X*' is a Hebraism that denotes one's 'dominant characteristic or affiliation ... a fundamental disposition' (Fowl, *Ephesians*, 69–70; see Acts 4:36, where Barnabas is named the 'son of encouragement'). So also 'children of wrath' in Eph. 2:3. Divine 'wrath' upon the 'sons [and daughters] of disobedience' is also found in 5:6.

against God. Fowl observes wryly that the 'children of disobedience' are quite obedient – just not obedient to *God*. 'The picture painted in 2:2 is of people who are in the thrall of forces opposed to God. Satan has captivated them; they are under Satan's dominion.'[74] Dead in sin. Immersed in sin. Soaked in sin. For 'all have sinned and fall short of the glory of God' (Rom. 3:23).

And those deliberate and conscious acts of disobedience on the part of mankind are portrayed as a purposeful 'walking' (Eph. 2:2; the Greek verb, *peripateō*, translated 'to walk', is a synonym for 'to live'), the rebellious engagement of a sinful and deviant way of life. This includes not only fornication, impurity, rape, murder and the more 'spectacular' sins, but also the various feelings and attitudes that arise from the human impulse to self-aggrandisement. As well, all the rivalries and hostilities that result when this god-complex is thwarted – selfish ambition, envy, jealousy, fits of rage, a contentious temper, not to mention those community ills that ensue, such as quarrels, dissensions and party intrigues. Accompanying these deliberate sins are guilt and shame and fear and alienation and defensiveness and anger and frustration and ambition and hatred and bitterness and confusion and hurt and every other struggle that scars and traumatises each human being in every human society. Deviant and dead!

> ... among whom [i.e., with all other fallen humans] we all also formerly lived in the lusts of our flesh, performing the desires of the flesh and of the mind.
> (Eph. 2:3)

Subsisting in the 'lusts of our flesh' and perpetrating the 'desires of the flesh and of the mind' together emphasise the anti-God stance and activities of unsaved humanity. Not only were the ones bearing the *imago Adam* pursuing evil, they were doing so voluntarily, obeying the evil instincts of their 'flesh' – that fallen aspect of every human that serves Satan and sin – and acting upon those desires with no regard for God.[75]

74 Fowl, *Ephesians*, 70.

75 See Chapter 3 for more on the 'flesh', the ethical entity in fallen humans, embracing both material and immaterial parts of their being, which is entirely opposed to God.

Humans, after the fall, did whatever they wanted, whenever they wanted and however they wanted. And all this 'by nature'; they did not need to be trained, educated or otherwise coached to sin:

> … and [we] were by nature children of wrath, as also [were] the rest. (Eph. 2:3)

And so 'by nature' humankind was deserving of wrath. Something had gone horribly wrong with the fall that warped the very 'nature' of humanity.[76] The inherent sinfulness of mankind is indicated in that expression 'by nature'.[77] Humans are thus born sinful and born dead. 'Unbelievers are "dead", not because of a succession of sins which brought death, but because they have never come alive as believers.'[78] And as a result, those 'sons [and daughters] of disobedience' became 'children of wrath', characterised by, and deserving only of, the wrath of an absolutely holy God.

All of this paints the hopeless predicament of humans, mired as they were in the depths of degrading evil. The entire sphere of the life of mankind was governed by evil that affected its environment ('the course of this world', 2:2) and its inclinations ('the desires of the flesh and of the mind', 2:3) and by the influences of a nefarious foe ('the ruler', 2:2) – a total pervasiveness of anti-God deviance in every aspect of humanity post-fall. Those who are sinful 'by nature' only produce sin. A dire situation, indeed!

God's goal was to be glorified in and through his creation, particularly by the ones he had created to be his vice-regents on earth, humans representing him. That was his design. But since the fall, that divine design has been afflicted by the human deviance of those born dead to God. The displeasure of God with this pernicious turn of events is patent:

> '"A son [and daughter] glorifies the father, and a servant the master. Then if I am a father, where is My glory? And if I am a master, where

76 No doubt, a primary result of the fall upon the human 'nature' was the introduction of the 'flesh'.

77 Also see Job 14:1–4; 15:14; Pss. 51:5; 58:3; Jer. 3:25; Rom. 5:12, 19; et cetera.

78 Best, *Critical and Exegetical Commentary*, 211.

> is My fear?" says Yahweh of Armies to you, priests who despise My name.'
> (Mal. 1:6)

The consequence for those born dead, who are thus not glorifying God, is divine condemnation for sin and all unholiness – eternal death away from the presence of God.[79] What, if anything, could be done to resolve this seemingly intractable crisis? This was a peril that would require nothing less than supernatural intervention to derail the natural history of this terminal illness of deviance afflicting humans. And intervene, God did!

79 But – and we are getting ahead of ourselves here – it must be borne in mind that those born dead but who have become alive by the grace of God in Christ through the Spirit now have the choice to glorify God or not to do so: there are consequences for either option, both in this life and hereafter, blessing or bane (though eternal death is not part of the latter for these children of God by faith). For the consequences of not glorifying God, see 1 Sam. 2:30 ('Yahweh declares, "... the ones glorifying Me I will glorify, and those despising Me, I will disgrace"'); Deut. 28:58–59 ('If you are not careful to do all the words of this law which are written in this book, to fear this glorious and awesome name, Yahweh God, then Yahweh will cause extraordinary blows on you and your descendants, blows great and ongoing, and sufferings adverse and ongoing'); Mal. 2:2 ('If you do not listen, and if you do not place upon [your] heart to give glory to My name', says Yahweh of Armies, 'then I will send upon you a malediction and I will curse your blessings'); et cetera.

2

Salvation

The cure

May they exult and rejoice in You –
all those who seek You;
may they say continually, 'May Yahweh be magnified' –
those loving Your deliverance.
But I am afflicted and needy,
may the Lord consider me.
My help and my saviour You are;
my God, do not delay.
(Ps. 40:16–17)

A few decades ago, a young Iranian woman, Kataun Safaie, applied for a visa to the US at the American Consulate in Frankfurt, Germany. Her plan was to join her recently married husband, Mahmoud Ayazi, an electrician in Sacramento, CA, who had moved from Iran to the USA eight years earlier. Her tourist visa was refused because the consular officer was unconvinced that she was not an impending immigrant who would overstay her visa, a State Department spokesperson explained.

So the newlywed couple took matters into their own hands. The petite Safaie stuffed herself (and a few bananas for nourishment) into a tan soft-sided suitcase, 26 inches × 33 inches × 10 inches, that Ayazi then checked in for his (solo) Lufthansa flight back to California. Tragically, when he went to claim the suitcase at Los Angeles International Airport after the nearly 12-hour flight across an ocean and two continents, Safaie was dead, likely crushed by numerous other pieces of luggage in the cargo bay of the aircraft.[1]

1 Morrison and Heffernan, 'Iranian's Suicide Solves Suitcase Mystery'.

Attempts to smuggle oneself into the kingdom of God are, likewise, doomed to failure: there is no plan humanly contrived that can cure the disaster of fallenness or correct the deviance of sinfulness. Only a supernatural rescue mission could counteract the eternally fatal ramifications of original sin and its repercussions for the glory of God. And that supernatural mission God undertook, to accomplish the *only* cure possible for the deathly malady!

Deliverance

We concluded Chapter 1 depicting the dire sickness incurred at the fall of humanity and its terminal consequence – death, eternal separation from God, the source of life. Ephesians 2:1–3 described the ongoing deviant state of mankind lost in sin. Clearly, doomed humans were not going to be able to glorify God as they were designed to do. How could they – lost in sin, forever separated from God in spiritual death? Ephesians 2 labels the disastrous and ruinous situation of these as being 'without Christ … having no hope, and godless in the world' (2:12): Christless, hopeless, godless! Certainly bereft of any God-glorifying capacity at all! If God created humans so that they may glorify him, then the fall of humankind would signify a derailment of God's plan, so to speak, an upsetting of his purpose. A failed God?

Researcher Sheena Iyengar, a professor at the Columbia Business School and author of *The Art of Choosing*, a recognised expert on decision-making, once said: 'I recently did a survey with over 2,000 Americans, and the average number of choices that the typical American reports making is about 70 in a typical day.'[2] By my calculations, that adds up to 25,550 decisions per year; if you live to be 75 that means you've made 1,916,250 choices in your life. And that's your life in a nutshell! I hate to remind us of this, but we and most of our almost 2 million choices and decisions are terribly faulty and error prone – the desperate efforts by Ayazi and his spouse disastrously proved this to be the case with that horrible chain of events described earlier. But not so God and his decisions and their execution. His plans never fail. His

2 Iyengar, 'How to Make Choosing Easier'.

undertakings always succeed. Surely, he must have foreseen what would happen in the fall and would devise a way to rescue these sinful humans from the dire predicament they had put themselves in? He had, and he would. For their sickness of sin God, and God alone, had a cure.

In fact, there was a hint, even in the narrative of the fall of the original humans, that God had created an escape route; we find it within the divine sentence upon the serpent:

> 'Enmity I will put between you [the serpent] and between the woman, and between your seed and between her seed; he – he will bruise you [on] the head, and you – you will bruise him on the heel.' (Gen. 3:15)

In light of the fact that the pronoun associated with 'seed', 'he', is singular, it is quite likely that a single 'seed' of the woman is in view in 3:15, particularly since that pronoun is somewhat redundant in that verse – the masculine singular subject is clearly understood from the conjugation of the Hebrew verb, *yshuphka*, '*he*-will-bruise-you'.[3] The Targums (Aramaic translations/paraphrases of the OT) explicitly schedule this ultimate victory of the 'seed' for the days of the 'King Messiah'.[4] What exactly did God do?

The grace of God (Eph. 2:4–7)

To examine God's deliverance of humankind from their dire straits, we continue in Ephesians 2.[5] This passage is, in effect, an account of how God's original plan to glorify himself through humans is recovered and regained, despite the failure (fall) of deviant humans. Here's the divine operation in a nutshell:

3 Hence my translation: 'he [independent pronoun] – he-will-bruise-you [conjugated verb]'. Elsewhere, when 'seed' indicates 'posterity' with a plurality of descendants, the associated pronouns are always plural (see Gen. 17:9; 15:3; 17:7–10; 48:11–12; et cetera); the pronouns are singular when a specific descendant is indicated (see 4:25; 21:13; 38:9; et cetera).

4 *Tg. Ps.-J.* and *Tg. Neof.* on Gen. 3:15. Of course, the NT assigns messianic significance to this passage in Gen. 3 (Rom. 16:20: Heb. 2:14; 1 John 3:8; Rev. 12:1–6, 13–17).

5 Much of the following discussion is taken from Kuruvilla, *Ephesians*, 52–65.

> God, being rich in mercy, because of His great love with which He loved us, even while we were dead in transgressions, co-enlivened [us] with Christ – by grace you have been saved – and co-raised and co-seated [us] in the heavenlies in Christ Jesus, in order that in the coming ages He might demonstrate the surpassing riches of His grace in kindness towards us in Christ Jesus; for by grace you have been saved through faith; and this not of yourselves, [but] the gift of God.
> (Eph. 2:4–8)

Finally, in 2:4–8, after the bleak description in 2:1–3 of humanity mired in the depths of degrading evil that renders them utterly incapable of glorifying God,[6] we come to the three main verbs of the single sentence that comprises 2:1–7, describing three divine undertakings, each prefixed with the Greek preposition *syn-* (= 'with') – syn*ezōpoiēsen*, syn*ēgeiren*, syn*ekathisen*: God 'co-enlivened' (or 'made alive') the saved with Christ, 'co-raised' them with Christ and 'co-seated' them in the heavenlies with Christ (2:5–6), referring, of course, to Christ's own exaltation, his 'raising' and his 'seating' at the right hand of God in the 'heavenlies' (described in 1:20 using two of the same verbs and the same celestial location as found in 2:4–7).[7]

Paul's goal here is to demarcate the striking contrast between the *past* state of post-fall, non-God-glorifying sinners[8] and the *present* state of post-cross, potentially-God-glorifying believers, comparing the consequences of human deviance and of divine deliverance, as it were (see Figure 2.1).

Incredibly, those 'dead' ones have become, by God's deliverance, 'co-enlivened [… with] Christ' (2:5), and 'children of wrath' (2:3) have become the children of God saved by grace through faith (2:4–7). Indeed, to underscore the dreadful plight of non-Christians prior to this divine intervention of grace, the wording of 2:1 ('while you were dead in your

6 Chapter 1 dealt with those verses.

7 I have translated the words beginning with *syn-* rather woodenly, prefixing the corresponding English words with 'co-' to reflect the preposition-affixed structure of those Greek verbs.

8 The word 'formerly' is employed twice in 2:2–3.

PAST (post-fall)	PRESENT (post-cross)
'dead' (2:1)	'co-enlivened [us with] Christ' (2:5)
Ruined 'in [*en*]' sins (2:1–2)	Raised 'in [*en*] the heavenlies' 'in [*en*] Christ' (2:6)
Intimately related to: 'course of this world' 'ruler of the authority of the air' '[ruler] of the spirit' (2:2)	Intimately related to: 'Christ' (2:5–6) 'in the heavenlies' (2:6)
Deviant 'by nature' (2:3)	Delivered 'by grace' (2:5, 8)
Subjects of divine 'wrath' (2:3)	Subjects of divine 'mercy', 'love', 'kindness' and 'grace' (2:4–8)

Figure 2.1

transgressions') is repeated almost verbatim in 2:5 ('even while we were dead in transgressions'). Notice also the contrast between 'by nature' (2:3; i.e., from the start, from birth and by constitution – congenitally unsound, unwhole and unhealthy) and 'by grace' (2:5, 8; by divine intervention, by rebirth and by gift, saved – cured to soundness, wholeness and healthiness). Those in the former state of deviance were doomed to suffer divine wrath (2:3), but those in the latter state of deliverance have now been destined as subjects of God's mercy, love, kindness and grace (2:4–8) for the purpose and ultimate destiny of God's glorification (as we will see below).

What happened 'in Christ' had nothing to do with what humanity had done, was doing or would/could do to extricate itself from the dire predicament it found itself in after the fall. No self-medicated cures would suffice for this disease. Deliverance was entirely God's work, as the word 'grace' indicates – undeserving merit credited to believers, a divine 'gift' (2:8) – all of it accomplished by God, with zero contribution from humanity.[9] It is not just '*His grace*' that was in operation, or 'His grace *in kindness*', or even the '*riches* of His grace in kindness': rather, it is the

9 The passive construction in 2:5, 'by grace *you have been saved*', is commonly labelled a 'divine passive', indicating that it is God's doing. Anglican Archbishop William Temple once said about God's deliverance, tongue in cheek: 'All is of God: the only thing of my very own which I can contribute to redemption is the sin from which I need to be redeemed' (*Nature, Man, and God*, 401). But while the salvation graciously offered is universal in its provision, it is not universal in its application, for the instrument of that salvation is faith on the part of the believer (2:8).

'*surpassing* riches of His grace in kindness' – a piling on of descriptors of divine grace in Christ that was demonstrated and donated to deliver undeserving humans.[10] Amazing grace, indeed! Such a wondrous work of God was necessary, for how else could these deviant sin-perpetrators be transformed into delivered God-glorifiers?

Thus, humans' bondage to the world, to its evil ruler and to the flesh post-fall (2:2–3) was broken by divine deliverance in Christ, post-cross. No longer does the child of God have to succumb to these influences of evil. This is astounding, indeed: 'sons of disobedience' and 'children of wrath', who were fraternising with the enemies of God, are now, as believers in Christ Jesus, afforded all the benefits and privileges that appertain to God's Son – '*co*-enlivened', '*co*-raised' and '*co*-seated' with him 'in the heavenlies'! What a shared destiny – what is true of Christ is now also true of believers! They have been moved from the past to the present, from one fate to another (2:6–7).

Indeed, it is only because of this identification of believers with Christ that divine deliverance was achieved ('in Christ' occurs in 2:6, 7, 10; besides the 'co-' words connoting the same notion). And it is the identification with their Saviour that restores the ability of these now-saved humans to meet their divinely-ordained destiny – the glorification of God. But this identification with Christ is not just a theoretical comparison or a hypothetical simulation – it is an actual union with Christ, and to that important concept, revealed in Romans 6, we now turn.

Baptism by Christ, in the Spirit, unto himself (Rom. 6:1–4)

For the remainder of this chapter (and for a significant portion of the next), we will examine Romans 6–8, the foundational portion of Scripture addressing the privileged station of those who have been saved by grace through faith in Christ – and are now in union with him – and

10 I am assuming here a foundational knowledge of salvific events (including the atoning work of the Saviour) and their theological ramifications; this work is not intended to be exhaustive in that respect. Our focus here will be upon scrutinising the chosen texts for what they say about the trajectory from sin to salvation (Chapters 1 and 2; and thence to spiritual empowerment and scriptural obedience, i.e., sanctification, in Chapters 3 and 4).

the practical ramifications thereof for the glorification of God.[11] But before we dive into this chunk of text, it will help to scrutinise briefly the layout of the epistle. One might remember that the citation of Habakkuk 2:4 in Romans 1:16–17 forms the key to the entire composition to the Romans: only the one who is 'righteous-by-faith' (i.e., justified by faith) will live.

> I am not ashamed of the gospel, for it is the power of God unto salvation to all who believe, to the Jew first and to the Greek. For in it the righteousness of God is revealed from faith unto faith, just as it has been written, 'The righteous-by-faith shall live.'
> (Rom. 1:16–17)

Romans 1–8 proceeds to explicate 'the righteous-by-faith shall live', with Romans 1–4 dealing with 'righteous-by-faith' (justification) and Romans 6–8 with 'shall live' (sanctification) (see Figure 2.2).[12]

Romans 1–4	Romans 5	Romans 6–8
'the righteous-by-faith		shall live'
Justification		*Sanctification*

Figure 2.2

The chapter between these two sections, Romans 5, is concerned with the reconciliation of humans with God, which understandably comes right before our text of interest, Romans 6–8, that focuses upon their sanctification – in union with Christ and empowered by the Spirit enabling them to glorify God. Thus, the believer is justified by faith (Romans 1–4), and reconciled to God (Romans 5), and enters a new sphere of life of union with Christ (Romans 6–8). The distribution of key words in the letter manifests this intent of the apostle (see Figure 2.3).

11 While union with Christ involves participation and identification with him, as well as incorporation into him (Romans 6; in this chapter) and their being bound to him (Romans 7; in the next chapter), this current work considers 'union' as a conglomeration of all those elements, without seeking to dissect out their nuances and differences. See Campbell, *Paul and Union with Christ*, 29.

12 The prepositional phrase 'by faith' modifies the 'righteous', as is evident in the juxtaposition of the two terms in both Hebrew (*tsaddiq be'emunto*) and Greek (LXX and NT: *ho de dikaios ek pisteōs*). See Nygren, *Commentary on Romans*, 86–90; Porter, 'Newer Perspective', 376.

Key Words and Their Distribution in Romans

Romans	1–5	6–8	9–16
'faith'	30	1	14
'believe'	9	1	11
'law'	*36*	*30*	*6*
'sin'	6	**36**	2
'death'	15	**40**	10
'flesh'	4	**15**	5
'Spirit'	3	**20**	6

Figure 2.3

Reflecting these focuses, 'sin' and 'death' [both *thanatos* and *nekros*] are prominent in Romans 6–8, though less so in Romans 8: for each of these three chapters, 'sin' occurs 16×, 15× and 5× respectively; and 'death' 21×, 10× and 9× respectively. So also 'Spirit' is predominantly located in Romans 6–8, but particularly in Romans 8: for each of the three chapters of Romans 6–8, 'Spirit' occurs 0×, 1× and 19× respectively. Indubitably, the significantly higher frequency of this word in Romans 8 makes this *the* chapter of the Third Person of the Godhead.[13]

We begin our examination of Romans 6–8 in this chapter, dealing here with Romans 6 (with a brief return to Ephesians 2 later). The entirety of Rom 6:1–7:6 concerns the matter that Paul introduces with a question in 6:1–2a:

> What then shall we say? Do we remain in sin, in order that grace may increase? May it never be!
> (Rom. 6:1–2a)

The issue of 6:1–7:6 is whether believers, delivered and cured from the disease, can remain in sin, in the same domain that non-Christians, doomed and afflicted by deviance, exist in. They cannot, Paul unequivocally declares, for two reasons – both introduced with verbatim

13 Romans 7 will be scrutinised in Chapter 3, and Romans 8 in Chapter 4. Also, 'law' occurs in about the same frequency in Romans 6–8 (30 times) as it does in Romans 1–5 (36 times). For becoming 'righteous-by-faith' (justification; Romans 1–4), the importance of 'faith' in opposition to 'law' is obvious, but the significance of 'law' for 'living' (sanctification; Romans 6–8) is vastly underrated (more about that later).

exclamations of incredulity on the apostle's part: 'or are you unknowing …?' (6:3a; 7:1a) (see Figure 2.4).[14]

REMAIN IN SIN? NEVER! (6:1–7:6)
'What then shall we say? … *Remain in sin?* … May it never be!' (6:1–2a)

'Or are you unknowing …?' (6:3a)
REASON #1: Union with Christ: Baptised unto Him (6:3–14)
Picture of baptism (6:3b–4a)

Exhortation to new life of obedience to God (6:15–23)

'Or are you unknowing …?' (7:1a)
REASON #2: Union with Christ: Bound to Him (7:1–6)
Picture of marriage (7:1b–3)

LAW IS SIN? NEVER! (7:7–23)
'What then shall we say? *Is the law sin?* May it never be!' (7:7)

Figure 2.4

Both reasons champion the union of believers with Christ: the first reason believers cannot remain in sin is because they are in *union with Christ*: *baptised unto him* (utilising the picture of baptism; 6:3–14). The second reason is because believers are in *union with Christ*: *bound to him* (utilising the picture of marriage; 7:1–6).[15] In between these two reasons is 6:15–23, a powerful exhortation to believers to lead new lives of faithful obedience to God, no doubt grounded and based on the surrounding theme of union with Christ.

Now on to Romans 6 in detail.

> What then shall we say? Do we remain in sin …
> (Rom. 6:1)

It is remarkable how Paul discusses 'sin' in the singular throughout Romans 6–7 and often elsewhere: 'sin' is pictured as the sphere in which sinners live (6:1), and as a power that is alive (7:9), that enters the human

14 I have translated the Greek *agnoeō* as 'unknow' to distinguish between the uses of this verb in 6:3 and 7:1 from the use of *ouk oida*, 'not know', in 6:16. That 6:1–7:6 is a complete section is clear: the following verse, 7:7a, commences a new section almost exactly as 6:1 did: 'What then shall we say? Is the law sin? May it never be!' (See Figure 2.4.)

15 That these two reasons are parallel in structure, illustrative picture and vocabulary will be seen when we tackle the second reason in Chapter 3.

realm (5:12) and dwells in the believer (7:17), that controls humans (5:13–19; 6:11, 13–14), that reigns (5:21; 6:12) and that enslaves (3:9; 6:6, 13–20, 22), prompting deeds of sin by deception (7:8, 11), effecting death (7:13; 8:10) and even dying and coming to life itself (7:8–9). In fact, it is also an evil employer paying wages to those in its abominable service (6:23).[16] It is quite personified, and rightly so, considering the role of Satan, the first sinful being and the one who, with his hordes, was (and is) the instigator for the first (and every subsequent) production of sins. 'Sin is not merely a series of separate acts nor an abstract principle, but a demonic power, a world ruler who claims the obedience of [humans] just as God does.'[17] Indeed, the very first time this nefarious notion, 'sin', is introduced in the Bible, it is depicted is as a personified entity:[18]

> … at the door sin, he is crouching; and his desire [for control] is towards you, but you must master him.
> (Gen. 4:7)

This pastoral and parental counsel offered by Yahweh to the first biblical murderer and fratricide, Cain, has some idiosyncrasies of text: 'sin' is feminine, but 'crouching' is a masculine participle – '*he* is crouching', and 'desire' has a masculine pronominal suffix – '*his* desire'; likewise, the object of the verb 'master' is masculine – 'you must master *him*'. Though Hebrew nouns that are feminine (here, 'sin') may occasionally be treated as masculine morphologically (and thus get masculine verbs and suffixes), there may be more going on here. The Hebrew verb, *rbts* ('crouch'), is related to the Akkadian *rābiṣu*, a male (usually) demonic entity that stood guard at entrances to buildings.[19] It is quite possible, then, that 'sin' in Genesis 4:7 is subtly being likened to a crouching demon – the shift from feminine noun ('sin') to masculine participle ('he is crouching') and the pronominal suffixes ('his', 'him') might very

16 This singular 'sin' is pointedly different from the plural 'sins' that denotes everything contrary to the holiness of God. Thus, at least in Romans 6–8, 'sins' is the product of 'sin' and its baleful divine glory-countering influence upon the beings God designed for glorifying him.

17 Tannehill, *Dying and Rising*, 16.

18 The discussion below is taken from Kuruvilla, *Genesis*, 81.

19 Kitz, 'Demons in the Hebrew Bible', 447–64.

well reflect the true character of 'sin'. And this (demonic) entity seeks to control humanity as God warned Cain.

Thus, we can conceive of two authorities seeking to influence humans: God, himself, from creation on, causing righteousness to be produced, but since the fall, 'sin' too – antithetical to the interests of God, militating against the directives of God, antagonistic to the purposes of God that he be glorified in his creation – causing 'sins', unrighteousness, to be performed (see Figure 2.5). And, in the lives of unsaved humans since the fall, 'sin' is the predominant authority. One might conceive of these two authorities as operating in two distinct realms: the realm of God under the rulership of deity, and the realm of 'sin' under the aegis of Satan, with the latter in ascendancy since the fall.

Figure 2.5

In Romans 5:20, the last verse of Romans 5 before our chapter of interest, Romans 6, Paul had announced that where sin increased, grace abounded all the more, making possible a reconciliation with God. But, he now avers, that does not mean that believers should remain in sin, in the domain of and under the control of the evil authority 'sin', as if increasing human sinfulness were the way to make divine graciousness abound.[20]

> What then shall we say? Do we remain in sin, in order that grace may increase? May it never be! We who died to sin, how shall we live in it? (Rom. 6:1–2)

It is absolutely not the case that once one is saved, one can live however

20 Or as W. H. Auden, the British-American poet, explained: 'Every crook will argue, "I like committing crimes. God likes forgiving them. Really the world is admirably arranged"' (*For the Time Being*, 123–4).

one desires because grace is free and grace is abundant. More sin ≠ more grace! And to that gross misunderstanding, Paul declares, 'May it never be!' Why not?

The first thing to catch here is that the apostle is addressing believers as those who have 'died *to* sin' (6:2). The ones who were once 'dead *in* sin' (Eph. 2:1) are now 'dead *to* sin'. As we saw in Chapter 1, in medical parlance, death is the lack of response to the environment and its stimuli. At the fall, deviant (sickly) humanity, in and through its sinning ancestors, Adam and Eve, became dead (i.e., non-responsive) to God and the things of God, rendering their God-glorifying ability null and void; they lived in the realm of 'sin' producing sins: 'dead *in* sin'. But here Paul declares that believers have now 'died *to* sin': they have been granted the possibility of being *non*-responsive to the overtures and enticements and persuasions of 'sin', the evil authority, for they are dead *to* it and therefore potentially non-responsive to it.[21] So, if every Christian has died to sin, how, Paul asks, can the Christian even think of remaining 'in sin' and living 'in it', breathing its air, living its lifestyle, obeying its diktats (Rom. 6:1–2)? With the strongest possible negation available to him in Greek ('May it never be!'), Paul declares that such a situation is impossible, because it is virtually an oxymoron. And he proceeds to make the case that this impossibility is because believers have been united with Christ (6:1–7:6). What is this union between Saviour and saved all about? The apostle proceeds to explain with two crucial modalities of this union with Christ that serve as two key reasons for not remaining 'in sin': the saved are *baptised* unto him (6:1–14) and they are *bound* to him (7:1–6).

First, their baptism into Christ:[22]

> Or are you unknowing that as many of us were baptised unto Christ Jesus, [it was] unto his baptism you were baptised?
> (Rom. 6:3)

21 As we will find out, having died *to* sin does not mean that believers do not sin, or that they do not follow that evil authority. It simply indicates that the people of God living in a post-resurrection dispensation now have a choice: they can follow either the divine authority (with their restored God-glorifying ability) or the demonic one (refusing to employ that restored ability). Hence believers are only *potentially* non-responsive to sin. For the still-present evil 'flesh' in them that induces them to sin, see below.

22 For the second modality of union with Christ, and the second reason for not living 'in sin', see Chapter 3.

Paul propounds 'baptism' as the first modality by which this union with Christ was accomplished. The verb 'to baptise' *literally* indicates an immersion into liquids.[23] With time, the term also took on *figurative* notions of submersion into non-fluid elements.[24] In the LXX, the Greek verb is used *literally* of Naaman dipping into the Jordan (2 Kgs. 5:14; also see Jud. 12:7; Sir. 34:30), and *figuratively* of one being plunged in corruption (Job 9:31 Aquila) and of being deluged by iniquity (Isa. 21:4). In the NT also, the verb *baptizō* and the cognate nouns *baptisma* and *baptismos* indicate a *literal* immersion in water in many of its uses.[25] As for the *figurative* uses of this verb and the nouns in the NT that focus on the baptism of believers (excluding other religious baptisms, such as unto John or unto Moses), the categorisation shown in Figure 2.6 is helpful for our purposes as we continue to examine Romans 6.[26]

As is evident, often the baptiser is Christ (though humans can be the agents of the literal act[27]), the medium into which the baptisand is

23 As in: taking a dip in the ocean (Plutarch, *Moralia: Superstition* 166); the sinking of ships (Polybius, *Histories* 1.51.6; Josephus, *Jewish Wars* 3.9.3); drownings, accidental or otherwise (Josephus, *Antiquities* 15.3.3); dipping into wine jars with drinking cups (Plutarch, *Life of Alexander* 67); immersing in brine during cooking (Nicander, *Fragment of a Work on Husbandry* 2); wool soaking in dye to colour it (Basil the Great, *On Baptism* 1.2.10); et cetera.

24 As in: being overwhelmed in troubled times (Dion Cassius, *Roman History* 38.27); being engulfed by grief (Libanius, *Epistle* 35); or by drunkenness (Plato, *Symposium* 176b); or by disease (Plotinus, *Ennead* 1.4); or by persecution (Josephus, *Jewish War* 1.27.1); or even by taxes or debt (Plutarch, *Life of Galba* 21); et cetera.

25 See Matt. 3:6, 7, 13–14, 16; 21:25; Mark 1:4–5, 9; 6:14, 24; 7:4; 11:30; Luke 3:3, 7, 12, 16, 21; 7:29, 30; 11:38; 12:50; 20:4; John 1:25–26, 28, 31, 33; 3:22–23, 26; 4:1, 2; 10:40; Acts 1:22; 8:12, 13, 36, 38; 9:18; 10:37; 11:16a; 13:24; 16:15, 33; 18:8, 25; 19:3–4; 22:16; 1 Cor. 1:13–17; 15:29; Heb. 6:2; 9:10.

26 In Mark 10:38–39, using both the verb and one of the nouns (also see Luke 12:50), the concept of 'baptism' concerns the way of suffering that is being modelled by Christ and which is to be followed by the disciple (the 'cup' symbolises suffering, as Mark 14:36 clarifies): this is not included in Figure 2.6. Also not included is Col. 2:12, where the passive voice of the verb suggests God as the baptiser of Paul's addressees, the baptisands (= the ones being baptised); however, the medium and purpose are not mentioned, though the prepositional prefix in '*co*-buried' and '*co*-raised' and the dative, 'with Him', seems to indicate a union with Christ in that verse – thus a figurative use of 'baptism'. The connotation of 'baptism' in Eph. 4:5 is unclear, though being part of a quasi-credal utterance, it is also likely to be figurative. See Conant, *The Meaning and Use of Baptizein*, 1–91. The 'fire' in Luke 3:16 could well be referring to the ministry of the Holy Spirit (Acts 2:3).

27 We can safely assume that when the baptiser is named (for, e.g., Philip or Paul), literal immersion in water conducted by that person (or his agent[s]) is in view in the text, but taking place simultaneously with the figurative understanding – baptism in the 'name' of Christ; thus I have included these verses in Figure 2.6, too.

immersed is the Holy Spirit, and the purpose is denoted by 'into the name of Christ/Trinity', or 'unto Christ' or 'unto one body' of Christ.[28]

TEXT	BAPTISER	BAPTISAND	MEDIUM	PURPOSE
Matt. 3:11	Christ	'you'	Holy Spirit fire	
Matt. 28:19	Disciplers	'nations'		Into the 'name' of the Trinity
Mark 1:8b	Christ	'you'	Holy Spirit	
Luke 3:16	Christ	'you'	Holy Spirit fire	
John 1:33	Christ		Holy Spirit	
Acts 1:5		'you'	Holy Spirit	
Acts 2:38		'each of you'		Into the 'name' of Christ
Acts 8:16	Philip	Samaritans		Into the 'name' of Christ
Acts 10:48				Into the 'name' of Christ
Acts 11:16b		'you'	Holy Spirit	
Acts 19:5	Paul	Ephesians		Into the 'name' of Christ
Rom. 6:3–4		'all'		Unto Christ
1 Cor. 12:13		'we all'	Holy Spirit	Unto one body
Gal. 3:27		'all'		Unto Christ

Figure 2.6

As far as these purposes are concerned, baptism 'unto Christ' and 'unto one body' in context clearly depict the Christian becoming a member of the body of Christ – a way of picturing the union with Christ that also results in the union with the community of Christians.[29] But what is it to be baptised 'into the name of Christ/Trinity'? A glance at some rabbinical texts utilising the idiom 'into the name …' provides clarity.[30]

28 The Greek preposition translated 'unto' and 'into' in these phrases varies, but the thrust essentially remains the same.

29 See 1 Cor. 12:13; 2 Cor. 13:14; Gal. 3:27; Eph. 4:3; Phil. 2:1; et cetera.

30 Granted, these documents are dated later than the NT, but they shed light on practices and employ language describing actions that seem to have been in existence long before.

For instance, the Talmud states that a slave could be baptised 'unto the name of [Aramaic *lshem*] a son of freedom', i.e., baptised into freedom thus becoming free (*b. Yebam* 45b; and likewise 46a, 47b[31]). Thus, 'unto the name' designates the affinity of the baptisand with the person/entity/notion so named. Likewise, baptism in the name of the Trinity (Matt. 28:19) 'places the person being baptised in a certain relationship with God'.[32] The employment of 'baptism in the name of ...' in the NT is likely the reuse of such a Semitic idiom, indicating an identification, a union, of the baptisand with the one whose name was being invoked, as also Gal. 3:27 seems to indicate. In sum, baptism into the name of Christ unites the baptisand with Christ. (There is no reason to see baptism into the name of the Trinity as any different: after all, two Persons, the Son and the Spirit, are explicitly involved in this transaction as we have already seen; undoubtedly the Father is, too.)

All that to say, the general pattern of describing NT baptism – and we are focusing on the figurative aspect alone – is that Christ baptises the baptisand in the Spirit, who is the sphere into which one is baptised and thus the divine means by which the union of the believer with Christ (and with the body of Christ) is accomplished. Needless to say, this is a momentous event co-incident with faith, regeneration and justification. It is essentially a reversal of the deviance of fallen humans, a remission of that disease, for it now renders these saved humans capable of glorifying God (as we will see below). The ritual of water baptism (the *literal* sense: in water) pictures that greater reality of Spirit baptism (the *figurative* sense: in the Spirit).[33] Through their once-for-all undergoing of *literal* baptism, the visible ritual, it is being publicly proclaimed that baptisands have already experienced the once-for-all *figurative* baptism, that greater

31 In another intricate transaction described in the Talmud, a female POW might be baptised by an owner 'unto the name of [*lshem*] slavery', i.e., into slavery thus making her a slave, and then be immediately baptised again 'unto the name of [*lshem*] freedom', i.e., into freedom now rendering her free. Such a doubly baptised person transits from the status of a prisoner to that of a slave, and then from the status of a slave to that of a free person, thus permitting the owner to marry her (*b. Yebam* 47b–48a). My translations from the Aramaic in all cases.

32 Strack and Billerbeck, *Kommentar zum Neuen Testament,* 1.1055 (my translation from the German).

33 The ritual of water baptism is, more often than not, concurrent with the reality of Spirit baptism unto Christ. Schreiner, *Romans,* 306, is right: 'unbaptised Christians were virtually nonexistent' in the early days of the Church. On a personal note, I got baptised eleven years after I got saved – ignorance of divine command being my only excuse.

invisible reality of their union with Christ accomplished in and by the Holy Spirit.[34] So for the rest of our discussion, by referring to 'baptism' I will mean the figurative sense of the word, the reality of the union of the Christian with Christ.[35] In sum, baptism is the Christ-performed and Spirit-mediated process by which the believer is placed in Christ and united with him (and therefore with his body also).

So what happens in baptism unto Christ that makes Paul vehemently deny the possibility of the believer remaining in sin (Rom. 6:1), and leading him to ask incredulously, 'Are you unknowing …'? The aspect of union with Christ that the apostle wants to focus on and emphasise in Romans 6, by employing the picture of baptism, is the identification of believers with the death and resurrection of Christ:[36]

> Or are you unknowing that as many of us were baptised unto Christ Jesus, [it was] unto His death you were baptised? Therefore, we were co-buried [with] Him through baptism unto death, in order that just as Christ was raised from the dead through the glory of the Father, so we too may walk in newness of life. For if we have become co-identified [with] the likeness of His death, certainly we will also be [co-identified (with) the likeness] of the resurrection.
> (Rom. 6:3–5)

Because of this union of believers with Christ via their baptism by him, in the Spirit and unto himself, they are 'co-buried' with Christ 'through baptism unto death' (6:4): he died, so they died. And now he lives, so baptisands, too, are to live in new life (more on this necessity for a

34 See Sawyer, 'In Christ', 55.

35 One notices that it is the passive form of the verb that is employed in Rom. 6:3, *ebaptisthēmen*, 'we were baptised' (×2) – a 'divine' passive, as it were, implying that God (in Christ) is the one who performs the act. So also the other passives in Rom. 6: 'we were co-buried' and 'was raised' (6:4), 'was co-crucified' and 'may be inactivated' (6:6), 'has been made righteous' (6:7), 'having been raised' (6:9), and 'having been freed' and 'you were enslaved' (6:18; these last two are also repeated in 6:22). All indicate the sovereign work of God in uniting the believer to Christ; there is no activity implied on the part of believers undergoing figurative baptism. No undertaking of self-medication or performance of auto-surgery by deviant humanity could accomplish what is described in Rom. 6.

36 Indeed, Jesus himself referred to his passion and death as a 'baptism' (Mark 10:38–39; 14:36; Luke 12:49–50).

newness of life below).[37] The bottom line here is that what pertains to Christ pertains to believers, by virtue of their union with him in baptism. They have been baptised to die to sin (in Christ), as Christ himself did, and they have also been raised from the dead to live new lives (also in Christ), as Christ himself does (notice the comparatives: '*just as* Christ ... *so* we too' in 6:4, and 'we will *also*' in 6:5, besides the 'co'-words that make the same correlation). Baptisands died with Christ: their former life under the old master, sin, has now ceased, and a fresh life under a new master, God, has commenced. Therefore, they should not be sinning! But there is more: the destiny of these new-life livers (a reflection of their being co-raised with Christ).

Destiny

The destiny of the delivered is carefully developed in the remaining verses of Romans 6 (and continued in the following two chapters of the epistle).

Baptismal union with Christ's death and resurrection (Rom. 6:4–14)

The subsequent, post-salvation life of believers hinges on the fact that in union with Christ (baptised unto him) it was not only with Christ's death that a believer was identified, but also with his resurrection: a new life has been inaugurated.

> Therefore we were co-buried [with] Him through baptism unto death, in order that just as Christ was raised from the dead through the glory of the Father, so we too may walk in newness of life. For if we have become co-identified [with] the likeness of His death, certainly we will also be [co-identified (with) the likeness] of the resurrection.
> (Rom. 6:4–5)

37 The phrase in 6:4 describing Christ's resurrection as being 'through the glory of the Father' is likely shorthand for God's glorious *power* that works in the raising of Christ and of believers. The juxtaposition (and equation) of divine 'glory' and 'power' (as here in Rom. 6:4) is also found in 2 Thess. 1:9; Heb. 1:3; and Rev. 15:8 (also see Matt. 6:13; 24:30; Mark 13:26; Luke 21:27; Rev. 4:11; 5:12; 7:12; 15:8 – all reflecting a Semitic idiom, as in Pss. 63:2; 145:11; et cetera).

Notice that an equivalence is being made between the outcomes of Christ's resurrection and that of believers – '*so we too* may walk in newness of life' (6:5; also see 1 Cor. 15:43; Phil. 3:21).[38] That is, their newness of life, resembling that of Christ, is to be a Christ-emulating walk of sanctification (see below): a participation with Christ in his death (and abandonment of the old walk of life) and a participation with his resurrection (with an adoption of the new walk of life). 'We were co-buried' (Rom. 6:4a) is an aorist expressing a participatory (i.e., identified with Christ) *actuality* – it has already happened. The corresponding 'so that we … may walk' (6:4b) is a subjunctive expressing a participatory (also an identification with Christ) *potentiality* – it is yet to happen, or it should be happening in an ongoing fashion.

> … knowing this, that our old person was co-crucified [with Christ], in order that the body of sin may be inactivated, for us to be slaves to sin no longer; for the one who died has been made free from sin. (Rom. 6:6–7)

The cognitive basis for such a participation, Paul argues, is a comprehension of ('knowing') the fates of the two entities named in 6:6: 'old person' and 'body of sin'. First, the 'old person' as opposed to the 'new person' is uniformly employed to Paul to designate the pre-conversion way of life of the believer (see Eph. 2:14; 4:22–24; Col. 3:9–11) – the believer's life-in-its-fallenness.[39] This 'old person' who has been 'co-crucified' (aorist) has, in another participatory *actuality*, died in union with Christ: the old relationship with the false authority, sin, is gone! Second, there is the 'body of sin'. While the believer has become a new person, there are still vestiges of fallenness that remain (and they

38 Just as Christ's resurrection was by the 'glory of the Father', i.e., by his power, so also is the resurrection and the new walk of believers: see Col. 1:10–11; 2 Pet. 1:3. More of divine empowerment for the new life in Chapter 3. 'To walk' is a Semitism that means 'to live', primarily in a moral and ethical fashion: see Gen. 17:1; Ps. 1:1; Isa. 33:16; Mic. 6:8; et cetera (all use the Hebrew *hlk*, 'to walk'); so also in the NT, employing the Greek *peripateō*, 'to walk': see Eph. 2:2, 10; 4:1, 17 (×2); 5:2, 8, 15; Col. 1:10; 2:6; 3:7; 4:5; et cetera.

39 'Old person' and 'new person' in Pauline discussions 'do not … speak of a change in nature, but of a change in relationship' – from an old life once subservient to the former authority, sin, to a new one submitting to the current authority, God (Moo, *Epistle to the Romans*, 373). Rather than specific species of anthropological entities, two contradictory and incommensurate ways of living are being indicated by these terms.

will, until the consummation of salvation in the eschaton). The 'body of sin' is the conglomerate of these leftovers, no doubt including the yet-unglorified physical body, as well as the irredeemable flesh (for which see Chapter 3) – both instruments still under the control of the tyrant, sin.[40] However, that entity's authority has been wrested away upon union of the believer with Christ (baptised unto him): the 'old person was co-crucified [with Christ]' (actuality: in the aorist), and the 'body of sin' is being 'inactivated' (potentiality: in the subjunctive).[41] Relieved from control of the evil despot (actuality), day by day, more and more, the believer is now being renewed and living out the baptismal union with Christ (potentiality). The Greek order of the words in Romans 6:6 clarifies this relationship between actuality and potentiality, both the result of a participatory union with Christ in baptism (see Figure 2.7).

'our old person'	
'was co-crucified'	*[participatory actuality]*
'in order that'	
'may be inactivated'	*[participatory potentiality]*
'the body of sin'	

Figure 2.7

Indeed, the first, participatory actuality, happened 'in order that' the second, participatory potentiality, might happen – 'in order … for us to be slaves to sin no longer' (6:6). That actuality is further described in 6:7: the saved person united with Christ has been 'made free *from sin*,'[42]

40 Obviously, Paul is not giving us anatomical or physiological components of the believer's self; it is unproductive to try to determine exactly what part of the person is where, doing what, when and how. For the present discussion it will suffice to consider that the believer no longer is to lead the old way of life (i.e., the 'old person'), but still carrying residues of the fall (encompassed in the 'body of sin').

41 The Greek verb, *katargeō*, translated 'inactivate', can be used with a much stronger sense of complete extinction, but that sense is usually restricted to events happening at the eschaton, as in 1 Cor. 6:13; 13:8, 10, 11; 15:24, 26; Eph. 2:15; 2 Thess. 2:8; 2 Tim. 1:10 (and perhaps 1 Cor. 2:6; 2 Cor. 3:7, 11, 13–14). 'The implication … [of the verb in Rom. 6:6] therefore is not of a final judgement already executed, but of a decisive step taken to "put out of action" … to "render powerless" … now and to ensure final destruction in the end' – an ongoing participatory potentiality because of the believer's union with Christ (Dunn, *Romans 1–8*, 319).

42 The verb translated 'made free from' is the Greek *dikaioō* with the preposition *apo*, 'from'. While it might be rendered 'made righteous from', in this context it likely has the sense of 'make free from' (as in Sir. 26:29; *T. Sim.* 6:1; Acts 13:38–39 [?]), thereby creating that clever parallel between freedom and slavery in Rom. 6:6–7.

as opposed to being 'slaves *to sin*' (6:6). Christ's baptism of believers has a goal, a destiny – 'in order that'[43] they may manifest their positional righteousness of status in their practical righteousness of subsistence, free from slavery to sin. This is what God has destined them for.

In sum, water baptism (i.e., the *literal* sense of the term) is the symbol, the ritual that testifies to the reality of a believer's union with Christ and with fellow believers through baptism (i.e., the *figurative* sense of the term) by Christ in the Holy Spirit and unto himself. Just as the wedding ring is not what marries one, baptism in water is not what saves a person; the former is an outward attestation of marriage and, likewise, the latter is a ritual proclamation and affirmation of baptism in the Spirit, the reality of union with Christ. But lest we forget, water baptism, the ritual, is not to be dismissed as being merely an outward proclamation of an actuality (neither is a wedding ring merely a sign of a changed marital status); it is also a solemn public commitment to a changed life, the potentiality. The apostle further develops this important ramification of union with Christ in the remainder of Romans 6.

> Now if we died with Christ, we believe also that we will co-live [with] Him …
> (Rom. 6:8)

In Romans 6:8 we once again see the participatory actuality in the aorist form of the verb, 'we died with Christ', resulting in the participatory potentiality in the future form, 'we will co-live with Him'. It is because of the former actuality that the latter potentiality is created. Figure 2.8 presents all those actualities (expressed in Greek aorists and perfects) and potentialities (expressed in Greek subjunctives and futures) that we have seen thus far.

> Now if we died with Christ, we believe also that we will co-live [with] Him, recognising that Christ having been raised from the dead is no longer to die; death is no longer lording [over] Him. For

43 Expressed in the Greek as a *hina*-clause.

[when] He died, to sin He died once for all; but [when] He lives, He lives to God.
(Rom. 6:8–10)

Participatory Status in Christ

Verse	Statement	Status
6:4	'we were co-buried' **AORIST**	*Actuality*
	'so we too may walk in newness of life' **SUBJUNCTIVE**	*Potentiality*
6:5	'we have become co-identified [with] the likeness of His death' **PERFECT**	*Actuality*
	'we will also be [co-identified (with) the likeness] of the resurrection' **FUTURE**	*Potentiality*
6:6	'our old person was co-crucified [with Christ]' **AORIST**	*Actuality*
	'in order that the body of sin may be inactivated' **SUBJUNCTIVE**	*Potentiality*
6:8	'we died with Christ' **AORIST**	*Actuality*
	'we will co-live [with] Him' **FUTURE**	*Potentiality*

Figure 2.8

There is an intriguing comparison that Paul makes in 6:8–10 between baptisands' lives, past (pre-union with Christ) and present (post-union with Christ), and with Christ's life, past (pre-death) and present (post-death). Before his resurrection, Christ *was* affected by sin: he bore it and he was susceptible to its sentence of death ('death … lording over Him' [6:9], though sinless himself). And similarly (at least as far as the comparison will allow), the past lives of believers were conducted 'in sin' (6:1–2), as 'slaves to sin' and as agents of sin (6:6–7): *in toto*, they were under the total control of this evil authority. Therefore, like Christ, they, too, were condemned by the sentence of death (6:1–2, 6).[44]

44 Spiritual death had already happened to fallen humans (as we have seen); physical death would inevitably follow for each of them.

But, Christ, after his resurrection in glory, is no longer vulnerable to the effects of sin ('Christ … is no longer to die' [6:9], for 'He died once for all' [6:10]): the death he suffered, as he bore the condemnation of the law for the sins of humanity, no longer had any overlordship of Christ after he rose again. And likewise (and the comparison can only go so far), for believers who have been united with Christ in baptism, there is the participatory potential of living anew in accord with God's demand for holiness, no longer under the tyranny of sin. Just as Christ 'lives to God' (6:10), no longer under the 'lording' of sin leading to death, so also believers are to live to God, free of the dictatorship of sin over their lives – free, enslaved no more![45]

Indeed, carrying the comparison between the death of Christ and that of his faithful ones further, Paul strikingly describes Jesus' death as being 'to sin' (6:10), using exactly the same phrase that he uses for believers' vicarious death (by virtue of their union to Christ): their death was also 'to sin' (6:2, 11). Thus, Christ both died *for sin* (unique to him: his atoning work) and also *to sin*, and in this latter aspect, he becomes the paradigm for believers, for they, too, have 'died to sin'.

Romans 6:11–13 develops the consequences for such a death and resurrection that believers share with the Lord they are united with in baptism.

> So you too consider yourselves [to] dead to sin, but living to God in Christ Jesus. Therefore let sin not rule in your death-destined body unto obedience to its desires, and do not be presenting your members to sin as instruments of unrighteousness, but present yourselves to God as those living from the dead, and your members to God as instruments of righteousness.
> (Rom. 6:11–13)

The apostle summarises the takeaway for believers baptismally identified with Christ with a 'so you too …': they also are to consider themselves

45 Though eternal death of believers is obviated by their union with Christ, physical death is still an agony that every human has to undergo. But, one day, the child of God will be removed forever from this harrowing remnant of the fall too, indeed even from the very presence of sin: 'we shall be like Him [Christ]' with glorified bodies (1 John 3:2). It is this 'not yet' aspect of salvation that necessitates a potential and partial, rather than an actual and complete, comparison of believers' current lives with that of their Saviour, Jesus Christ.

'dead to sin' but 'living to God' (6:11[46]) – the same notions that had been used to describe Christ's death and life in 6:10. The Christian is not to 'consider'[47] *sin* dead, but only to 'consider' *oneself* dead to sin (as Christ himself is to sin; 6:10). The dethroning of that evil authority, sin, is not in the portfolio of believers; that overthrow has already been accomplished. Now they are only asked to manifest that defeat and demonstrate that coup by their new lives manifesting their union with Christ in baptism. Never are the children of God to seek to win their own freedom (self-medication) from the enslavement of that nefarious ruler. That liberty (cure) has already been achieved through Christ, but it has to become 'real-ised' or actualised in their lives. That is to say, believers 'living to God in Christ Jesus' (6:11) – united with him in baptism by Christ, in the Spirit, unto his body – are to 'consider' the truth that they are no longer under the inevitable control of the erstwhile reigning lord and false authority, sin, that was manifesting its reign in their '[once-]death-destined body'.[48] Not that they *cannot* sin, but that they do not *have to* sin.

Earlier we discussed the two authorities ruling in two distinct domains: that of God and that of sin/Satan. The transfer of believers from the latter realm to the former one was accomplished by the work of Christ and applied to them at their union with Christ (Gal. 3:27–29). Now believers are dead to the old authority, sin, and alive to the new authority, God. No longer enslaved to that evil and false authority, baptisands are henceforth to manifest their liberty in Christ, living in the control of the good and true authority, God (see Figure 2.9).

The influence of the despotic ruler results in sins; the influence of the divine ruler results in righteousness. It is so that the latter regency may prevail that believers have been united with Christ – baptised unto him. And it is only by this new life of righteousness, overcoming the insalubrious effects of the disease of the fall, that humans can glorify God – their destiny since the day of creation. So how then are they to live glorifying God?

46 Likely another pair: participatory actuality ('dead [adjective] to sin') and participatory potentiality ('living [present participle] unto God').

47 I.e., to reckon with that truth.

48 Or 'mortal' body, but I wanted us to be reminded that the Greek adjective *thnētos*, 'mortal', is closely related to *thanatos*, 'death'; hence: 'death-destined body' (this also shows up in 8:11; and there is 'death-destined flesh' in 2 Cor. 4:11).

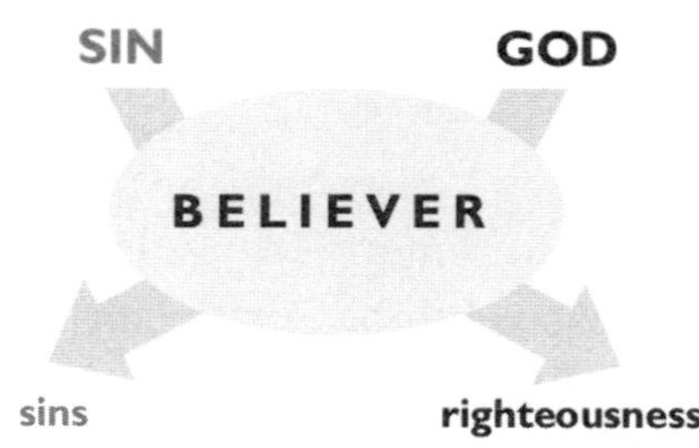

Figure 2.9

Despite the defeat of sin by the work of the Lord Jesus Christ, the triumph of salvation in all of its phases will be consummated only in eternity, and therefore there is still the possibility that believers may, in their earthly lives here and now, allow the evil authority to lord over them,[49] though they do not have to. So baptisands are given a choice and a responsibility: 'they must not let sin go on reigning unopposed over their daily life, but must revolt in the name of their rightful ruler, God, against sin's usurping rule'.[50] Those united to Christ in baptism are to *not* present their body parts to sin and to sin's rule as its tools and devices working sins; rather they are to present themselves to God and to God's rule as his agents and entities working righteousness (Rom. 6:13). And all this because of their baptismal union with Christ and the potentiality of new life resulting therefrom. Indeed, it is because this new life is a potentiality (and not an inevitable actuality[51]) that this warning shows up: believers are to work daily to make that participatory potentiality a participatory actuality, increasingly manifesting that newness of life in Christ, moment by moment, day by day (6:12).[52] This living for Christ under the authority of God gets a summative assessment:

---

49 Through the 'flesh', for the workings of which, see Chapter 3. And, of course, the final comeuppance of Satan and his hordes is also yet to happen, explaining their ongoing baleful leverage over believers.

50 Cranfield, *Critical and Exegetical Commentary*, 1: 316–17.

51 Not till eternity future.

52 I am with Dunn on this: 'Moral effort is in no way antithetical to faith; it is rather the outworking and expression of faith' (*Romans*, 350 [italics removed]), notwithstanding the fact that divine effort significantly aids human effort, by means of the Holy Spirit (more on that from Romans 8, in Chapter 3 of this work).

> For sin will not lord [over] you, for you are not under law but under grace.
> (Rom. 6:14)

The possibility of living a new life for Christ, dead to sin and body parts dedicated to God for righteousness, is spelled out as a participatory potentiality in the future: 'sin will not lord [over] you'. Paul's employment of the verb 'lord', the Greek *kyrieuō*, is hardly accidental; it hints at the true *kyrios*, the 'Lord', of the believer. Of course, that contrast between the two authorities, the evil 'lord', sin, and the good 'Lord', has already been made.

But there is a crux in 6:14: the declaration that believers are 'not under law but under grace'. It is highly unlikely that Paul is deprecating the OT law here.[53] After all, it is *God's* Law (3:2; 7:22, 25; 8:7; 9:4; Gal. 3:19), so how could it be bad, overruled or abolished? Cranfield describes the common understanding of the law as being abrogated as a 'modern version of Marcionism' that regards biblical history as 'an unsuccessful first attempt on God's part at dealing with man's unhappy state [by giving the law], which had to be followed later by a second (more successful) attempt [by removing the law]' – a 'theologically grotesque' view.[54] A more viable option is to see 'under law' here in Romans 6:14 as shorthand for 'under [the condemnation of] law' for sin – the law's condemnation of the sinner to death, the 'sting' of sin (1 Cor. 15:56).[55] So for Paul to say in Romans 6:14 that believers are 'not under law' means that they are no longer under its condemnation for sin (sin = breaking of the law; 8:1 affirms Christians' freedom from this condemnation). In other words, 'as those living from the dead' (6:13) – i.e., as those who are no longer dead, as they effectively were while 'under [the condemnation of]

53 For the apostle's positive view of the law in this epistle, see 2:12–13, 17–18, 20, 25–27; 3:21, 31; 7:12, 14, 16; 8:4; 13:8–10. Besides, Paul frequently appealed to various individual OT laws in his letters (Rom. 7:7; 13:8–10; 1 Cor. 9:8–9; 14:21; Gal. 5:14; Eph. 6:1–3; 1 Tim. 5:18; for such citations elsewhere in the NT, see Jas. 2:8, 11; 1 Pet. 1:15–16; et cetera).

54 Cranfield, *Critical and Exegetical Commentary*, 1: 862.

55 Cranfield, *Critical and Exegetical Commentary*, 1: 320. Other texts that seem to be negative about law, but are in actuality referring only to the condemnation thereof for sin, include: Rom. 7:9–11; 1 Cor. 9:20; 2 Cor. 3:6–9; Gal. 3:13, 23; 4:4–5, 21; 5:18. Also see Rom. 4:15 for a statement about the law resulting in divine wrath; clearly this is also the condemnation pronounced in the law for sin. For a detailed exposition of the relationship between the Christian and biblical law, see Kuruvilla, *'Applicable,' not 'Obeyable.'*

law' for sin, but as those who are alive because they are now 'under [the deliverance of] grace' from sin – they are no longer under the lordship of sin (6:14).[56] Altogether one may conclude that 'not under law' in 6:14 does not indicate the abandonment of the law *qua* law (as divine demand from God dictating how his children should live, in accordance with his own character[57]). Rather, a contrast is being made between those 'under law' who were therefore once dead (because of the condemnation of law) and those 'under grace' who are now alive (because of deliverance from the condemnation of the law by the gracious work of God in Christ).[58]

This is a good place to stop and survey the entirety of 6:1–14 with its carefully balanced structure (see Figure 2.10). It is bookended on either side by 'what then …' (6:1a, 15a) and by 'grace' (6:1b, 14b). This extended section begins with a bemused exclamation by Paul about believers living in sin (*A*), followed by an incredulous question about believers being unknowing about their union with Christ in baptism (*B*). At the centre of the scheme is a christological segment (*C*), itself centring upon the 'walk in newness of life' (6:4b), which is the force of the apostle's argument in 6:1–14. This new 'walk' is surrounded on either side by notations of the death and resurrection of Jesus Christ, the ground and basis for that new life. This segment is followed by a statement about the ramifications of knowing about this work of Christ (*B′*, echoing 'death' as in *B*), and the chiasm concludes with an exhortation about how believers, therefore, ought to live (*A′*).[59]

---

56 That 'death' lorded over Christ once (6:9) also substantiates this reading: it was as the Saviour bore law's *condemnation* for the sins of humanity that 'death' become master over him; but once atonement for sins was made, and condemnation of the law paid in full, death had no hold upon Christ. There is also 7:6 that asserts that by the Lord's atoning work, believers themselves 'have been released from the law, having died to that by which we were being held'. That is to say, they were (like Christ) once subject to the law's condemnation as sinners, but now have gained their freedom by their vicarious death in Christ by which they have been 'released from the law['s condemnation]', under which 'we were being held'.

57 See Chapter 4, where God's 'righteous requirement' (Rom. 8:4) is found to be synonymous with divine demand.

58 That 'death' (both *thanatos* and *nekros*, as well as their cognates) occurs 21× in Romans 6 (only 10× in Romans 7, and 9× in Romans 8), leads one to further equate the antithesis of 'under law' vs 'under grace' in 6:14 with the corresponding antithesis of dead (because condemned, and dead like Christ who bore the law's condemnation) vs living (because delivered, and enlivened like Christ who was resurrected).

59 Also see, for a somewhat similar chiastic structure, Gonzalez, 'Romans 6:1–14', 73–4. All the words derived from 'die' reflect the Greek root, *thanatos*, except as noted. Parallel elements in the various sections of the structure are denoted by italics.

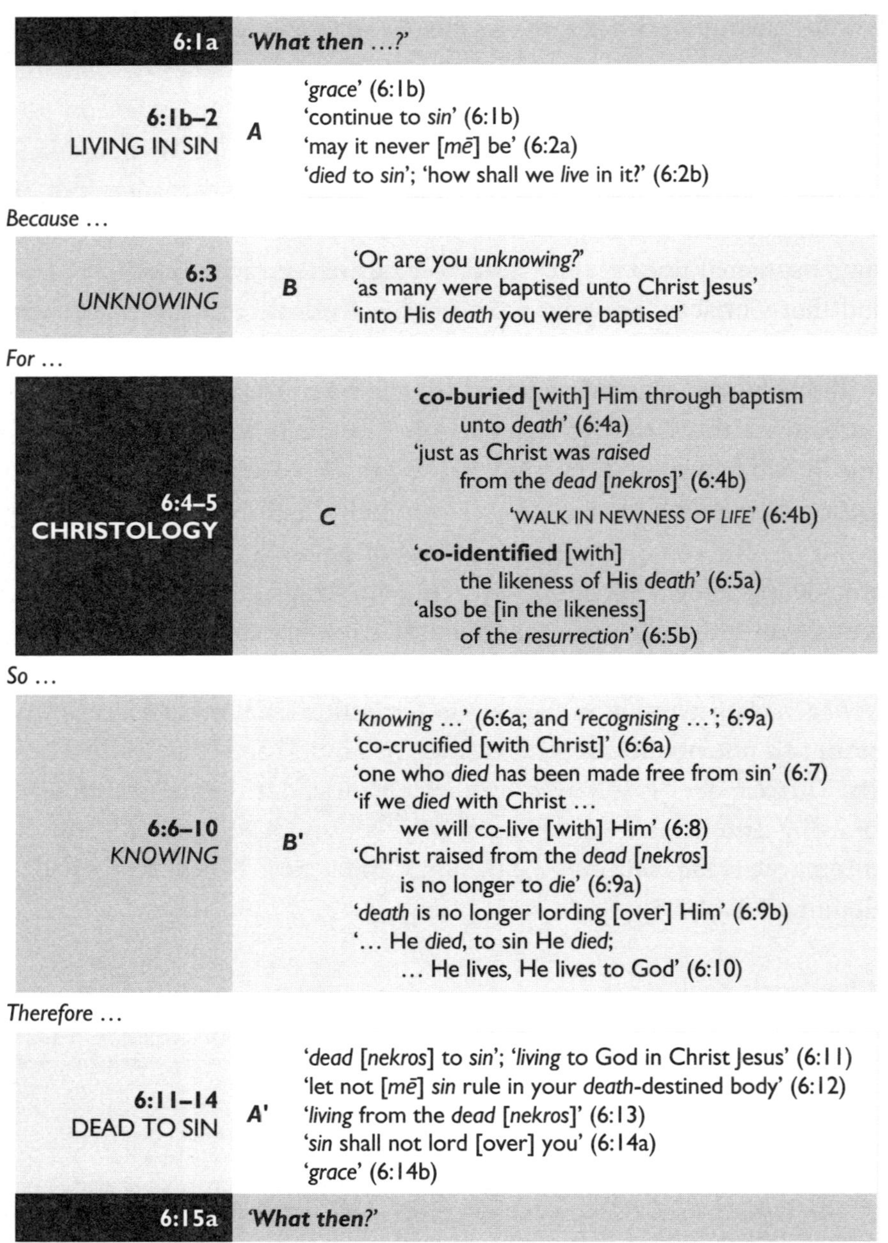

Figure 2.10

The section, 6:1–14, is almost narratival, as I have attempted to show by the italicised words linking each segment in Figure 2.10 and the paraphrase of Paul below:

> If you have experienced the grace of salvation, how can you 'continue to sin' to 'live in it'? *Because,* 'are you unknowing' that you have been united with Christ when you were 'baptised'? *For,* that union with Christ involves being 'co-buried [with] Him' and 'co-identified' with Him – with His 'death' as well as with his 'resurrection' [participatory *actuality*]. *So*, you should be 'knowing' of your baptismal union with Christ – 'co-crucified [with Christ]' – and that Christ is 'no longer' susceptible to 'death lording [over] Him', and that he 'lives to God'. *Therefore,* you, too, should 'co-live [with] Him', for 'sin shall not lord [over] you'; instead, because of God's 'grace' that has delivered you from the condemnation for sins, you should be yielding yourself to God for 'righteousness' [participatory *potentiality*].

In other words, the potential to glorify God by living to him – the capacity that was lost in the fall – has now been restored to believing humanity, because of the work of Christ. It is the responsibility of believers (in the power of the Spirit and by the agency of Scripture; see Chapters 3 and 4) to make this potentiality an actuality.

The new life of the baptised (Rom. 6:15–23)

Beginning at 6:15, Paul comes full circle, returning to where he had started in 6:1, with a question and a vehement 'No!' in answer:

> What then? Shall we sin because we are not under law but under grace? May it never be!
> (Rom. 6:15)

In 6:1 the apostle's strong negation reflected his disagreement that 'where sin increased, grace multiplied even more' (5:20). In other words, one should absolutely not remain in sin in order that grace may abound. But here in 6:15, his rebuttal is in response to a potential misunderstanding of his acknowledgement that 'we are not under law' (6:14, 15) and that, therefore, baptisands united with Christ can keep on sinning in their new life disregarding divine demand (God's law).[60] Most certainly not, the apostle expostulates. He then proceeds to underscore the importance of believers' new lives lived in obedience to God and to his law whereby they fulfil the human destiny to live changed lives (and thus glorify deity, as we will see).

> Do you not know that the one to whom you are presenting yourselves as slaves unto obedience – slaves you are to the one you are obeying, either of sin unto death or of obedience unto righteousness?
> (Rom. 6:16)

We have already seen the two authorities over humankind: the evil one, sin, and the good one, God. Humanity, Paul declares, is always under one or the other, subject either to sin or to God. Being a slave to sin results in death (for unsaved humans). But there has been a dramatic change for the saved. They are now united with Christ by baptism. Therefore, the authority to which they submit has now shifted from sin to God. Here in 6:16, the antithesis of enslavement to sin (the lot of the unsaved) is enslavement to obedience (the lot of the saved): 'slaves … of sin unto death' vs 'slaves … of obedience unto righteousness'.[61] It is incumbent upon these baptisands to be obedient to God, 'unto righteousness', i.e., becoming progressively righteous as they are sanctified.[62]

> But thanks [be] to God that [though] you were slaves of sin, yet from the heart you were obedient to the form of teaching to which you were handed over, and having been freed from sin, you were enslaved to righteousness.
> (Rom. 6:17–18)

60 That misunderstanding is not rare in the modern day: the law is abolished! (Though, of course, those subscribing to that misconstrual would never advocate sinning as did the apostle's hypothetical interlocutor[s].)

61 No doubt the thralldoms of believers, to obedience (6:16) and to righteousness (6:16, 18), are equivalent manifestations of enslavement ultimately to God, the good authority (6:22).

62 This 'righteousness' is not the divine declaration of righteousness of 6:7 – justification, positional righteousness that is already the possession of baptisands. Rather, this refers to the ongoing process of holiness – sanctification, practical righteousness that is, hopefully, being increasingly attained throughout life.

And it was to increasingly manifest this bondage to righteousness in their new lives that these erstwhile slaves of sin in their old lives were 'handed over' to the teaching of another authority, God, so that they may be obedient from the heart (6:17), thus becoming progressively sanctified.[63]

One has by now noticed the flexibility in Paul's use of 'righteousness': besides being an obvious antonym to 'unrighteousness' (6:13), it is also directly opposed to 'sin' (6:18; and see 6:20[64]), to 'death' (6:16), and to 'impurity' and 'lawlessness' (6:19). As well, it appears to be equivalent to 'God' (see 6:22). Thus, 'righteousness' is effectively a metonym for all that is happening to the believer in the process of sanctification, culminating in eternal life.[65] This – the sanctification of those in union with Christ by baptism – is the focus of the remainder of Romans 6; in fact, the theme of sanctification is continued further through Romans 7 and 8.

In sum, humans are always slaves, to one lord or to another Lord. The question is: Who will be their master? Paul continues:

> (I speak in human terms because of the weakness of your flesh.) (Rom. 6:19a)

Presumably, Paul's parenthetical apology in 6:19a is for his ironic mixing of metaphors – images of slavery to sin with those of slavery to righteousness, as well as images of freedom from sin with those of freedom from righteousness (6:18–22).[66] But the contrast between the two kinds of slavery is clear in 6:19b–22:

63 'Form of teaching' refers to the teaching that is to be obeyed, that will result in righteousness and sanctification, i.e., divine demand (or, as we will see in 8:4, God's 'righteous requirement'). Schreiner, *Romans*, 336, suggests that the word 'form' was used to qualify teaching because this instruction '"molds," "shapes," and "transforms" those who are delivered over to it'.

64 There is also 5:21, that opposes 'grace may reign through *righteousness* unto eternal life' to '*sin* reigned [implied: "through unrighteousness"] in death'.

65 See Dunn, *Romans*, 335.

66 The 'weakness of … flesh' combined with 'human terms' indicates that Paul is referring to an incapacity to understand on the part of his addressees – not necessarily the result of a moral failure as 'flesh' later in the epistle connotes. This failure of comprehension moved the apostle to stretch everyday language to limits that seemed almost contradictory, necessitating his excuse in 6:19a.

> For just as you presented your members as slaves to impurity and to lawlessness unto [further] lawlessness, so now present your members as slaves to righteousness unto sanctification. For when you were slaves to sin, you were free to righteousness. Therefore what fruit did you have then from the things you are now ashamed of? For the outcome of those things is death. But now having been freed from sin and enslaved to God, you have your fruit unto sanctification, and the outcome, life eternal.
> (Rom. 6:19b–22)

On the one hand, slavery to sin becomes even more sinful ('lawlessness unto [further] lawlessness'); on the other, slavery to righteousness becomes even more righteous ('righteousness unto sanctification'). This contrast is further depicted in 6:20–22 in terms of 'fruit' and 'outcome' (see Figure 2.11).[67]

	Status		'Fruit'	'Outcome'
6:20–21	*Then:*	'slaves to sin' 'free to [or "from"] righteousness'	shame	death
6:22	*Now:*	'freed from sin' 'enslaved to God'	sanctification	eternal life

Figure 2.11

Needless to say, sanctification culminating in eternal life (the trajectory of *Now*) ought to be the ongoing life-pattern of the believer (and not that of *Then*).[68] And so Paul ends the chapter with another encouragement:

> For the wages of sin is death, but the gift of God is life eternal in Christ Jesus our Lord.
> (Rom. 6:23)

The evil employer, sin, doles out dues – death; but the good Creator, God, grants the gift – eternal life, not a wage earned but a donation of grace.

67 Modified from Moo, *Epistle to the Romans*, 407.

68 Of course, eternal life is assured. But whether sanctification happens in this life, or how much of it happens, is contingent.

In sum, sinners, slaves to sin, were effectively dead by the condemnation pronounced by the law. But believers, united with Christ in baptism, are now enslaved to God, made alive. The destiny of such Christ-united baptisands and the goal of God's deliverance is that these saved (cured) ones, now headed for eternal life, increasingly bear the fruit of righteousness in the process of ongoing sanctification – their destiny. Then, and only then, are they able to fulfil their God-ordained design to glorify God.

Destination good works (Eph. 2:8–10)

What does this 'fruit unto sanctification' (Rom. 6:22) look like in the lives of those united with Christ in baptism? Returning to Ephesians 2 will provide some specificity to those products of righteousness. As we have already seen, this chapter commenced with how these saved ones used to 'walk' in their unsaved state of death:

> And while you were dead in your transgressions and sins, in which you formerly *walked* according to the course of this world, according to the ruler of the authority of the air, [the ruler] of the spirit that is now working in the sons of disobedience.
> (Eph. 2:1–2)

But now notice how 2:10 ends this section – with another 'walk' prescribed for the people of God:

> ... for His workmanship we are, having been created in Christ Jesus for good works that God prepared beforehand, in order that we may *walk* in them.
> (Eph. 2:10)

Thus 2:1–10, that began with how they once used to 'walk' in their unsaved state (2:1–2), concludes with how they now should 'walk' in their saved state (2:10) – doing 'good works'. The parallels between the two walks are unmistakable (in the Greek order of the words) (see Figure 2.12).

Thus, 'good works' in 2:10 is the diametric opposite of 'transgressions

2:1–2	'in transgressions and sins	*in* [*en*] which	you formerly *walked*'
2:10	'for good works	... *in* [*en*] them	we may *walk*'

Figure 2.12

and sins' in 2:1.[69] In other words, God saves humankind from one sphere of living (in sin, under its evil authority) to another (doing good works, under divine authority), i.e., to be 'holy and blameless' (1:4). The destiny of God's people to be holy in new living, that we saw in Romans 6, is now further specified as the doing of good works.[70] This is the goal of God's redemption, so that through these good works God may be glorified (as we will see) – thus accomplishing the ultimate end of all things and the fulfilment of God's original design. In other words, though salvation is not '*of* works' (Eph. 2:9), salvation is '*for* works' (2:10). Works are not the ground of salvation, but the goal thereof – salvation's fruit, not its root; salvation's effect, not its cause.

What exactly are 'good works', and how do they relate to this new life of those united with Christ in baptism, to result in the glory of God? The term is common in Scripture.[71] In Matthew 5:16, the people of God are exhorted to perform good works:

> 'In this way, let your light shine before people, in such a way that they may see your *good works* ...'
> (Matt. 5:16)

'In this way' follows immediately after the Beatitudes that pronounce blessedness upon God's people who respond in a variety of ways to a variety of life situations by their dispositions (poverty of spirit, mourning, yearning for righteousness, purity of heart and suffering of persecution)

69 There is also the contrast of an evil one influencing non-Christians ('ruler of the authority of the air' and of the 'spirit that is now working in the sons of disobedience', 2:2) with a good One influencing believers ('His workmanship we are, having been created for good works that God prepared beforehand', 2:10).

70 A *hina* ['in order that']-clause in 2:10 makes this purpose of redemption clear.

71 Particularly so in the Pastoral Epistles. In these letters, it occurs in a variety of verbal forms in 1 Tim. 2:10; 3:1; 5:10a, 10b, 25; 6:2, 18a, 18b; 2 Tim. 2:21; 3:17; Titus 1:16; 2:7, 14; 3:1, 8, 14 (and Titus 2:5, which describes doers of 'good works'). Thus, every chapter of Titus and almost every chapter of the two epistles to Timothy contain the concept in some form or other. See Kuruvilla, *1 and 2 Timothy, Titus*.

and by their deeds (of gentleness, mercifulness and peacemaking) (Matt. 5:3–9).[72] But good works consist not only of dispositions and deeds; Titus 3:8–9 expands the category to include discourses, too:

> … these things I want you to confidently assert, so that those who have believed God will be careful to engage in *good works*. These things are good and profitable for people. But avoid foolish controversies and genealogies and strife and quarrels about the law, for they are unprofitable and futile.
> (Titus 3:8–9)

Stressing the importance of God's people engaging in 'good works' that are 'good and profitable' (3:8), Paul describes other undertakings that are, instead, 'unprofitable and futile', such as 'foolish controversies', 'genealogies', 'strife' and 'quarrels about the law' – all dealing with discourses that are markers of evil works (see Figure 2.13).[73]

	Exhortation	Object	Value
3:8	'be careful [*proistēmi*]'	'good works'	'good' and 'profitable'
3:9	'avoid [*periistēmi*]'	worthless 'strife' [= evil works]	'futile' and 'unprofitable'

Figure 2.13

Likewise, one may also comprehend the nature of 'good works' from 2 Timothy 2:21:

> Therefore, if anyone purifies himself from these things, he will be a vessel for honour, being made holy, beneficial for the Master, prepared for every *good work*.
> (2 Tim. 2:21)

72 Elsewhere, good works are also depicted as dispositions and deeds ('doing good') towards enemies (Luke 6:33–35), and when being treated harshly (1 Pet. 2:20); they include other kinds of deeds, as well (in 3:16–17).

73 Besides two adjectives in the value column that are antonyms, there is also the clever deployment of two verbs in the exhortation section that are both derived from the same root, *histēmi*.

The 'these things' from which such a 'good work-er' must be purified were listed in the preceding verses, 2:16–18, as 'profane empty chatter' and 'word[s]' that 'eat away like gangrene'. So again, discourses are also part of good works. But in the following verse, 2:22, the apostle adds that 'youthful lusts' must be fled from, too, and that, instead, one is to 'pursue righteousness, faith, love, peace'. Thereby, good works also include dispositions (and probably corresponding deeds, as well).

Elsewhere, Paul commends the wealthier individuals in Timothy's congregation to 'do good' and to be rich in 'good works … generous and sharing' (1 Tim. 6:18). Also notice that the office of overseer in 1 Timothy 3:1 is itself recognised as a 'good work' – all indicating deeds as integral constituents of good works. Then, in 1 Timothy 5:9–10, Paul approves of putting godly women on the list of widows, i.e., those with …

> … a testimony for *good works*, if she has raised children, if she has practised hospitality to strangers, if she has washed saints' feet, if she has aided the afflicted, if she has pursued every *good work*.
> (1 Tim. 5:10)

Notice how the apostle begins and ends the list with 'good work(s)', with the items in between indicating what those are (see Figure 2.14).

'having a testimony for ***good works***'
'raised children'
'practised hospitality to strangers'
'washed saints' feet'
'aided the afflicted'
'pursued every ***good work***'

Figure 2.14

Putting it all together, then, good works include dispositions, deeds and discourses, and these good works please God:

> … walk worthy of the Lord, pleasing him in all things, in all *good work* bearing fruit and growing in the knowledge of God, empowered in all power according to His glorious might.
> (Col. 1:10–11)

This delight of God in 'all' things, i.e., in 'all' the fruit-bearing good works of believers strengthened by 'all' power of God's 'glorious might', signifies the importance of these good works comprehensively engaged in by the children of God.[74] Likewise, 1 Peter 2:15 declares that 'good works' (also described here in parallel as 'doing good', in contrast to what '*evil*doers' engage in) is unequivocally 'the will of God':[75]

> Beloved, I exhort you … to abstain from lusts of the flesh which war against the soul. Keep your behaviour among the Gentiles good, in order that, though they slander you as evildoers, from observing your good works they may glorify God … For such is the will of God – by *doing good* to silence the ignorance of foolish people.
> (1 Pet. 2:11–12, 15)

A summative understanding of good works in the NT thus involves dispositions, deeds and discourses. In thought, in word and in deed, God's people are to manifest good works, the will of God that brings pleasure to God. This is the essence of new life in Christ, their destiny.

> [Jesus Christ] gave Himself for us in order that He may redeem us from all lawlessness and purify for Himself a people for His very own, zealous for *good works*.
> (Titus 2:14)

Once again we see the goal of God's salvation – the destiny of believers: to manifest 'good works'.[76] Paul reiterates later in Titus that good works have to be an outcome of conversion:

---

74 Note also that these good works are performed in the power of God ('His glorious might'); this notion of divine empowerment for the new life and destiny of believers will be addressed in Chapter 3.

75 Evidently the 'lusts of the flesh' of 'evildoers' (1 Pet. 2:11) are being contrasted to the 'good' behaviour of God's people – i.e., their '*good* works' and their 'doing *good*'. (In fact, 'doing good' also meets with the approbation of civic rulers; 2:14.)

76 Note that the contrast in Titus 2:14 is between 'lawlessness' and 'good works', where one might have expected 'lawfulness'. No doubt, then, 'good works' = 'lawfulness'. Thus, to do good works is what it means to be obedient to divine will = lawfulness (what I have elsewhere called 'faith-full obedience'; see Kuruvilla, *Privilege the Text!*, 151–209; also see Chapter 4 of the current work). The passage continues in 2:15–3:1, reiterating the importance of good works and impressing upon leaders the gravity and priority of preaching every 'good work'

> ... when the kindness and mankind-love of God our Saviour appeared, He saved us, not by works which we ourselves did in righteousness, but according to His mercy ... *in order that*, being made righteous by His grace, we might be made heirs according to the hope of eternal life. This statement is trustworthy; and concerning these things I want you to confidently assert, *in order that* that those who have believed God may be careful to engage in *good works*.
> (Titus 3:4–8)

Thus the apostle makes the point that though 'works' do not save, salvation should lead to 'good works' (a notion we have already established from Eph. 2:8–10). So as described in Titus 3:4–8 salvation in Christ (justification) has two outcomes: relating to life in the hereafter and to life in the here-and-now, as noted by the duplicated 'in order that'-clauses: 'in order that ... we might be made heirs according to the hope of eternal life' (3:7; in the future: glorification), and 'in order that those who have believed God may be careful to engage in good works' (3:8; in the present: sanctification). The apostle then summarises the section, once again urging 'good works' to be manifested by God's people – it is these that make them fruitful, fulfilling the destiny for which they were called (3:14):[77]

> Now our people must also learn to engage in *good works* to meet pressing needs, in order that they may not be unfruitful.
> (Titus 3:14)

That doing good works is to be an essential and integral part of the life of the Christian can, therefore, not be understated. The apostle John creates an antithesis between 'the one doing evil' and 'the one doing

in the body of Christ: 'These things speak and urge and reprove with all authority. Let no one disregard you. Remind them ... to be ready for every *good work* (3:1).

77 Here the focus is on deeds, 'to meet pressing needs', no doubt because of the exigencies of the context of Titus 3, where Paul is dealing with behaviour in society (3:1–15; see Kuruvilla, *1 and 2 Timothy, Titus*, 222–9). At any rate, the *hina* ['in order that']-clause in 3:14 once again points to the critical role of good works in rendering one fruitful.

good' emphasising the importance of good works (and the seriousness of neglecting them):

> Beloved, do not imitate what is evil, but what is good. *The one who does good*, he is of God; the one doing evil, he has not seen God.
> (3 John 1:11)

That is quite a declaration: only 'the one doing good' is 'of God' and 'has seen God'! What an indictment of those *not* engaging in good works, and a powerful inducement to God's children to undertake them. Good works, in the form of dispositions, discourses and deeds, are therefore incontrovertibly essential to the economy of God; their performance is the destiny of every believer united to Christ in baptism. And it is the means by which God is glorified – his divine design and ultimate goal for his creation. Jesus himself declared it to be the case, as we have already seen:

> 'In this way, let your light shine before people, in such a way that they may see your *good works*, and glorify your Father, the One in heaven.'
> (Matt. 5:16)

Not to mention other writers in the NT who come to the same conclusion:

> For this also we pray always for you, in order that our God may count you worthy of [your] calling, and fulfil [your] every desire of *goodness* and the *work* of faith with power, by which the name of our Lord Jesus may be glorified in you, and you in Him, according to the grace of our God and the Lord Jesus Christ.
> (2 Thess. 1:11–12)

> Keep your behaviour among the Gentiles good, in order that, though they slander you as evildoers, from observing your *good works* they may glorify God in the day of visitation.
> (1 Pet. 2:12)

> Now may the God of peace, who brought up from the dead the great Shepherd of the sheep through the blood of the eternal covenant,

> Jesus our Lord, equip you in all *good* [things] *to do* His will, [He] doing in us what is pleasing before Him, through Jesus Christ, to whom be glory forever [and forever]. Amen.
> (Heb. 13:20–21)

To reiterate: good works, encompassing dispositions, discourses and deeds, is the destiny of the people of God and the reason why they were united to Christ by baptism.[78] And thus is the design of God realised – his glory. No wonder Paul advocates that a child of God be 'an example of good works' (Titus 2:7). With the deliverance of salvation comes the restoration of the capacity to glorify God that was lost in the fall. Now, by the grace of God that saved believers and united them to Christ (as they were baptised by Christ, in the Spirit, unto himself), that ability has been reconstituted, and now ought to be manifested in their new lives of sanctification, in the form of good works!

Needless to say, such fruit-bearing and sanctification in the form of good works is accomplished by humans only by a divine operation of grace, for God it is who has 'prepared beforehand' those 'good works' for his chosen to perform, as Ephesians 2:10 asserts. That God's grace is involved in both justification (2:8–9) and sanctification (2:10) is clear from the syntax of 2:8–10: notice the parallel statements employing 'for' and 'so that' (see Figure 2.15), both pairs of utterances expounding the great and abounding grace of God in Christ to his people (2:7) so that they may accomplish their destiny to do good works.[79]

This is what all humans were created for (as we saw in Chapter 1) – God's design. In fact, the verb used here in 2:10, 'create' (*ktizō*), is employed in Ephesians only of the first creation of the universe (3:9) and for this second creation of a new peoples (2:10, 15; 4:24).[80] The first creation ended up failing to glorify God. Now, with the second creation,

78 See Rom. 6:4, 6; 7:4; 8:3–4; Eph. 2:10; Titus 2:14; 3:4–8, some of which we have already scrutinised; all of them explicate the same notion with identical *hina* ('in order that')-clauses.

79 See Chapter 3 for more on the divine empowerment of good works in sanctification. Believers' glorification, too, is of God's grace, as Eph. 2:6–7 indicates (also see 1 Cor. 1:3–6; 1 Pet. 1:10, 13).

80 Incidentally, the cognate of *ktizō* is also found in Rom. 1:20 as a noun, along with the only other instance of *poiēma* ('workmanship', also in Eph. 2.10) in the NT – both denoting the (first) creation of the universe.

2:7	**'... the surpassing riches of His grace in kindness towards us in Christ Jesus'**
2:8	'*for* [*gar*] by grace you have been saved through faith'
2:9	'*in order that* [*hina*] no one may boast'
2:10a	'*for* [*gar*] His workmanship we are, having been created ... for good works'
2:10b	'*in order that* [*hina*] we may walk in them'

Figure 2.15

saved believers, united to Christ in baptism, have been granted the ability to glorify God by good works (cured from the affliction of the fall). The construction in 2:10 is quite emphatic that this is God's doing – 'for his workmanship we are'. God is certainly doing an amazing thing to fulfil his divine design for glory. And the role of believers in this design is nothing less than a participation in the glorification of this great God, through their sanctification, their performance of good works – their destiny.

One might think that all is well that ends well, now that this second creation has happened and believers are rendered once again capable of glorifying God by good works. But one would be wrong in so presuming, because the story is not over yet. All believers are keenly aware that sin continues to be an ever-present reality in their lives – even as they remain in union with Christ post-baptism. Why is that still the case, and what can be done? We will take up this thorny problem and its divinely provided solution in Chapter 3.

3

Spirit

The healer

Teach me to do [what is according to] Your favour,
for You [are] my God;
Your good Spirit, may He lead me on level ground.
... I [am] Your servant.
(Ps. 143:10, 12)

Peter Benjamin Parker, aka Spider-Man, is, in his daily life, Everyman, perhaps even 'Every Christian'. Parker is common born and becomes a superhero not because of anything he has done or aspired to, but because of something that happened to him supernaturally: he was bitten by a radioactive spider. In one issue of the comic series, Spider-Man confesses: 'For whatever I am – whatever I've become – the good – whatever good I've done [is] with the powers fate gave me'.[1]

But he is a flawed individual, afflicted with all kinds of problems: he has trouble paying his bills, he struggles to maintain stable relationships with loved ones and he is plagued by lust and self-aggrandisement. Parker is also cowardly: despite having superpowers, he did nothing to prevent the murder of his Uncle Ben by a criminal, a tragedy that has haunted this hero with shame all his life.[2] But that event dramatically changed (cured?) him. It was after that calamity that Spider-Man decided to use his superpowers to fight crime (his version of 'good works'?). That only provokes his enemies, with one particular demonic

1 Lee, *Amazing Spider-Man* 181: 16. To stretch the theological analogy beyond breaking limits, I have to add that at the grave of his uncle, to whom he owed much, Spider-Man confesses in the same issue: 'You died that Spider-Man might be born.' Also see Richardson, 'Gospel According to *Spider-Man*', 694–703; and Palumbo, 'Marvel Comics Group's Spider-Man', 67–82.

2 Lee, *Amazing Fantasy* 15: 14.

killer, the Green Goblin, tormenting Spider-Man and his family on personal and psychological levels. All this angst makes the arachnid hero's identity crisis constant and intense: 'All my life I've had trouble knowing myself – always wondering who – or what – Spider-Man really is! I've been fighting myself ever since the day I first became Spider-Man.'[3]

This is all not very different from the experience of a saved human. Having been born in, and having lived in, 'transgressions and sins' since the fall of humanity, 'Every Christian' once was, in deviance, incapable of living up to the demand of divine design to glorify God, afflicted with the curse of sin. But the grace and mercy and love and kindness of God worked deliverance, uniting the believer to Christ in baptism – an act entirely of divine initiative, nothing whatsoever to do with the exertions of the baptisand: a divine cure. 'Every Christian' now had a destiny to be sanctified doing good works, and thereby the original creation design was potentially restored: the capacity to glorify God. But the fact is that 'Every Christian' still falls victim to the evil authority, sin, that still has its hooks in that individual who continues to produce sins. This, as we shall see from Romans 7, is the conflicted experience of all believers of all times and in all places.

How does one comport this continuing malignant detriment with the magnificent deliverance that God has already effected? Is there something more that those united with Christ in baptism need in order to do good works that glorify God (rather than the evil works of sin that fail to do so)? Does not the Bible say that '[God's] divine power has given us all things [necessary] for life and godliness' (2 Pet. 1:3)? Whence this power? What is its effect? How will it keep 'Every Christian' from falling prey to the tyranny of sin and sinning? These questions occupy us in Chapter 3.

First, we return to Romans to address the discordant issue of believers in union with Christ, baptised unto him, *but* continuing to sin.

3 Lee, *Amazing Spider-Man* 149: 23.

Discord

As was seen in Chapter 2, the entirety of Romans 6:1–7:6 concerns the issue that Paul introduced with a question in 6:1–2a: 'What then shall we say? Do we remain in sin, in order that grace may increase? May it never be!' Believers cannot remain in sin, Paul emphatically asserted, and then he proceeded to explain why not, giving two reasons, both relating to believers' union with Christ. The first reason, in 6:3–14, began with 'or are you unknowing ...?' (6:3a). There the apostle explained that believers could/should not remain in sin because they had been united with Christ – baptised unto him (employing the picture of baptism). The second reason, in 7:1–6, begins with a verbatim repeat of 6:3a: 'Or are you unknowing ...?' (7:1a), signalling that this section provides another reason why believers ought not to remain in sin: because they are in union with Christ – *bound to* him (employing the picture of marriage). These two explanatory sections parallel each other, as is evident in the structure, questions, illustrative pictures and the common vocabulary employed in 6:3–14 and 7:2–6 (see Figure 3.1). And in between these two reasons for not remaining in sin comes 6:15–23, a strong exhortation to believers to, instead, lead new lives of faithful obedience to God.[4]

Bound to Christ (Rom. 7:1–6)

Let's dive in:

> Or are you unknowing, brothers [and sisters] (for I am speaking to those who know the law), that the law lords over a person as long a time as he lives?
> (Rom. 7:1)

4 The central section, 6:15–23, recapitulates the preceding Reason #1 (6:3–14) with verbal repetitions ('righteous', 6:7; 'unrighteousness', 6:13; and 'righteousness', 6:13, are all carried over as 'righteousness', 6:16, 18, 19, 20). This central section also anticipates the proceeding Reason #2 (7:1–6), also with verbal repetitions ('fruit', 6:21, 22, anticipates 'fruit-bearing', 7:4, 5). Thus, 6:15–23, looking, as it were, both backwards and forwards, serves as the hinge of the larger section 6:1–7:6. That this hinge is integral to the whole is also evident in that it, too, begins with a double question and an asseveration ('What then? ... May it never be!' [6:15], as also do 6:1 and 7:7), and is followed by a third question relating to the knowledge (or lack thereof) on the part of the apostle's readers about a vital truth ('Do you not know ...?' [6:16], as also in 6:3 and 7:1, though different verbs are used in these cases: 'Are you unknowing ...?').

REMAIN IN SIN? NEVER! (6:1–7:6)
'What then shall we say? … *Remain in sin?* … May it never be!' (6:1–2a)

'Or are you unknowing …?' (6:3a)
REASON #1: Union with Christ: Baptised unto Christ (6:3–14)
(*syn* and *syn*-words: 6:4–6, 8)

Picture of baptism (6:3b–4a)
'*died* with Christ' (6:8; see 6:4–10)
'raised from the dead' (6:4b)
'*newness* of life' (6:4c)
'slavery' to sin no longer (6:6)

Exhortation to new life of obedience to God (6:15–23)

'Or are you unknowing …?' (7:1a)
REASON #2: Union with Christ: Bound to Christ (7:1–6)
('another's' / 'another man's': 7:3 [×2], 4)

Picture of marriage (7:1b–3)
'*die* to the law['s condemnation]' (7:4, 6)
'raised from the dead' (7:4)
'*newness* of Spirit' (7:6)
'slavery' to God (7:6)

Figure 3.1

And with that, Paul commences to provide the second reason why believers ought to be living new lives of holiness, commensurate with their cured status in Christ. He starts by returning to a discussion about the sway of the law, something he had already mentioned in 6:14, 15: believers are 'not under law'. We had noted that this meant that believers were no longer under the *condemnation* of the law. The apostle continues with this notion here; in fact, a comparison between 6:1–22 and 7:1–6 confirms our assessment of 'law' as being shorthand for 'law's condemnation' (see Figure 3.2).[5]

The correspondence between 'sin' and 'law['s condemnation]' depicts them as quite equivalent, at least in outcome: 'sin' describes the authority that causes the production of sins; 'law' describes the condemnation incurred as a result of such production of sins. To both 'sin' and to 'law['s condemnation]' believers have died. Both 'sin' and 'law['s condemnation]' have lost their control over the objects upon which they act. Both have

5 See Moo, *Epistle to the Romans,* 409.

'Sin'	'Law['s Condemnation]'
'died to *sin*' (6:2)	'made to die to the *law*' (7:4)
'body of *sin* … inactivated [*katargeō*]' (6:6)	'released [*katargeō*] from the *law*' (7:2, 6)
'*sin* shall not lord [over] you' (6:14)	'*law* lords over a person' only till death (7:1)
'freed from *sin*' (6:18, 22)	'free from the *law*' (7:3)

Figure 3.2

been deposed from their ruling thrones. From both, believers are now freed, united as they are with Christ in baptism. All that to say, the law's condemnation of sin-produced sins has been declawed and defanged, for Christ took on that condemnation of the law – death.

Paul then offers a picture of marriage (corresponding to the picture of baptism he had given in Romans 6:3b–4a), to explain the second reason why believers ought not to remain in sin:

> For the married woman is bound by law to her living husband; but if her husband dies, she is released from the law of the husband. Then therefore, while her husband is living, if she becomes another man's, she shall be called an adulteress; but if the husband dies, she is free from the law, not to be an adulteress when becoming another man's. Therefore, my brothers [and sisters], you also were made to die to the law by the body of Christ, in order that you may become another's, of the One raised from the dead …
> (Rom. 7:2–4a)

At its core, the illustrative example conveys the principle that death, when it affects one who is under a particular law, nullifies the hold of that law upon its subject. But scholars have had a tough time reconciling and making congruent the illustrative picture with the corresponding theological reality. So a reassessment is in order, and it will lead us to a better understanding of Paul's second reason why believers ought not to remain in sin.[6]

6 And, as well, it will generate a greater appreciation of this marvellous piece of inspired writing by the apostle. I, therefore, start my interpretation of this text (indeed, of any text)

Let's scrutinise 7:1–6 carefully. First things first: there are only two individuals in 7:1–6 who *physically* die – the 'husband' (7:2, 4) and Christ (indicated by 'body'[7] and by being named as the one who is 'raised from the dead', 7:4).[8] This being the case, we have ground to equate these two deceased individuals – the 'husband' who dies and Christ who died. It goes further: the death of the 'husband' released the woman from 'the law of the husband' (7:2; i.e., the condemnation of civic law for adultery), and the death of Christ released believers from the law of God (i.e., the condemnation of divine law for sin), because they were 'made to die to the law by the body of Christ' (7:4) (see Figure 3.3).[9]

Illustrative Example (7:2–3)	Theological Reality (7:4)
'Husband' dies, releasing 'woman' from 'the law of the husband' (i.e., civic law's condemnation of adultery).	Christ dies, releasing believers from the law of God (i.e., divine law's condemnation of sin).

Figure 3.3

Then there is the woman: she, who was unfaithful to her living husband, was condemned by civic law as an 'adulteress' (Greek *moichalis*; 7:3). This is quite similar to the case of all humanity being unfaithful to Yahweh their Creator since the fall, and to their being condemned by divine law as 'adulteresses' against God.[10] This now makes Yahweh equivalent to the 'living husband'; but we have already seen Christ as equivalent to the 'husband' who died. Of course, since Christ is a Person of the Trinitarian

---

with a first instinct of charity to the author, and assume his illustration fits precisely with the reality he is talking about. My claim here is that, while illustrations, being what they are, can never be a perfect analogy, the reading of the illustration in this current work makes for a better fit with the theological truth of Rom. 7:1–6 than has been propounded thus far.

7 *Habeas corpus!*

8 Believers, on the other hand, are only '*made* to die' (7:4; a passive verb, signifying, as we have seen in Chapter 2, their vicarious, not actual, death [in Christ]).

9 Also see Gal. 2:19 for Paul's 'dying to the law['s condemnation]', and 3:13, for Christ's role in redeeming believers 'from the curse of the law, becoming a curse for us'.

10 The same label *moichalis*, 'adulteress', is used of deviant humanity: LXX Hos. 3:1; Ezek. 16:38; and Jas. 4:4. As well, there are the many references in the OT to Israel engaging in 'prostitution' with anti-God entities. Interestingly enough, the name of the Canaanite god *Ba'al* can also mean 'husband' in Hebrew (Deut. 24:4; Jer. 3:14; et cetera; and Jer. 7:9 LXX has both *Baal* and *moichaomai* ('commit adultery').

Godhead (= Yahweh), such an understanding poses no major difficulty.[11] But it also enables us to see (as we already did in Chapter 1) that all humanity was created to be 'bound'[12] to Yahweh, the Triune God, to whom they were originally in relationship, and to whom they owed their allegiance by virtue of his being their Creator who designed them for his glory. Isaiah 54:5 explicitly makes this creation-relationship an espousal: 'Your husband is your Maker, Yahweh of Armies is His name, and your Redeemer is the Holy One of Israel, called God of all the earth.'[13] It is because that original 'spousal' relationship between Creator and created humans was (and is still intended to be) sacrosanct and inviolable that the latter's post-fall pursuit of, and entanglement with, false deities and authorities inimical to God were equivalent to adultery against this divine Husband. Now we can add to our comparison of example to reality (see Figure 3.4).

Such a freedom from civic law's condemnation of adultery enables the woman to marry 'another man' (Rom. 7:3 [×2]). And freedom from divine law's condemnation of sin facilitated believers to be married (= 'bound'; 7:2) to 'another', i.e., Christ, 'the One raised from the dead' (7:4). This reading, of course, necessitates that Christ be seen as the one who died to release believers from the condemnation of divine law and also as the one who subsequently united them to himself. In effect, with regard to the illustration, he becomes both the husband who died *and* the

11 One might simply consider 'God' as the living husband *and* 'God' as the one who died, though the Persons of the Godhead are different in each case: the Trinity in the first (Yahweh), the Son in the second (Christ).

12 Borrowing the verb used in Rom. 7:2.

13 Marital metaphors in the OT describing the relationship between Yahweh and his people, and in the NT for the notion of Christ being united to his bride, the Church, the body of believers, are, of course, well-attested. In the OT, see Song of Songs; Isa. 62:5; Jer. 2:1–3:14; 13:20–27; 31:32; Ezek. 16; 23–24; Hos. 1–3. That the Creator is espoused to mankind is not at all surprising in a corpus where this relationship between deity and humanity is frequently described with words redolent of marriage covenants: e.g., Hebrew *lqch*, 'to take' (Exod. 6:7; Deut. 4:34; Jer. 3:14; et cetera); *yd'*, 'to know [intimately]' (Hos. 2:20; 5:4; Amos 3:2; and perhaps Ps. 36:11); *chsq*, 'to love' (Deut. 7:7; 10:15 – the verb has an erotic sense in Gen. 24:8; Deut. 21:11); *sgullah*, 'own possession' (Exod. 19:5; Deut. 7:6; 14:2; 26:18; Ps. 135:4 – the LXX uses the Greek *periousios*, also found in Titus 2:14); Greek *epistrephō*, 'to return', to indicate the rejoining of the profligate people of God to their faithful and forgiving deity (LXX: Jer. 4:1–2; Hos. 2:7; 3:5; 6:10; 12:6; 14:1–2; and in the NT: Acts 3:19; 14:15 [embracing God as Creator, citing Exod. 20:11; Ps. 146:6]; Acts 15:19; 26:18, 20; 28:27 [citing Isa. 6:10 LXX]; 2 Cor. 3:16; 1 Thess. 1:9; 1 Pet. 2:25). Of particular interest in our context of Romans 7 is the use of the Hebrew verb, *qnh*, 'to acquire/purchase', used for marriage (as in Ruth 4:10): it connotes the sense of binding or possession of the wife by the husband and, not surprisingly, it is also used for the relationship of Yahweh and his people (Deut. 32:6; Ps. 74:2; Isa. 1:3).

Illustrative Example (7:2–3)	Theological Reality (7:4)
Woman is married to her husband.	Humans are espoused to their God, Yahweh –
	the Creator.
Woman is condemned as 'adulteress' against husband by civic law.	Humans are condemned as 'adulteresses' against Yahweh by divine law.
'Husband' dies releasing 'woman' from 'the law of the husband' (i.e., civic law's condemnation of adultery).	Christ dies releasing believers from the law of God (i.e., divine law's condemnation of sin).

Figure 3.4

new husband of the widowed woman. But this is good theology: Christ died to set sinners free, *and* Christ, now raised, is espoused ('bound') to his saved ones.[14] Thus we discover that there is quite a precise analogy between example and reality, not just in its parts, but in its entirety (see Figure 3.5).

The points of seeming incongruity between illustrative example and theological reality (reflecting the inadequacy of the former) are only that: the 'husband' is Yahweh (in the first darkest shaded box on top in Figure 3.5), but he is not the one who dies – it is Christ who does; and the 'another [man]' who is espoused to freed believers is also Christ – but now as 'the One raised from the dead' (in the second darkest shaded box at the bottom of Figure 3.5). Or, to put the whole thing simply, and without distinguishing the Persons of the Trinity: God was espoused to humans (at creation); they committed adultery against him (at the fall and thereafter); God died for them; and God espoused them to himself

14 For this relationship of Christ to believers, see 2 Cor. 11:2; Eph. 5:23–32; Rev. 19:7–9; 21:9 (and the several references to the Church as the 'body of Christ'); and for Christ as the groom, see Matt. 9:15 (= Mark 2:19–20 and Luke 5:33–39); Matt. 22:2–13; 25:1–13; John 3:29; 2 Cor. 11:2–3 (with Paul as the groomsman); Eph. 5:21–33; Rev. 19–21. It must be noted that Ps. 45:6–7, addressing Yahweh, the God-King pictured as a bridegroom of his people-queen, is cited in Heb. 1:8–9, addressing Christ (see Kuruvilla, *Psalms 45–100*, 1–9).

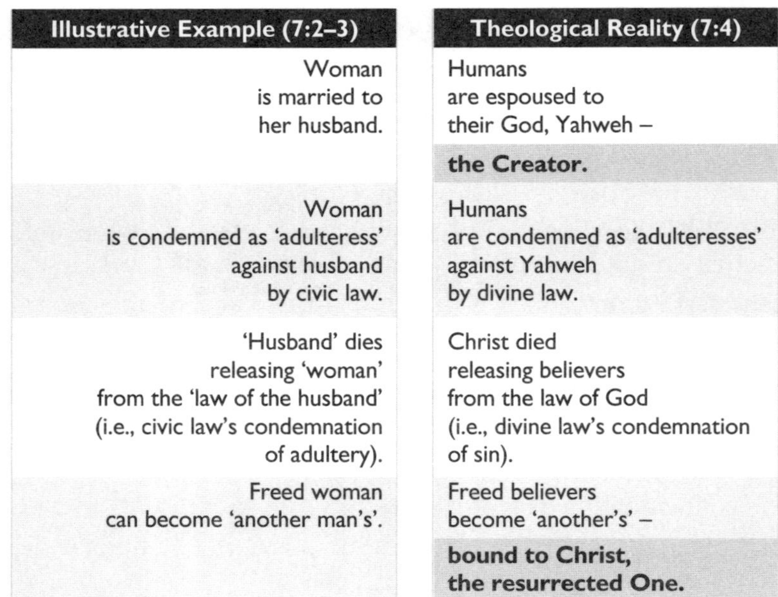

Illustrative Example (7:2–3)	Theological Reality (7:4)
Woman is married to her husband.	Humans are espoused to their God, Yahweh – **the Creator.**
Woman is condemned as 'adulteress' against husband by civic law.	Humans are condemned as 'adulteresses' against Yahweh by divine law.
'Husband' dies releasing 'woman' from the 'law of the husband' (i.e., civic law's condemnation of adultery).	Christ died releasing believers from the law of God (i.e., divine law's condemnation of sin).
Freed woman can become 'another man's'.	Freed believers become 'another's' – **bound to Christ, the resurrected One.**

Figure 3.5

after the resurrection.[15] Thus even the seeming imperfection of the illustration is overcome by the clever employment of the picture of marriage, generating a noteworthy equivalence between example and reality.

And thereby we have Paul's second reason why believers should not remain in sin (6:1–2a): with the picture of marriage, believers are bound to Christ, possessed by him, for now they have 'become another's', a personal espousal and ownership (7:4). The consequence of this binding to Christ of the people he redeemed[16] is clear: they owe their possessing deity total loyalty, complete allegiance and unremitting service – all to this end: 'that we may be fruit-bearing to God' (7:4b).

> Therefore, my brothers [and sisters], you also were made to die to the law by the body of Christ, in order that you may become another's, of the One raised from the dead, in order that we may

15 Such an understanding of the marvellous grace of God can never be gotten from 7:1–4 without seeing this remarkably perfect fit between illustration and reality as proposed here.

16 Or the repossession by Yahweh of the people he '(re)created' (the latter verb is adapted from Eph. 2:10; see Chapter 2).

be fruit-bearing to God. For when we were in the flesh, the sinful passions were working through the law in our members unto fruit-bearing to death.
(Rom. 7:4–5)

The only other option is to be 'fruit-bearing to death'.[17] Pre-conversion, sinful activity resulted in the law's condemnation of the sinner to eternal death and separation from God. It was 'by the law['s condemnation]' that this 'fruit-bearing to death' ensued (7:5). After all, 'the sting of death is sin, and the power of sin is the law' (1 Cor. 15:56): sin uses its 'power [of attorney!]', the 'law', to 'sting [i.e., condemn]' sinners so as to cause 'death'. Paul is thus contrasting the past life natural to sinners (who are facing the law's condemnation of death; Rom. 7:5) with the present life expected of the saved (who are freed from the law's condemnation of death), now that they are united with Christ – bound to him (7:4). The textual elements are deliberately ordered (in the Greek), with alliterations and paralleled items (see Figure 3.6).

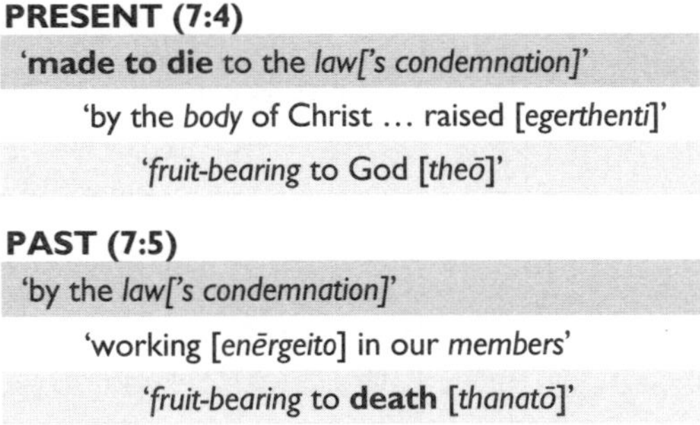

Figure 3.6

Dying and death begins and ends the organised structure of 7:4–5, though they are very different kinds of death, of course. The first is a vicarious and liberating experience, via the death of Christ that removed the law's condemnation of sin; the second is a direct and penalising experience of eternal death and separation from God, the result of the law's condemnation of sin. The 'raised [*egerthenti*]' body of the Saviour

17 These two options are not dissimilar to the contrasting assertions in 6:21 (the 'fruit' of sinful activity is 'death') and in 6:22 (that 'fruit' of sanctified living is 'life eternal').

facilitated 'fruit-bearing to God [*theō*]'; but the 'working [*enērgeito*]' of sinners' body parts only furthers 'fruit-bearing to death [*thanatō*]'.

In other words, the law provides no help, no resources and no power for living the new life of those united to Christ, but only condemns sinners.[18] But now, as believers who have 'become another's' (7:4) – bound to Christ – they have the potential for producing fruit unto God, and they should do so. No more 'remaining in sin' for them (6:1). But how exactly does that happen? If the law did not offer any aid in that direction, how are believers going to be 'fruit-bearing to God' (7:4) and produce 'fruit unto sanctification' (6:22)? The solution is in 7:6 (and developed further):

> But now we have been released from the law, having died to that by which we were being held, therefore to be slaves in newness of Spirit and not in oldness of letter.
> (Rom. 7:6)

Believers 'have been released from the law['s condemnation of sin], having died to that by which we were being held [i.e., "the law('s condemnation)"]' (7:6). And the goal for this deliverance from law's condemnation is explicitly stated: that the saved ones may 'be slaves in newness of Spirit and not in oldness of letter' (7:6). What exactly is this letter-vs-Spirit antithesis? It cannot imply that the 'letter' (= law) is unspiritual: after all, the author of God's word (including God's law) is the same Holy Spirit. Indeed, the apostle explicitly labels God's law 'spiritual' (7:14). So what does he mean here in 7:6? Second Corinthians 3:6, where the same letter-vs-Spirit antithesis is found, clarifies what is intended.

> [God] made us adequate as ministers of a new covenant, not of letter but of Spirit, for the letter kills, but Spirit enlivens. But if the ministry of death, in letters carved on stones, came with glory … how will the ministry of Spirit not be with more glory? For if the

18 That is not an imperfection of the law; it is simply that helping and resourcing and empowering the people of God to meet the divine demand of the law is not in its portfolio.

> ministry of condemnation has glory, much more does the ministry of righteousness abound in glory.
> (2 Cor. 3:6–9)

Notice the precise contrasts here in the antithesis between 'letter' and 'Spirit' (see Figure 3.7).

'Letter' [= Law]	'Spirit'
'kills' (3:6)	'enlivens' (3:6)
'ministry of death' (3:7)	'ministry of Spirit' (3:8)
'came with glory' (3:7)	'will … be with more glory' (3:8)
'ministry of condemnation' (3:9)	'ministry of righteousness' (3:9)
'has glory' (3:9)	'much more … abound[s] in glory' (3:9)

Figure 3.7

On the one hand, we have the killing by the 'letter', the killing referring to the condemnation of the law of sin, explicitly called 'the ministry of condemnation' (= 'the ministry of death'; 2 Cor. 3:7, 9a). On the other, we have the enlivening by the Spirit who empowers obedience, explicitly labelled 'the ministry of righteousness' (= 'ministry of Spirit'; 3:8, 9b). It must be noted that *both* 'ministries' are said to have 'glory' (though the latter has 'more' and 'much more … abound[s]' in glory; 3:8–9). That clearly indicates that the 'letter'/law is not abrogated – it *does* have a role (to direct life according to God's demand and to condemn failures for non-compliance), and it *does* have 'glory' (it is divinely intended to accomplish its purpose for the ultimate end of all things, the glory of God). So, in the entirety of this discussion in Romans 7 (and in 2 Corinthians 3) there is no indication whatsoever that the law is abolished, inactivated or otherwise rendered effete: the 'release from the law' (Rom. 7:6) is only emancipation from its condemnation, as has oft been stated in the present work.

So, returning to Romans 7, here is the short answer to the question of how believers are enabled to produce fruit of sanctification Godward (6:22; 7:4):[19] by the obedience-empowering ministry of the enlivening Holy Spirit, who is mentioned in Romans 6–8 for the first time here in

19 The long answer, so to speak, comes in Romans 8 (below).

7:6. Appropriate enough, for it is here that we see, also for the first time, the incapacity of law to empower sanctification. The law can only decree obedience and denounce disobedience; it offers no aid to the children of God to obey the law. It simply sets rules and dispassionately condemns the transgression (and transgressors) of those rules. So while the law is in itself not sinful or evil – after all, it is a divine instrument to accomplish deity's purposes – it does not help the child of God keep the law of God. But God does not abandon his people – who are baptised and bound to Christ – to their own inadequate artifices and paltry contrivances as they seek to live obediently unto him and thus glorify him. Rather, this benevolent and loving deity grants his children an incredibly gracious provision to keep his law – in the empowering Person of the Holy Spirit (as 7:6 has hinted, and as Romans 8 will detail).

And so, with 7:6, Paul concludes the extended section he had begun in 6:1: 'What then shall we say? … Remain in sin? … May it never be!' (6:1–2a). And in answering this question, he has given two reasons. Reason #1: Believers are united with Christ, baptised to him (6:3–14); and Reason #2: Believers are united with Christ, bound to him (7:1–6). In between the two reasons was, as we have seen, a powerful excursus in the form of an exhortation to believers to live a new life of obedience to God (6:15–23) (see Figure 3.8).

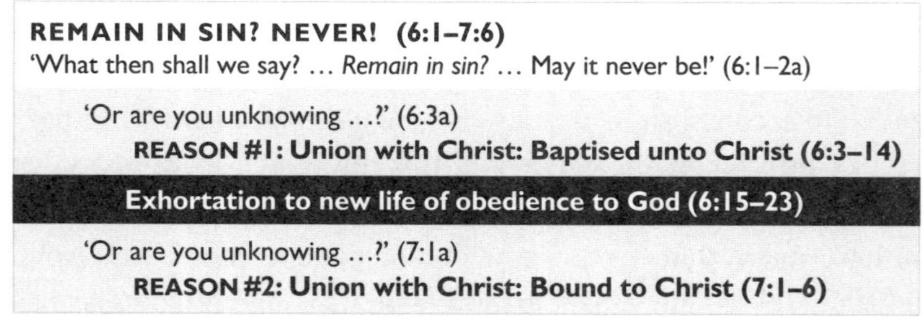

REMAIN IN SIN? NEVER! (6:1–7:6)
'What then shall we say? … *Remain in sin?* … May it never be!' (6:1–2a)

'Or are you unknowing …?' (6:3a)
REASON #1: Union with Christ: Baptised unto Christ (6:3–14)

Exhortation to new life of obedience to God (6:15–23)

'Or are you unknowing …?' (7:1a)
REASON #2: Union with Christ: Bound to Christ (7:1–6)

LAW IS SIN? NEVER! (7:7–8:30)
'What then shall we say? *Is the law sin?* May it never be!' (7:7)

Figure 3.8

Sin, law and sins (Rom. 7:7–13; Gen. 2–3)

With 'law' also showing up in 7:1–6, an obvious question is raised in the mind of the reader, one that Paul expresses and immediately negates in

7:7a:[20] 'What then shall we say? Is the law sin? May it never be!' And so, for the remainder of Romans 7 and most of Romans 8 (7:7–8:30), Paul proceeds to refute that false assumption of the law's sinfulness.

> What then shall we say? Is the law sin? May it never be! But I did not know sin except through the law; for I would not have known about desiring, if the law did not say, 'You shall not desire'.
> (Rom. 7:7)

No, the law is not sinful (a notion we have already encountered). In fact, it is 'through [i.e., "by means of"] the law' that one understands what sins are, comprehending what is not part of God's moral will and divine demand, and discerning what is contrary to God's nature (exemplified here in 7:7 by one of the Ten Commandments). Rather, it was sin using law as its sting, so to speak, that provoked the performance of sins:

> But taking opportunity through the commandment, sin worked in me all [kinds of] desires; for apart from the law, sin is dead. And I was once alive apart from the law, but with the coming of the commandment, sin came to life and I died. And I found that, to me, the commandment unto life, it was unto death; for sin, taking opportunity through the commandment deceived me and through it killed [me].
> (Rom. 7:8–11)

Paul proceeds to depict the utilitarian (and lethal) relationship between sin and the law by means of an artistic structure (see Figure 3.9).

No, the law is certainly not sinful. On the contrary, it is 'sin' – personified again as the evil, despotic authority that has total, unfettered control over non-Christians – that hijacked God's law and used it nefariously as its tool to stimulate in them all kinds of evil desires (*A*; 7:8a).[21]

---

20 As he had done for the earlier question in 6:1, thus marking 7:7 as the start of a new section.

21 'Sin' was using the law to 'work [from *katergazomai*]' in non-Christians evil 'desires' 'through the commandment' (7:8a), quite similar to the description of 'sinful passions ... working [from *energeō*; notice the shared Greek root, shaded] through the law' to bring about death (7:5). 'Through the law/commandment' occurs in 7:5, 7, 8, 11, 13.

	A	**Sin through Law → Desires**		
		'... taking opportunity through the commandment, sin worked in me all [kinds of] desires'		**7:8a**
PRE-LAW	B	**Sin Dead**	'for apart from the *law* sin is *dead*.	**7:8b**
		'I' Alive	And I was once *alive* apart from the *law*'	**7:9a**
POST-LAW	B'	**Sin Alive**	'but with the coming of the *commandment*, sin was *enlivened*	**7:9b**
		'I' Dead	and I *died*. ... *commandment* unto life, it was unto death'	**7:10**
	A'	**Sin through Law → Deceit, Death**		
		'... sin, taking opportunity through the commandment, deceived me and through it killed [me]'		**7:11**

Figure 3.9

Paul then proceeds to contrast the situations pre-law and post-law (*B* and *B'*; 7:8b–10). If there were no law (pre-law state), there would be no sin – 'sin is [effectively] dead. And I was once alive' (*B*; 7:8b–9a). The apostle is likely referring to the pre-law (and pre-fall) dispensation in the Garden of Eden, the situation that existed *before* the giving of God's commandment regarding consumption of fruits (Gen. 2:16–17), hypothetically placing himself in that arena. But with the coming of the law ('commandment'; post-law state), matters took a dreadful turn: 'sin was enlivened and I died' (*B'*; Rom. 7:9b–10). What was intended to keep people *from* dying (7:10b; by their abiding by God's law and thereby avoiding its condemnation unto death) became an instrument of sin to drive people *to* dying (7:9–10a; by their breaking God's law and incurring its condemnation unto death). How exactly the arrival of law on the scene enticed people to disobey it is described in the fall that took place in the Garden of Eden: the 'deception' accomplished by sin referred to in 7:11 is undoubtedly being depicted as parallel to the 'deception' of the serpent (LXX Gen. 3:13).[22] Though we have examined that devastating

22 Employing the same Greek word, *exapataō*, as also in 2 Cor. 11:3; 1 Tim. 2:14.

event in Chapter 1, a return to those precincts is helpful to capture Paul's trajectory of thought in Romans 7, particularly his reasoning for the law as an (involuntary) agent enlivening sin.[23]

The catastrophe of the fall of humankind is described in Genesis 3, juxtaposing the promulgation of divine law (prohibiting consumption of the tree of the knowledge of good and evil) with the rebellious act of non-compliance to that divine law by humans. If eating the fruit tree of life would have led to immortality (3:22), it is reasonable to assume that consuming the fruit of the tree of the knowledge of good and evil would have led to a knowledge of good and evil. Wenham makes the case for 'knowledge of good and evil' being divine wisdom, 'a wisdom that is God's sole preserve' (Job 15:8–9; Prov. 30:1–4).[24] Indeed, the fact that God himself acknowledged that the trees he caused to grow in the Garden of Eden were 'desirable in appearance and good for food' (Gen. 2:9) suggests that Eve's evaluation of the tree of the knowledge of good and evil as 'good for food' and 'attractive to the eyes' (3:6) was neither erroneous nor illegitimate. Rather, the problem lay with her focus upon the tree's third attribute – 'desirable to make [one] wise', equivalent to 'knowing good and evil', the peculiar feature of this tree.

Thus, the emphasis of the author of Genesis is not on the substance or content of knowledge (what particularly was good or evil), but rather on humans seeking moral autonomy to decide what was good and what was evil, the making of moral judgements without privileging divine law. One remembers that the attributes of the fruit of the tree of the knowledge of good and evil that the woman extols in 3:6 are also shared by God's word, as Psalm 19 made clear ('reliable, making wise the simple', 'pure, enlightening the eyes' and 'sweeter than honey', 19:7, 8, 10; see Chapter 1), once again substantiating the thesis that such wisdom as was sought by mankind in Eden was being pursued apart from God and his law. And so it is not accidental that, in the accusatory and judgemental phase of the fall narrative, the tree of interest is not designated by Yahweh as the 'tree of the knowledge of good and evil'; instead, he labels it 'the tree of which I commanded you not to eat', a description that is repeated

23 Much of the following discussion is taken from Kuruvilla, *Genesis*, 62–7.

24 Wenham, *Genesis 1–15*, 63–4.

(Gen. 3:11, 17). The focus is upon the command of God, the demand of God that had been repudiated – God's law rejected by humans. They had decided that they would be the arbiters of morality: what to eat and what not to, what to do and what not to, what to abide by and what not to. This was nothing but an attempt to usurp the dominion of God.

But how did sin 'take opportunity through the commandment' (Rom. 7:8, 11) to deceive? What was that 'opportunity' afforded by God's law for sin to work its malignant purpose? Drawing from the account of the fall in Genesis 3 (shaded light in Figure 3.10), we find that it was humanity's disdainful distrust and dangerous disregard (shaded dark and in italics in Figure 3.10) of particular divine attributes embodied in the law (in bold and in small capitals in Figure 3.10) that caused the calamity of the fall (as it always does).

God's wisdom, truthfulness, holiness, sovereignty, goodness, love and justice – all grounded in the promulgation of divine law – are challenged and disavowed. Each of those potential assertions by sinners listed in Figure 3.10 is a satanic falsehood and a self-deception provoked by sin (the personified entity), the indirect results of the 'coming of the commandment' that stoked and kindled the production of sins. God's law was indeed 'the power of sin' (1 Cor. 15:56).

But to reiterate (and to return to Romans 7), it was not the law *per se* that was sinful, and neither was it the law's condemnation that killed, but sin that exploited the law ('taking opportunity through the commandment', Rom. 7:8, 11) for its lethal purposes and thereby wrought divine consequences upon all anti-God rebellions. 'Sin used the law as its instrument … to effect death … Sin is the *ultimate* cause of death. The law is the *instrumental* cause, but it is not itself blameworthy, for it is inherently good.'[25] Sin is the culprit, and 'the commandment unto life' became '[the commandment] unto death' (7:10). To ensure no misunderstanding of this critical notion, the 'goodness' of the law is asserted again in 7:12–14:

> Therefore, the law is indeed holy and the commandment holy and righteous and *good*. Then did what is *good* become death to me? May it never be! But sin, in order that it may manifest [as] sin,

25 Schreiner, *Romans*, 372 (emphases original).

through what is *good* worked death in me, in order that sin may become exceedingly sinful through the commandment. For we know that the law is spiritual.
(Rom. 7:12–14a)

WISDOM OF GOD

'God is not serious about his law – that's only a suggestion: I can sin freely.'

Serpent's questioning of God's communiqué to man and woman (3:1)
Serpent's conversion of God 'commanding' (2:16) to God 'saying' (3:1)
Woman's abetting the serpent's conversion of command to statement (3:3)

TRUTHFULNESS OF GOD

'God is lying about consequences – they're only empty threats: I'm going to sin.'

Serpent's contradiction of God 's command:
'no – you will surely [not] die' (3:4) *vs* God's 'you will surely die'

HOLINESS OF GOD

'God is not bothered by sins – he couldn't care less: I can keep on sinning.'

Woman's identification of the tree by its location, not significance (3:2)
Woman's alteration of God's command:
'lest you die' (3:3) *vs* God's 'you will surely die' (2:17)
Serpent's promise of positive outcomes (3:5b)

SOVEREIGNTY OF GOD

'God is not in charge – there's no need for submission: I can do what I want.'

Serpent's 'God' in (3:1b–7 [×3]) *vs* narrator's 'Yahweh God' (3:1a, 8–23 [×9])
Woman's acquiescence to the serpent's use of 'God' (3:3)

GOODNESS OF GOD

'God is not interested in my best – I must help myself: I'll just disobey him.'

Woman's alterations of God's command:
'we may eat' (3:2) *vs* 'you may *freely* eat' (2:16)
'from … the tree …' (3:2) *vs* 'from *every* tree …' (2:16)
'not eat from eat *or touch it*' (3:3), adding severity to the law of 2:16–17

LOVE OF GOD

'God is a jealous control-freak – I need to be in charge of myself: I'll ignore him.'

Serpent's attribution of a base motive to God for his law (3:5a)

JUSTICE OF GOD

'God cannot punish me – it's never my fault: I'll continue in my own sinful ways.'

Man's passing the blame onto the woman and onto God himself (3:12)

Figure 3.10

With a triple iteration that God's law is 'good' (7:12–13), Paul refutes any deprecation of the law (see Figure 3.11).

'Did what is good become death to me? May it never be!'

'*sin, in order that* it may be manifest [as] *sin,*	*through what is good*
worked death in me,	
in order that sin may become exceedingly *sinful,*	*through the commandment'*

'For we know that the law is spiritual.'

Figure 3.11

Sin was the problem (and, of course, the sinner, too, namely the sinner's 'flesh' – see below). That evil authority, sin, utilised law ('what is good' [×3]; 7:12–13) to manifest itself and accomplish its wicked goal of producing sins that culminate in the death of the sinner (7:13). No, the 'good' law is not sinful and neither does it cause death – 'may it never be!' After all, 'we know that the law is spiritual' (7:14a). And with that we have yet another appreciation of divine law and its essential 'spiritual' nature and quality.

So here are all of Paul's positive affirmations about the law in Romans: it is 'holy', 'righteous', 'good' (7:12–13 – 'good' thrice; also see 7:16[26]); it is 'spiritual' (7:14[27]); and it is assuredly not sin (7:7). Paul exclaims that he does not 'nullify the law' but 'establishes the law' (3:21); in fact, he 'delights in the law of God' (7:22; see below). What is the 'law of God' (7:22, 25; 8:7; and 3:2 has 'the oracles of God') ought certainly not be disdained or neglected, divinely intended as it was to ordain and govern a life of blessing with God (7:13).[28]

The 'flesh' (Rom. 7:14–25)

So, yes, the law is good and spiritual, et cetera, but there is a problem: the breaker of the law!

> For we know that the law is spiritual, but I – *of the flesh I am*, having been sold [as a slave] into sin.
> (Rom. 7:14)

26 In 7:16, the Greek adjective *kalos*, 'good', is employed, instead of *agathos* as in 7:12–13.

27 I.e., 'it derives from the Spirit (given by inspiration), embodies the Spirit, manifests the Spirit' (Dunn, *Romans 1–8*, 387), and, as we shall see, its performance is empowered by the Spirit. Thus, Holy Spirit is the 'Healer', the doctor-teacher who guides, directs and instructs believers baptised unto, and bound to, the Son, by the grace of the Father.

28 See Pss. 19:7–10; 93:5; 119; Ezek. 20:11; Luke 11:28; Rom. 10:5.

Despite the fact that a believer is cured from the affliction of sin, there is a devious spanner in the works – the 'flesh' that threatens to render the saved one a law-breaker, 'sold [as a slave] into sin'.[29] What exactly is the 'flesh', and how does this entity pervert one into a slave to sin?

But first a much-debated crux of in 7:14–25 must be addressed: Who is the 'I' in this passage? Paul has already used the first-person plural five times in 7:4–7a when addressing believers ('brothers [and sisters]' in 7:1, 4[30]). And his conceding that the law is 'holy and righteous and good' (7:12) makes it quite clear that the use of the first-person singular in 7:7b–13 indicates one who is a believer. But how about the rest of the chapter, 7:14–25? Is it the same believer writing autobiographically, or could it be that the apostle is penning these verses from the viewpoint of a non-Christian? Though scholars have tossed this issue back and forth, there are several reasons to hold that that the referent in 7:14–25 is also a believer, and that what Paul describes there is characteristic of the life of a child of God:

1. The shift from the Greek aorist verbs of 7:7–13 (here are their frequencies: aorist = 15; present = 1) to the present verbs of 7:14–25 (present = 37; aorist = 0).
2. The person referred to in 7:14–25 delights in God's law (7:22), seeks to obey it (7:15–20) and serve it (7:25), desiring liberation from 'this body of death' (7:24); such a mindset is uncharacteristic of a non-Christian (for whose inclination see 3:11; 8:7).
3. This individual 'wishes' to do good (7:15, 16, 18, 19 [×2], 20, 21).
4. The 'inner person' and 'mind' of the person in question are inclined towards God (7:22, 23, 25).[31]
5. Paul's confession that he is 'of the flesh' (Greek *sarkinos;* 7:14) can very well indicate a characteristic of the believer, as in 1 Corinthians

29 The verb, when used of persons, has the connotation of being sold into slavery, hence my translational gloss: see LXX Lev. 25:39, 42; Deut. 15:12; 28:68; Esth. 7:4; Ps. 105:17; Isa. 50:1; 52:3; Jer. 34:14.

30 The content of this section, especially 7:4, 6, also confirm that he is indicating believers with the first-person plural.

31 Only believers seem to possess such an 'inner person' (2 Cor. 4:16; Eph. 3:16), or a renewed 'mind' (Rom. 12:2). This is unlike the 'mind' of a non-Christian (Rom. 1:28; Eph. 4:17; Col. 2:18 [specifically labelled 'mind of the flesh', or 'fleshly mind']; 1 Tim. 6:5; 2 Tim. 3:8; Titus 1:15).

3:1 (also using *sarkinos*; these 'fleshly' ones are explicitly labelled 'infants in Christ' – believers).

6 The discussion of the person's conflicted state (Rom. 7:25b) comes *after* the mention of deliverance (7:25a).

7 Besides, the placement of 7:14–25 after the larger section of 6:1–7:14 (i.e., after the discussion of believers' union with Christ: baptised to him and bound to him) also indicates that it must be about believers.

8 If this text were describing the apostle's pre-conversion state of mind – troubled and irresolute – it would appear to contradict his unwavering and steadfast orthodox zeal as a non-Christian pictured in Philippians 3:6.

9 That discord of 'wishing' to do good, but 'doing' what is not good, rings true to life, as all children of God can, no doubt, attest.

10 This rather distressed and divided phase of life depicted in Romans 7:14–25 is also consistent with the angst described in Galatians 5:17 ('the flesh [has] desires against the Spirit, and the Spirit against the flesh') which, in context, describes what is characteristic of believers.

11 The question 'who will liberate me?' (Rom. 7:24) need not necessarily indicate a hoped-for justification in the future, anticipated from the vantage point of a non-Christian. The same verb, 'liberate', is used in the future tense in 2 Timothy 4:18 (and in 2 Cor. 1:10) to designate glorification in the future for Paul, an already justified person.

12 Such an interpretation of Romans 7:14–25 is seconded by several church fathers and ancients.[32]

So, when all is said and done, Paul seems to be talking about a believer in 7:14–25 with first-person singular verbs and expressing his own 'deep sense of personal involvement, his consciousness that in drawing out the general truth he is disclosing the truth about himself', as well as about every child of God on this side of eternity.[33]

32 For instance, Methodius, *Discourse on the Resurrection*, 1.2.2–3; Ambrose, *On Abraham*, 2.6.27; Augustine, *Retractions*, 1.22.1; 2.27; Luther, *Lectures on Romans* (on Rom. 7:14–25); and Calvin, *Commentary on Romans* (on Rom. 7:14–23).

33 Cranfield, *Critical and Exegetical Commentary*, 1: 343–4.

And with that, the first contrast between flesh and Spirit (in a believer) in Romans shows up in 7:14.

> For we know that the law is spiritual, but I – of the flesh I am, having been sold [as a slave] into sin.
> (Rom. 7:14)

The law that is 'spiritual', inspired by the Spirit, can only be comprehended by the help of the Spirit and obeyed by the power of the Spirit (as we will see from Romans 8). And so the 'I', the Spirit-indwelt Paul (and Every Christian), can assent to the goodness of this spiritual law (7:16), delight in it (7:22) and be a slave to it (7:25). But what of the 'flesh'? What is that entity and how is it undermining sanctification and the destiny of believers to do good works, and, ultimately, the divine design of humanity for God's glory?

While 'flesh' (Greek *sarx*) can indicate the physicality of living beings (as in 'flesh-and-blood'; see Rom. 1:3; 2:28; 4:1; 9:5; Gal. 4:13), or even denote humanity in general (Rom. 3:20; 1 Cor. 1:29; Gal. 2:16), in Romans 7–8 it is the immoral facet of humans that is in focus. It is the diametric opposite of what it means to be in the Spirit, indicated by the antitheses 'not in the flesh, but in the Spirit' (8:9, 12[34]), and 'works of the flesh' *vs* 'fruit of the Spirit' (Gal. 5:16–26).[35]

The flesh is that entity in humans that is the engine of their deviance and the dynamo of its evil passions and lusts (Rom. 13:14). And so, as an agent of the evil taskmaster, sin (7:14), the flesh rejects God's law (8:3), and most certainly does not please him (8:7–8). At the end of it all, the flesh is incorrigible and irredeemable, irrevocably evil and immutably opposed to God. This is why the declaration that 'nothing good dwells in me, that is, in my flesh' (7:18) is equated to the assertions that 'sin … is dwelling in me' (7:17, 20), that 'in me evil is present' (7:21), and that an evil 'law … is in my members' (7:23).[36] These verses indicate that the flesh is very

34 Also see 8:4–13; Gal. 3:3; 4:29; 5:16–17, 19–23; 6:8; Phil. 3:3.

35 Barclay, *Flesh and Spirit*, 21, puts the contrast between 'work' and 'fruit' neatly: 'A work is something a [hu]man produces for himself; a fruit is something produced by a power which he does not possess. [A hu]man cannot *make* a fruit.'

36 See Figure 3.15, below, for this evil 'law'.

present in believers, too.[37] And it is 'with the flesh' that humans serve sin (7:25). Indeed, 'the flesh is exactly the bridgehead through which sin invades the human personality. The flesh is like the enemy within the gates who opens the way to the enemy who is pressing in through the gates.'[38] It is, in effect, a traitor in believers, that owes allegiance to that old master and evil authority, sin, and it is thus the powerhouse of their sin-production. Even though sin does not have absolute control over the children of God – after all, united with Christ, baptised and bound to him, they are 'dead to sin' (6:11) – by means of the traitorous flesh, sin can cause the downfall of believers as they carry out sins.[39] The flesh is part of humans until they die, and will never be resurrected,[40] and so, for believers, the only way to counteract the downward and sin-driven impulses of the flesh is by the upward and God-driven power of the Holy Spirit (Gal. 5:16, 24) – the Spirit-empowered shunning of the flesh (Rom. 8:12–13).

In sum, the 'flesh' is an integral facet of all fallen humanity – delivered and undelivered. For non-Christians there is only one allegiance, to sin, via the flesh (and they have no other choice but to be subservient to sin's working through the flesh). For believers, indwelt by the Holy Spirit upon their union with Christ, there are now *two* authorities attempting to exert control over them: the evil authority, sin, causing the production of sins through the flesh, and the good authority, God, causing the production of righteousness through the Spirit (and believers have a choice as to which authority they submit to).

---

37 Though the 'old person' (6:19) – the believer's life-in-its-fallenness, that whole way of life before salvation – is gone, the entity called 'flesh' persists in believers. The difference between believers and non-Christians – both possessing the flesh – is that the former now have a choice to obey sin or to obey God; the latter do not. Those united with Christ (baptised unto and bound to him) are indwelt by the Holy Spirit, who empowers them to resist the sinful impulses of the flesh.

38 Barclay, *Flesh and Spirit*, 20, 21–2.

39 This potential undoing of believers is, of course, not a loss of salvation, but it does affect the filial relationship of children to their heavenly Father, and subverts the divine design of humans for God's glory.

40 Unlike the 'flesh', the 'body' is redeemable (Rom. 8:23), it can be an instrument for glorifying God (Rom. 12:1; 1 Cor. 6:19–20; Phil. 1:20) and it will be resurrected (Rom. 8:11; Phil. 3:21). Indeed, 1 John 3:2 specifies that 'when He appears, like Him we will be' – like Christ who in his impeccability does not possess this sin-serving and sin-compelling entity, the flesh. While the Bible is silent about the source of the flesh, it might well be an entity that became constitutionally part of humankind with the fall.

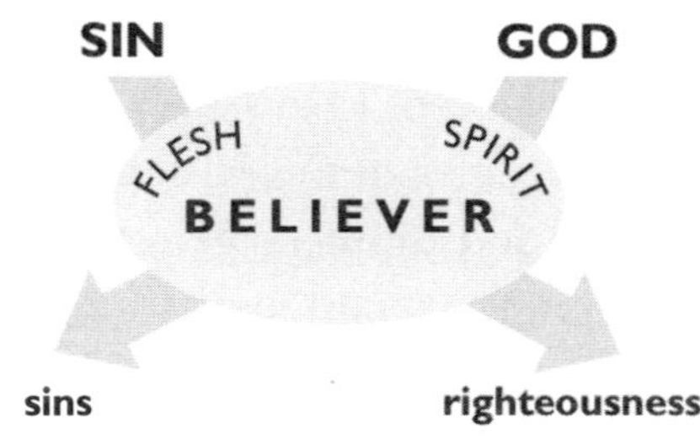

Figure 3.12

Again, non-Christians are 'in the flesh' (7:5), i.e., they live in the realm of the flesh, under the control of sin, with no choice but to submit; believers on this side of eternity also possess the flesh, but they do have a choice, because they have help in the battle against that entity – the indwelling Spirit (see Figure 3.12).[41] Thus the Christian, in the current dispensation, is torn between two competing authorities – sin via the flesh, and God via the Spirit – the source of the discord voiced by Paul in 7:14–25.

> For what I am working [out] I do not know; for what wish, this I do not practise; but what I hate, this I do. But if what I do not wish, this I do, [then] I assent with that law that [it is] good.
> (Rom. 7:15–16)

The struggle of the Christian with the flesh is expressed once again in multiple subject+predicate iterations of Paul's autobiographical struggle. With these repetitions of 'wishing' and 'doing' (and they are continued in 7:17–21), it is as if the apostle is confessing: 'I am completely and comprehensively conflicted, inside and outside, left and right, above and below!' And that would be true, because at every step of the way, at every instant, the flesh, the traitor within, prevails upon the child of God to succumb to the lure of sin, causing the performance of sins. There is no way believers' self-propelled wishing good or hating evil can result in righteousness. Sinning is the only possible outcome for believers who are attempting to counter, on their own, the compulsions of the treacherous

41 Believers on the other side of eternity are, of course, glorified and the flesh is no longer with them; and they are forever removed from the presence of sin – praise God!

flesh serving the evil authority, sin.[42] Indeed, their 'working [out]', and 'practising' and 'doing' what is not known, not wished and not loved – this very discord is proof positive of the existence of another law, God's law, that is 'good' (7:15–16) and antithetical to whatever sin tempts them to do through the flesh.[43] So Paul continues:

> But now, no longer am I the one working it, but sin which is dwelling in me. For I know that nothing good dwells in me, that is in my flesh; for the wishing is present with me, but the working of good is not. For I do not do the good I wish [to do], but the evil I do not wish, that I practise. But if what I do not wish, this I do, [then] no longer am I the one working it, but sin which is dwelling in me. I find then the law in me, the one wishing to do good, that in me evil is present.
> (Rom. 7:17–21)

Considering the repetitions of the verbs 'work', 'wish' and 'do', one spies an artistic patterning (in the Greek word order) in 7:15–21 (see Figure 3.13).[44]

7:15	'work', 'wish', 'do'
7:16	'wish', 'do'
7:17–18	'work,' 'wish,' 'work'
7:19	'wish,' 'do,' 'wish'
7:20a	'wish', 'do'
7:20b–21	'work', 'wish', 'do'

Figure 3.13

42 So in this aspect believers resemble non-Christians as sin-performers – no victory for either over the flesh if they employ their own resources (non-Christians, of course, have only their own resources to employ).

43 Paul's argument is that he would rather love and practise good – what the law commands. After all, he who wished to do 'good' (7:19) had already labelled the law 'good' (7:12, 13, 16). Besides, discussing sinfulness, he declares that 'nothing good' is in him, neither is the 'working of good' (7:18). In short, there is the law of God and it is 'good'; and there is another law operating via sin and the flesh, and it is evil.

44 There are also repetitions of the verbs 'practise' (7:15, 19), 'dwell' (7:17, 18) and 'present' (7:18, 21), as well as of the nouns 'good' (7:16, 18 [×2], 19, both *kalos* and *agathos*) and 'evil' (7:19, 21).

It appears that the author is literarily depicting, in this (organised) jumble of multiple verbal recurrences, the discord he (and every believer) is experiencing: it is intense and it is frustrating!

But is sin 'dwelling in me' (7:17)? Weren't those in union with Christ done with sin – after all, they were said to be 'dead to sin' and 'alive to God' (6:11)? Alas, what is positionally true has not yet become practically manifest, for as long as that traitor, the flesh, is part of believers' lives, sin, the evil master, through that wicked turncoat, continues to have a toehold in the lives of the children of God. Notice the synonymity of the statements in 7:17–21: 'sin … in me' (7:17, 20) = 'nothing good … in me … in my flesh' (7:18) = 'in me evil is present' (7:21b). The situation is not only discordant but also dire! Yes, believers may have been transferred from one authority (an evil one, that of sin) to another (a good one, that of God), but the flesh accompanied them in that domain displacement, and that irredeemable and corrupt entity continues to submit to and work for that erstwhile evil authority, sin. No wonder it is through the flesh that sin is 'dwelling in me' (7:17, 20).

And the discord within Christians – their wanting to do 'good', but being unable to do so because of the pull of the flesh, and in the end succumbing to sin and evil – is, as we saw, generated when these children of God try to fight the treacherous flesh with their own resources. In that battle, they will not triumph: the flesh, under the control of the evil authority, always wins, as it does in non-Christians for whom there is no such conflict, angst or discord as is described for Christians in Romans 7. This inner dissent and strangling inconsistency arises only in those individuals united to Christ, baptised unto him and bound to him. That's when the tug-o'-war commences: 'I want to do good – following God; but I end up doing what I don't want to do – following sin with my flesh!'[45]

Yes, Paul does confess that it is not he, but sin dwelling in him (via the flesh) that is 'working' (7:17, 20). That may sound as if the flesh is not part of the believer, but something adventitious and auxiliary, an external

45 It is only after one gets into Romans 8 that this discord is potentially obviated. Now it is the indwelling Holy Spirit fighting the flesh (Gal 5:16–17): sin does not always have to win now, unless it and the flesh are allowed to by the believer. As 'even in the renewed [i.e., believers], this control of the Spirit is never perfect, as the flesh even in them retains much of its original power, they are forced to acknowledge that they too are carnal' (Hodge, *Epistle to the Romans*, 359).

add-on that wreaks havoc and causes chaos, but not of the essence of an individual. This, however, would be far from the truth: Paul's assertions are simply dramatic flourishes to underscore the dividedness within himself. This discord is so intense that, for rhetorical purposes, in order to depict that clash of wills (so to speak), the apostle claims that 'no longer am I the one working' (7:17, 20). But the fact is that this 'worker' of sin and evil is Paul himself (as is Every Christian), and '*I* am working', '*I* practise' and '*I* do' (7:15, 16, 19) provide that corrective. All that to say, believers themselves, *in toto*, are guilty sinners when they succumb to sin; the flesh is not simply a disjointed slice of them, or something outside and peripheral to them. A schismatic anthropology that dissects and disunites the flesh as being separate from the whole person is not the apostle's thesis here, nor is it anywhere in Scripture. Rather, Paul affirms that it is the 'I' who is the guilty party, as the confessions of 7:15, 16, 19 articulate. The flesh is an integral part of that fallen 'I' of every child of God on this side of eternity.

What about 'the law in me' (7:21)? How is that different from God's own law? To get to the bottom of this, notice (see Figure 3.14) the equation of 'law in me' (7:21a) with notations of other indwelling wickednesses.

7:17	'sin'	'dwelling in me'
7:18	'nothing good'	'dwells in me ... in my flesh'
7:20	'sin'	'dwelling in me'
7:21a	'[evil] law'	'in me'
7:21b	'evil'	'in me ... is present'

Figure 3.14

So, compounding the equation seen earlier, if 'law in me' (7:21a[46]) = 'sin ... in me' (7:17, 20) = 'nothing good ... in me ... in my flesh' (7:18) = 'in me evil is present' (7:21b), then this 'law' of 7:21a must be an anti-God element – an evil 'law' of sin (as the gloss in 7:21a '[*evil*] law', in Figure 3.14, points out), which is opposed to the 'good' 'law of God' (7:22). This evil law promulgated by the evil authority, sin, sees to it that evil is worked, practised and done by believers through their flesh (7:20–21, 23), despite their wishing to abide by the good law promulgated

46 Also described in 7:23 as '*another law* in my members'.

by the good authority, God. 'Sin's exercising such authority over us is a hideous usurpation of the prerogative of God's law … a terrible travesty, a grotesque parody, of that authority over us which belongs by right to God's holy law'.[47]

> For I delight in the law of God in the inner person, but I see another law in my members, waging war against the law of my mind and making me captive to the law of sin which is in my members. Wretched person that I am! Who will liberate me from this body of death? But thanks be to God through Jesus Christ our Lord. Then therefore, I myself, with the mind, am being a slave to the law of God, but with the flesh to the law of sin.
> (Rom. 7:22–25)

Notice, in 7:22–25, the synonyms for the good law (of God) contrasted with those for the evil law (of sin) (see Figure 3.15).[48]

	Good Law of God	Evil Law of Sin
7:22–23a	'*law* of God in the inner person'	'another *law* in my members'
7:23b	'*law* of my mind'	'*law* of sin which is in my members'
7:25	'*law* of God'	'*law* of sin'

Figure 3.15

Again, the discordant situation appears hopeless, with the evil law of sin, working through the flesh, seemingly winning the battle. A frustrating predicament indeed, and a plight from which there seems to be no possibility of extrication for this 'wretched person' desiring liberation from 'this body of death' (7:24[49]), at least not in Romans 7. However, even before Paul lands in Romans 8 where the resolution to this discord is found, there is a strong hint here in 7:25a that the requisite

47 Cranfield, *Critical and Exegetical Commentary*, 1: 364.

48 'Mind' (7:23) and 'inner person' (7:22) are also synonymous here (as is also the renewed 'mind' of 12:2).

49 The 'body of death' in 7:24 is equivalent to 'body of sin' (6:6) and to 'death-destined body' (6:12; 8:11), as well as to 'members', i.e., body parts (6:13, 19; 7:5, 23) – all collectively the physical instrument of the flesh (under the governance of sin) for the production of sins.

emancipation has been granted 'through Jesus Christ our Lord', a freedom from sin and a freedom unto obedience that will be expounded upon in the next chapter of Romans.

And so the apostle closes Romans 7 summarising his distressing situation in 7:25b: as a believer he is doubly a slave – not only to the law of God with his 'mind'/'inner person' (7:22, 23, 25: his wishing to serve God and do good), but also to the law of sin with his 'flesh' (7:5, 14, 18, 25: his succumbing to serve sin and do evil) – accounting for the debilitating discord that ensues.[50] Thus, the good law of God has its counterpart in the evil law of sin: the two authorities, God and sin, are locked in skirmish over the believer, with their own law and agent (Spirit and flesh, respectively) (see Figure 3.16).

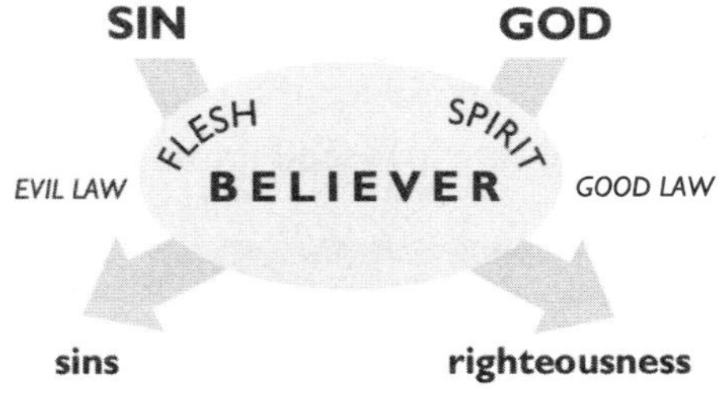

Figure 3.16

In sum, believers, baptised and bound in union with Christ, are no longer under the power of sin; in fact, they are dead to it. But there still remains a traitor within the camp – the flesh – causing a raging civil war within them. Although they may delight in the good law of God (7:22), the children of God are oft overcome by the evil law of sin because of the pervasive influence of their flesh (and the utter inadequacy of their own resources to fight sin and the flesh). All that to say even after being united with Christ in salvation, cured, believers are not free from sin's nefarious workings through their flesh: a relapse of the disease is a possibility (though not terminal, i.e., no loss of salvation is envisaged). Indeed, it is because they are in God's domain now that there is an intense discord and the resulting discomfiture at their incapacity (with their own

50 Whereas, as was mentioned, as a non-Christian he was only a slave to one authority – the evil one – and subject to the law of sin.

contrivances) to achieve their destiny to be sanctified for good works, so as to glorify God as he designed them to do.

What can ameliorate this helpless and hopeless situation? Christians cannot be relying on their own strength (totally insufficient) for sanctification, just as they could not for their justification (equally effete). Divine aid and grace were required for justification, and divine aid and grace are required for sanctification. And, yes, that assistance is forthcoming, hinted at in 7:25 and detailed in Romans 8, dealing with the Third Person of the Trinity, the divine doctor who guides, empowers and facilitates the obedience of the children of God to the law of God for the glory of God.[51]

Doctor

Romans 8 is unique in this letter: the Holy Spirit shows up four times in Romans 1–7[52] and six times in Romans 9–16,[53] but nineteen times in Romans 8, more than once in every two verses of this chapter.[54] This is undoubtedly a discussion that is intensely Spirit-related. It connects with the first mention of 'Spirit' in 7:6, that had noted almost in passing that believers united with Christ (baptised and bound to him) were to serve him as 'slaves in newness of Spirit and not in oldness of letter' (7:6). Now Romans 8, resuming that thought, commences with a restatement of the fact that 'there is now no condemnation to those in Christ Jesus' (8:1), i.e., they are no longer under law's condemnation for sins = 'oldness of letter' (7:6b). The apostle then proceeds with an explanation of what exactly it means to serve God, 'walking according to the Spirit' (8:2–30 [see 8:4], taking 29 verses – the main topic of the section), i.e., obedience under the 'doctor-ship' (direction, superintendence and empowerment) of the Spirit = 'slaves in newness of Spirit' (7:6b) (see Figure 3.17).

Romans 7, as we have seen, diagnoses a less-than-ideal situation: believers experiencing the discord of the tussle between flesh and mind.

51 'Doctor', the title of the next section, comes from the Latin, *docêre*, 'to teach', though, of course, the medical connotation is obvious (and intentional).

52 Rom. 1:4; 2:29; 5:5; 7:6 (six times if one adds 'spiritual', in 1:11; 7:14).

53 Rom. 9:1; 14:17; 15:13, 16, 19, 30 (seven times if one adds 'spiritual', in 15:27).

54 Rom. 8:2, 4, 5 (×2), 6, 9 (×3), 11 (×2), 13, 14, 15 (×2), 16, 23, 26 (×2), 27. The chapter in the NT with the next highest frequency is 1 Cor. 12, with eleven occurrences of 'Spirit' in thirty-one verses, slightly more than once in every three of its verses.

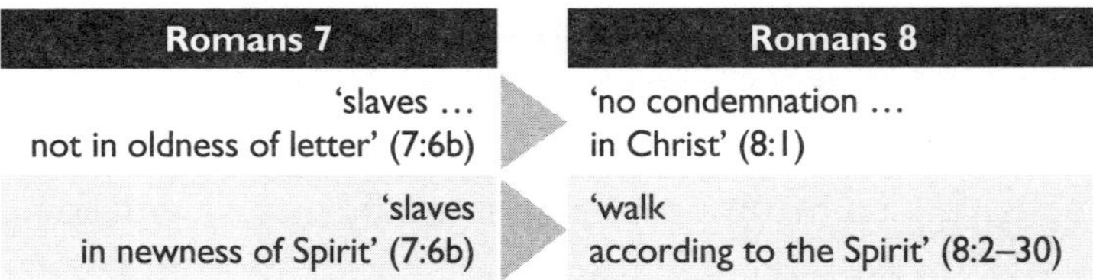

Romans 7	Romans 8
'slaves ... not in oldness of letter' (7:6b)	'no condemnation ... in Christ' (8:1)
'slaves in newness of Spirit' (7:6b)	'walk according to the Spirit' (8:2–30)

Figure 3.17

But Romans 8 prescribes the solution to this angst, and depicts the ideal situation: believers walking in obedience to God, by the empowerment of the Spirit that overcomes the flesh. The still-present flesh is to be subjugated by the power of the Spirit to whom the believer is yielded.

Spirit-directed sanctification (Rom. 8:1–30)

> Therefore there is now no condemnation to those in Christ Jesus.
> (Rom. 8:1)

Because of what was accomplished by Jesus Christ in his atoning work of salvation, 'there is now no condemnation [of the law] to those who are in Christ Jesus'. No doubt it is God's justification of sinners that is accomplished through Christ, but that is not the end of the story. What Paul adds in 8:2–4 makes clear that God's sanctification of believers is also a crucial outcome of, and integral to, what Christ has wrought.

> For the law of the Spirit of life has set you free in Christ Jesus from the law of sin and of death.
> (Rom. 8:2)

Freedom accomplished, not only from eternal punishment for sins (justification), but also from ongoing production of sins (sanctification): 'the law of the Spirit of life has set you free in Christ Jesus' (8:2). That this relates to sanctification is evident from the employment of the verb, 'set you free'. There have been only two other instances in Romans of that verb thus far, both times used with relation to 'sin' and to 'sanctification': '*having been freed* from sin, you were enslaved to righteousness ... unto sanctification' (6:18–19); and '*having been freed* from sin ... [believers are now] enslaved to God' producing 'fruit unto sanctification' (6:22). Since these referred to sanctification – emancipation from sin and enslavement to righteousness – that is, no doubt, also the import of the parallel in 8:2. Of course, this is obvious from the contrast between what set believers free ('the law of the Spirit of life') and what they have been freed from ('the law of sin and of death'). Both these 'laws', the good one and the evil one, respectively, were encountered earlier in various forms (see Figure 3.18).

	Good Law of God	Evil Law of Sin
7:22–23a	'*law* of God in the inner person'	'another *law* in my members'
7:23b	'*law* of my mind'	'*law* of sin which is in my members'
7:25	'*law* of God'	'*law* of sin'
8:2	'*law* of the Spirit of life'	'*law* of sin and of death'

Figure 3.18

Note the parallels in 8:2 between those two laws: each has a head noun and a twinned series of genitives that picture the diametric opposition between the two laws.

The genitives function identically in each set (see Figure 3.19). Genitives of Source indicate that the laws are sourced in (or are produced by) either the Third Person of deity, the Spirit, or the personified entity, sin. Genitives of Destination, on the other hand, indicate that those laws lead to (or produce) abundant life in the presence of God,[55] or death away from the presence of God on the other.[56]

	Genitives	
Noun	***Source***	***Destination***
'law	of the Spirit	of life'
'law	of sin	and of death'

Figure 3.19

55 Such a collocation of 'law' and 'Spirit' and 'life' recalls 7:10, 14 (where the law 'unto life' is described as 'spiritual'; also see 2 Cor. 3:6). 'Law of God' will show up again in Rom. 8:7, with 8:6 juxtaposing 'Spirit' and 'life'.

56 See Wallace, *Greek Grammar*, 100–1, 104–7, 109–10, for these genitival categories.

Because this antithesis between the evil law and the good law is oriented to sanctification, Paul explicitly labels the good law in 8:2 not as the 'law of God' as one might have expected (and as he had done earlier: 7:22, 25), but as the 'law of *the Spirit*', the specific divine agent of sanctification.[57]

The role of the Holy Spirit in sanctification is essential, for the flesh, the agent of sin and the instrumental cause of sinfulness, present and viable even in believers, cannot be overcome with one's own resources: the 'mind'/'inner person' will never achieve victory over the 'flesh', as was seen in Romans 7. Yes, believers have been 'set free' from the condemnation of sin (8:2; also see 6:18, 22), but this liberty does not mean that the evil law operating through the flesh is inactive; it only indicates that those united to Christ are now free not to succumb to that tendency. Though there has been a change of realm and a transfer of believers to a new domain, saved individuals can still yield, if they so wish, to the evil authority of the old regency, via the treasonous flesh still operating within them. But the happy truth is that, as believers, victory over the flesh is now made possible, because the indwelling Spirit, the doctor, works in and through them, prescribing the instructions (Scripture; see Chapter 4) and directing the operation of sanctification by empowering them to defeat the flesh. How the Third Person of the Godhead enables the sanctification of believers is next on the apostle's agenda.

> For what the law was unable [to do], in that it was weak through the flesh, God [did]: sending His own Son in the likeness of sinful flesh and for [a] sin [offering], He condemned sin in the flesh, in order that the righteous requirement of the law may be fulfilled in us who walk not according to the flesh but according to the Spirit.
> (Rom. 8:3–4)

A dual weakness plagues believers in this age, as mentioned in 8:3a. First, there is the weakness of the flesh: it is an incorrigible and irredeemable

57 Of course, priming the reader for a sanctification orientation, the law had already been tagged 'spiritual' in 7:14. On the other side of the opposition, perhaps the 'law of the flesh' would have been a better contrast to the 'law of the Spirit' (rather than 'law of sin'), for the flesh is the immediate agent of unholiness. However, this would have created the problem of having to assign source (or production) of the evil law to an entity that is part of the believer, the flesh. While the *performance* of sins may rightly be slotted as the portfolio of the flesh, the demonic originator of evil (and of the evil law) existed before humanity appeared on the scene at creation.

entity, a faithful agent of sin, exercising its baleful influence in believers to cause them to produce sins succumbing to the operation of sin's evil law and in opposition to God's good law. Second, there is the incapacity of God's law itself: though sourced in God, it is limited in its function – to detail divine demand and to condemn all who break it – and it offers no help to believers to obey God. But what the law could not do, God succeeded in doing, through the work of Christ who took on humanity, 'in the likeness of sinful flesh' (literally, 'in the likeness of the flesh of sin'[58]) and, in his impeccability, condemned sin (8:3b[59]). God's work in Christ is described in a chiastic way in 8:3b, 'sin' being shut off inside, by mentions of Christ's humanity (his 'flesh') functioning as bookends, and his decisive act of condemnation of sin at the centre (see Figure 3.20).

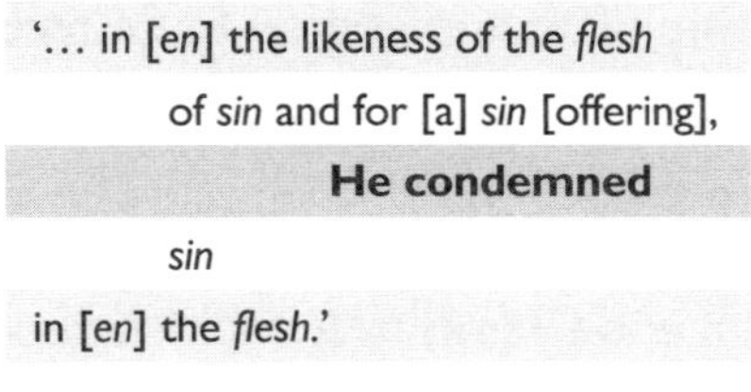

Figure 3.20

And with that work of God in Christ (8:3b, the situation of the *present*; see Figure 3.21), the law's incapacity and the weakness of the flesh (the dual problems – the situation of the *past*) are directly, dramatically and diametrically contrasted with the result of divine work (the situation of the *future*[60]): the keeping of the law's requirement by the saved ones not walking subject to the flesh – and here is the greatest difference between past and future (in bold in Figure 3.21) – but *in submission to the Holy Spirit.*

58 I have retained the literal version for the figure below to bring out the chiastic structure of that statement of God's work in Christ.

59 There are over forty occurrences of the Greek phrase *peri hamartias* (8:3) in the LXX, the vast majority of them dealing with the sin offering in the Mosaic Law (LXX Exod. 32:30; Lev. 4:3 [×2], 14, 28, 35; 5:6 [× 3], 7 [× 2], 8, 9, 10, 11 [× 2], 13; et cetera), as well as in Heb. 10:6, 8; 13:11. Thus, my translation of *peri hamartias* in Rom. 8:3: 'for [a] sin [offering]'.

60 'Future' because this is, again, a participatory *potentiality*, indicated by the subjunctive in 8:4, 'may be fulfilled'. Though help is available in the form of the Holy Spirit, it is not guaranteed that believers will follow that divine doctor; they could still revert to living according to the flesh. Hopefully, by God's grace, the fulfilment of the law's requirements is being/will be accomplished, more and more, day by day, in the lives of God's people (more on this potentiality becoming actuality in Chapter 4).

PAST (8:3a)	PRESENT (8:3b)	FUTURE (8:4)
'*law* was unable to do'	**Work of God in Christ**	'righteous requirement of the *law* may be fulfilled'
'weak … through the *flesh*'		'in us who walk not according to the *flesh*,
		but [walk] according to the Spirit'

Figure 3.21

In context, then, the 'righteous requirement of the law' is the divine demand of God, i.e., all that is commanded in his good law.[61] 'The use of the singular [for "righteous requirement" (and for my phrase "divine demand")] is significant. It brings out the fact that the law's requirements are essentially a unity, the plurality of commandments being not a confused and confusing conglomeration but a recognizable and intelligible whole, the fatherly will of God for His children.'[62] And, indeed, the fulfilment of God's 'righteous requirement' was the goal of deliverance:[63] this, as we have seen before, is the destiny of believers – obedience and holiness in the doing of good works (that include dispositions, discourses and deeds), so that the ultimate design of God, his glory, might be accomplished in them.[64] And such a destiny can be arrived at only with

61 Also see 1:32 ('righteous requirement of God') and 2:26 ('righteous requirement of the law', as here in 8:4).

62 Cranfield, *Critical and Exegetical Commentary*, 1: 384.

63 As expressed in the Greek *hina*-clause that commences 8:4: 'in order that …' Also see the identical connection in 7:4: deliverance 'in order that [*hina*] we may be fruit-bearing to God' (and, of course, the whole exhortation to the same end in 6:15–23). Also see Rom. 6:4, 6; Eph. 2:10; Titus 2:14; 3:4–8, all of which undergird the same notion of the goal of deliverance with *hina*-clauses.

64 The link between the work of God in Christ and the work of the Spirit is not explicitly stated, but were Christ's atonement for believers' sins, past and present and future, not accomplished, there would be no meaningful sense in which God's 'righteous requirement' could ever be fulfilled by them. Without the work of Christ, there would always be unatoned-for sins lurking in the past, not to mention such unpaid-for actual sins being committed in the present, as well as potential unforgiven sins being engaged in, in the future. Such arrears of sins would, in the final analysis, gainsay the claim that God's 'righteous requirement'/divine demand was fulfilled or fully met by his children. In addition, there is also Christ's sending of the Holy Spirit upon believers for their sanctification (John 14:15–26; 15:26; 16:7), a momentous occurrence that could happen only after the atonement was accomplished. Not that the Spirit was uninvolved in justification: Rom. 8:11 explicitly attributes the resurrection of Christ – and of believers — to the work of the Holy Spirit (see Rom. 1:4; Heb. 9:14; and perhaps, 1 Pet. 1:18). Also see John 3:5–6; 16:8–11; Rom. 8:5–9, 15; 15:18–19; 1 Cor. 3:16; 6:11; 12:13; 2 Cor. 3:17; Gal. 3:14; Eph. 1:13–14; Titus 3:5. Of course, the baptism by Christ of the believer in the Spirit is also coterminous with justification. But here in Rom. 8:3–4 it is the sanctifying work of the Spirit that is in view.

the aid of the divine doctor, the Holy Spirit, without whom there is only incapacity, weakness, frustration and failure.

In sum, God's goal with the work of Christ and that of the Spirit in the lives of his people is explicitly stated in Romans 8:3–4. Those once incapable of obeying divine command in the flesh would now be enabled to do so in the Spirit for, after their union with Christ, believers 'walk not according to the flesh but according to the Spirit' who, as the doctor and director of their sanctification, empowers them to abide by God's moral will (which itself was inscribed in the sacred writ by the inspiration of the selfsame Third Person of the Godhead).[65] The inability of the law and the weakness of the flesh were overcome by what God did! 'What God's gift of His Spirit has brought about … is nothing less than a beginning of the fulfilment of the divine purpose of Christ's work, namely, the establishment of God's law in the life of believers', their destiny for good works, and ultimately the design of God for his glory.[66]

Such empowerment of believers by the Spirit does not mean that obedience to divine demand involves no responsibility on the part of the believer. Not at all. Rather, it is a 'both … and …' situation, as often described in Scripture, for example, in Hebrews 13:20–21: 'Now may the God of peace … equip *you* with every good thing *to do* His will, *He doing in us* what is pleasing before Him, through Jesus Christ, to whom be glory forever.' Notice how the 'doing' is both human responsibility ('you' do) and divine prerogative ('He' does).[67] In fact, such a joint 'doing' is also part of God's promise in Ezekiel 36:27: 'My Spirit, I will put within you, and *I will do* it such that in My statutes you will walk and My judgements *you* will keep so as *to do* [them].'[68]

---

65 This notion is echoed also in Col. 1:10–11 where Paul prays that the people of God will 'walk worthy of the Lord, pleasing him in all things, in all good work bearing fruit and growing in the knowledge of God, empowered in all power according to His glorious might'. Likewise, 2 Pet. 1:3: '[God's] divine power has given us all things [necessary] for life and godliness.' This divine power is that of the Holy Spirit.

66 Cranfield, *Critical and Exegetical Commentary*, 1: 372. This, readers will notice, is not very different from what was seen in Eph. 2:10 as the goal of God for his saved people: to do good works for the glory of God.

67 Both verbs translate the Greek *poieō*, 'do', a wordplay of great significance that, unfortunately, most English translations fail to do justice to.

68 Another equally fateful translational neglect of the Hebrew *'sh*, 'do', in English versions.

Paul continues in Romans 8:

> For those who are according to the flesh set their minds on things of the flesh, but those according to the Spirit, on the things of the Spirit. For the mindset of the flesh is death, but the mindset of the Spirit is life and peace, because the mindset of the flesh is hostility towards God, for to the law of God it does not submit, for neither is it able [to do so], and those who are in the flesh are unable to please God. But you – you are not in the flesh but in the Spirit, if indeed the Spirit of Christ dwells in you. But if anyone does not have the Spirit of Christ, this one is not His.
> (Rom. 8:5–9)

The contrast between flesh-directed non-Christians and Spirit-directed Christians is clearly stated. The former do not submit to God's law and, in fact, are unable to do so; the latter, it is implied in an unstated premise (phrases in brackets in the unshaded box in Figure 3.22), are submissive to divine demand and, because of the indwelling Spirit, are actually capable of being so.

Flesh-directed Unbelievers	Spirit-directed Believers
'according to the flesh' (8:5a)	'according to the Spirit' (8:5b)
Minds set on 'things of the flesh' (8:5a)	Minds set on 'things of the Spirit' (8:5b)
Result: 'death' (8:6a)	Result: 'life and peace' (8:6b)
'hostility towards God' (8:7a)	Indwelt by 'the Spirit of Christ' (8:9)
Non-submissive to God's law (8:7b) Incapable of such submission (8:7b)	[Implied: *Submissive to God's law*] [Implied: *Capable of such submission*]
Unable to please God (8:8)	Bound to Christ [and pleasing to him] (8:9)

Figure 3.22

Paul explains the consequences of the lifestyle of non-Christians, who have their minds set on 'the things of the flesh': these individuals are destined for eternal separation from God, death, and they are in a state of hostility towards God. But believers, who have their minds set on 'things of the Spirit' receive 'life and peace',[69] and they, indwelt by the

69 No doubt, this 'life and peace' will be enjoyed both in the here-and-now and in the then-and-there.

Spirit, are in a state of allegiance to God. The contrast is strengthened by the emphatic second-person plural pronoun referring to the children of God, 'But *you* – you are not in the flesh but in the Spirit' and indwelt by him (8:9a). Those without this Third Person are decidedly not God's, not Christ's, not the Spirit's (8:9b). On the other hand, those with the Spirit are Christ's – this sense of possession harks back to the notion of believers 'bound' to Christ, to 'become another's', i.e., Christ's (7:1–4). The long and short of it is that non-Christians do not please God; Christians, with the Spirit and bound to Christ, do.

But the affirmation of 'death' for non-Christians vs 'life and peace' for Christians (8:6) raises an obvious issue: believers die, too. Even though the 'death' in 8:6 refers to eternal death (exclusively for non-Christians), the issue still remains: *both* non-Christians and Christians do die physically as a result of the fall. Lest this pose a problem for his readers, Paul clarifies with a parenthetical remark, 8:10–11:

> (And if Christ is in you, even though the body is dead because of [your] sin, yet the Spirit is life because of [Christ's] righteousness. And if the Spirit of the One who raised Jesus from the dead dwells in you, the One who raised Christ from the dead will also give life to your death-destined bodies through His Spirit dwelling in you.) (Rom. 8:10–11)

The contrast in 8:10 (see Figure 3.23) makes it clear that while the 'sin' of Christians leads to physical death – 'the body is dead' (as is the case for non-Christians, too, of course[70]) – it is the 'righteousness' of Christ that makes possible the resurrection of their 'death-destined bodies', through the Spirit, one day, soon and very soon.[71]

'the body	is dead	because of [your] sin'
'the Spirit	is life	because of [Christ's] righteousness'

Figure 3.23

70 The present tense, 'body *is* dead' in 8:10 is parallel to 'death-destined body' in 8:11, indicating that the body is already under the sentence of death (in the present), and that death will ensue in due course (in the future).

71 It is obvious that in 8:10 the 'sin' referred to is that of humans (hence the gloss 'your'); that

Thus, the wages of sin, at least its partial payment, is extracted from the believer – death, physical (8:10, 11, 38) but not eternal (8:2, 6).

After this parenthetical statement on the unavoidability of physical death and the inevitability of physical resurrection for believers in Christ, through the Spirit, Paul returns to his exhortation regarding the new life of those in union with Christ. Once again, a contrast is created between non-Christians, who do not have the Spirit, and Christians, who do (and whose sanctification is directed by him):

> Then therefore, brothers [and sisters], we are under obligation not to the flesh to live according to the flesh – for if according to the flesh you live, you will certainly die; but if by the Spirit you put to death the practices of the body, you will live. For all who are led by the Spirit of God, these are the children of God.
> (Rom. 8:12–14)

The distinction between the lifestyles of non-Christians (*A*, *B*, *C*; see Figure 3.24) and Christians (*C′*, *B′*, *A′*) is apparent in their lives and this difference is cleverly schematised in the chiastic structuring of 8:12–14 (see Figure 3.24).[72]

UNBELIEVERS

A	'we are under obligation not to the **flesh**'		
B	'to live according to the **flesh**'		
C	'if according to the *flesh*	you ***live***,	you will certainly ***die***'

BELIEVERS

C'	'if by the *Spirit*	you ***put to death*** the practices of the body,	you will ***live***'
B'	'for all who are led by the Spirit of **God**'		
A'	'these are the children of **God**'		

Figure 3.24

the 'righteousness' is that of Christ is more than likely, in view of the juxtaposition of 8:11 that follows (hence the gloss 'Christ's').

72 Of course, *A* refers to believers, but the negation clearly implies that non-Christians *are* 'under obligation … to the flesh'. Also of note, the present tenses of 'if you *live*' and 'if you are *put to death*' (with the conditional, 'if', 8:13; as also in 8:9 [×2], 11) simply indicate the

Both *A–B* and *B′–A′* include a double mention of 'flesh' and 'God', respectively. The significance of this comparison is that believers, God's children, are under obligation to him (not to the flesh), to obey his good law, as directed by his indwelling Spirit. For them, the outcome is life abundant and eternal. The responsibility of the believer is also clearly demarcated: to 'put to death the practices of the body', the instrument of the flesh that is itself an agent of sin.

And Paul joyously continues the trajectory of the filiation of believers to their God: they are his children, because of the 'Spirit of adoption' – the divine agent that relates God's people as children of their heavenly Father.[73]

> For you did not receive the Spirit of slavery unto fear, but you received the Spirit of adoption by whom we cry, 'Abba, Father!'
> (Rom. 8:15)

There is no need for fear, anxiety or worry about the seeming impossibility of ever being able to please God (8:8).[74] For believers can do so, because upon their adoption by God they have received the divine Spirit, who now directs their sanctification on the path of obedience to God's 'righteous requirement' towards holiness befitting the children of a holy Father. The apostle adduces two witnesses to this truth of divine adoption[75] – the Holy Spirit and the spirits of believers, together 'co-testifying' to this divine adoption:

> The Spirit himself co-testifies with our spirit that we are the children of God, and if children, also heirs, even heirs of God and co-heirs with Christ, if indeed we co-suffer [with Him] in order that we may also be co-glorified [with Him].
> (Rom. 8:16–17)

manifestations of the underlying status of the subjects as non-Christians and Christians, respectively. There is no suggestion of loss of eternal life for the latter; rather, it points to the ongoing continuance of their 'putting to death' sinful practices.

73 No doubt this is linked to union with Christ – baptised by Christ and bound to him – *in the Spirit* (described in Romans 6–7).

74 Or even the fear of death, the nearest antecedent crisis that might well provoke apprehension.

75 Perhaps this is a nod to the OT requirement of two witnesses in forensic settings to establish the truth of matters in question (Deut. 19:15). Also see 1 John 3:24 and 4:13 for this Spirit-sourced testimony to deity's abiding with believing humanity.

What an assurance for children: 'God is your heavenly Father!'[76] And if believers are children of God, then they are heirs of the Father; and if they are heirs, then they are co-heirs with the Son.

But this 'co-heir'-ship with Christ introduces another gloomy note into this otherwise mostly cheerful symphony of events: co-heirs of Christ not only share his glory but also his suffering ('co-suffering [with Him]'; 8:17). One suspects that the topic of suffering is not unrelated to Paul's recent mention of physical death in 8:10–11, the necessary consequence of the fall that is the fount of all suffering. Yet, that agony of believers 'co-suffering' with Christ is soon to be eclipsed by their 'co-glorification' with him. Since the apostle has addressed the justification of believers already in this letter, and is concluding his discourse on their sanctification here, it makes sense to touch upon the final act of the epic drama as well: the glorification of the saints of God in Christ, and the eternal hope thereby engendered. The remainder of this section (before the apostle's powerful conclusion in 8:31–39) addresses this endpoint further.

> For I consider that the sufferings of the present time are not worthy [to be compared] to the soon-coming glory to be revealed to us. For the anticipation of creation for the revelation of the children of God is being eagerly awaited.
> (Rom. 8:18–19)

Yes, there is going to be suffering, but the 'sufferings of the present time' are incommensurate with the eternal glory of the saints. And that glory is expressed in three different ways, with sequential word-repetitions chain-linking the trio: 'the soon-coming *glory* to be *revealed* to *us*' (8:18), 'the *revelation* of the *children of God*' (8:19) and 'the *glory* of the *children of God*' (8:21). No doubt this glory of the children of God redounds to the glory of God, a mutual glorification of sorts (though, of course, the latter is foundational to the former):

76 'Abba' transliterates *Abba*, Aramaic for 'father', a term of endearment – connoting more 'dear father' than 'Daddy' (Schreiner, *Romans*, 419) – used by Jesus himself to address the heavenly Father (Mark 14:36; also see Gal. 4:6).

> For this also we pray always for you, in order that our God may count you worthy of [your] calling, and fulfil [your] every desire of goodness and the work of faith with power by which the name of our Lord Jesus may be glorified in you, and you in Him.
> (2 Thess. 1:11–12)

That is to say, in the glorification of God's people, God is himself being glorified, for it is his glory that his people reflect (or 'remanate', to use Edwards' term).[77] 'As the image of God, man[kind] was created to reflect, express and participate in the glory of God, in miniature, creaturely form. Restoration to this is effected through the Spirit's work of sanctification, in which he takes those who have distorted God's image in the shame of sin, and transforms them into those who bear that image in glory.'[78] Psalm 8:5 describes with wonder the glory possessed by humans at creation (and defaced in the fall, though not effaced), God sovereignly enabling them, as rulers, to represent deity to the rest of the world and thus bring him glory: 'You make him lower than God by a little, and with glory and splendour You crown him.'[79]

The design of God for humanity is, in and through its sanctification destiny directed by the doctor-teacher Spirit, soon coming to pass: the glorification of God (and of his people) draweth nigh! And so, despite believers' ongoing struggles with the flesh and with sin – not to mention the debilitations and depredations caused by the fall: all manner of suffering including physical death – believers continue to hope for that finale, God's glorification (and theirs). And so does the rest of creation: 'With poetic boldness and with a penetrating prophetic insight Paul sees the whole splendid theatre of the universe together with all sub-human life within it as eagerly awaiting the time when the sons of God will be made manifest in their true glory.'[80] Thus, it is not only the children of

---

77 See Chapter 1 for Edwards' thesis on the glorification of deity. God's choice of his people for 'for salvation through sanctification by the Spirit and faith in the truth' is so that they will gain 'the glory of our Lord Jesus Christ' (2 Thess. 2:13b–14). This is echoed in Col. 3:4: 'When Christ, our life, is revealed, then you also will be revealed with Him in glory.' As well, in Phil. 3:21: '[The Lord Jesus Christ] will transform our humble body into conformity with His glorious body.'

78 Ferguson, *The Holy Spirit*, 139–40.

79 As we saw in Chapter 1.

80 Cranfield, *Critical and Exegetical Commentary*, 1: 412–13.

God who have been caught in the disequilibrium of the fall and its consequent suffering – the entirety of creation has also been so burdened, no doubt explaining its eager anticipation of what is to come:

> For to futility creation was subjected, not willingly, but because of the One subjecting it – in hope that creation itself also will be set free from the slavery of corruption unto the freedom of the glory of the children of God. For we know that the whole creation co-groans and co-suffers until now. And not only this, but also we ourselves, having the firstfruits of the Spirit – we ourselves also groan within ourselves, eagerly awaiting the adoption as children, the redemption of our body.
> (Rom. 8:20–23)

Creation (the non-human part thereof) did not end up this way because of what it had done; after all, besides the demonic reptile, it was not a 'willing' participant of the fall of humans. Rather it was God, the Creator and Judge, who decreed the dire consequences of, and severe penalties for, the invasion of sin into all that God had formed and called 'good' (8:20). And so, all creation now 'co-groans and co-suffers' with the children of God (8:22), 'eagerly awaiting' the fulfilment of human redemption (8:23), for that momentous end will also have an equally all-pervasive and eternally salubrious effect upon the rest of creation.

Paul makes it clear that one of the critical elements of this closing act of salvation yearned for by believers is the 'redemption of our body' (8:23). That 'death-destined body' (8:11; also see 6:12) will finally be redeemed. This redemption refers to the consummation of salvation upon glorification, the ultimate victory over death and all suffering. On that day there will be an appropriate 'co-glorification' with Christ of those who are 'co-heirs' with him, the children of God,[81] but who now 'co-suffer' with him (8:17).

The anguish and agony generating this 'groaning' of believers is particularly acute because they have partaken of the Holy Spirit who has

81 'We know that when He appears, like Him we will be, because we will see Him just as He is' (1 John 3:2).

produced 'firstfruits' (8:23): the results produced by the Holy Spirit are being enjoyed already, though the fullness of the harvest, so to speak, is yet to come. In other words, the people of God '*received* the adoption as children' of God, through the working of the Spirit (8:15) – it has happened. But paradoxically, believers now are only '*eagerly awaiting* the adoption as children' (8:23) – it is yet to happen. It is a 'both … and …' situation, or better, an 'already … but not yet …' state, thus generating a temporary, but painful, disconnect between the bane of 'now' and the bliss of 'then'. Nevertheless, the hope of that last day, when the promise of God of a bumper crop for his people is fulfilled, is certain. Yes, the fructification of salvation is sure and near.

> For in hope we were saved; but hope that is seen is not hope; for what one sees – why hope [for it]? But if for what we do not see we hope, with endurance we eagerly wait [for it].
> (Rom. 8:24–25)

With a neat structure, Paul underscores the 'already' ('we were saved'; 8:24a) and the 'not yet' ('we eagerly wait [for it]'; 8:25b): these two elements are separated by an alternated scattering of 'hope' and 'see' (see Figure 3.25).[82]

'For in hope we were saved'
'hope' [*noun*]
'see' [*verb*]
'hope' [*noun*]
'see' [*verb*]
'hope' [*verb*]
'see' [*verb*]
'hope' [*verb*]
'… with endurance we eagerly wait [for it]'

Figure 3.25

This is as if to say: 'For in hope we were saved … [and] with endurance we eagerly wait [for it].' And, yes, 'hope' will become 'seen', 'hope' will

82 A deliberate patterning is evident also in the grammatical properties of these words separating the 'already' and the 'not yet' (as shown within brackets).

turn to 'sight' and 'hoping' will be converted to 'seeing', more and more, day by day! In sum, salvation has begun, and is in the process of being consummated, therefore Paul exhorts: 'Hang in there "with endurance"!'

> And in the same way, the Spirit also co-supports our weakness; for what we may pray for as [we] ought, we do not know, but the Spirit Himself intercedes [for us] with inexpressible groanings, and the One who searches the heart knows what the mind of the Spirit is, because He intercedes for the saints according to God['s will].
> (Rom. 8:26–27)

Creation groans (8:22), believers groan (8:23) and now we are told that the Spirit groans, too (8:26). This post-fall dispensation is surely an age of groaning! But what does it mean for the Spirit to be groaning 'in the same way' (and to whom is he groaning)?

To figure this out, one needs to go back to the last-mentioned direct activity of the Holy Spirit in our text – in 8:16. After that verse, in which the Spirit was the subject of the verb 'co-testify', the next instance of the Third Person of the Trinity getting a verb is here in 8:26. What is striking is that in both those texts, 8:16 and 8:26, the verbs indicating the Spirit's action are *syn*-affixed ones: *symmartyreō*, 'co-testify', in 8:16; and *synantilambanō*, 'co-support', in 8:26. The 'co-testifying' suggests a quasi-verbal activity on the part of the Spirit and, not surprisingly, 'co-supporting' does too – it is an intercession with 'groanings' – as the structure of 8:26 depicts: the actions in *A*, *C* and *A′* are all likely to be verbal in nature (see Figure 3.26).

A	'the *Spirit* also co-supports			**LIKELY VERBAL**
	B	*our* weakness;		
		C	for what we may pray for as [we] ought,	**VERBAL**
	B'	we do not know,		
A'	but the *Spirit* Himself intercedes … with groanings'			**VERBAL**

Figure 3.26

So the two actions of the Holy Spirit described in 8:16 and 8:26 are, in a sense, speeches, the first directed to believers (assuring them that they are the children of God, in 8:16), and the second directed to God (endorsing to him that these believers are the children of God, in 8:26). In other words, the Spirit is reminding believers that God is their Father, and he is also reminding the Father (in a manner of speaking) that believers are his children! (See Figure 3.27.)

'Children, this is your Father God!'

8:16	'The Spirit *co*-testifies with *our* spirit that [*hoti*] we are *children* of *God*'

'Father God, these are Your children!'

8:26–27	'The Spirit even *co*-supports *our* weakness … because [*hoti*] He intercedes for the *saints* according to *God*['s will]'

Figure 3.27

What could be more powerful, moving, efficacious or reassuring for suffering saints, the children of the Father God, who, in these trying days, are awaiting with hope and endurance the consummation of their deliverance?[83] But Paul is not done yet! He now turns to the Father's overarching purpose for his children:

> And we know that to those who love God, all things co-work unto good, to those who are called according to [His] purpose.
> (Rom. 8:28)

Those children of the Father are labelled by the apostle as 'those who love God', sons and daughters who love their divine parent – a reiteration of the filial status of all believers.[84] These God-lovers (i.e., all God's children) are privileged humans, for 'all things co-work' synergistically and fittingly for the end result of the 'good' of these individuals, who are additionally tagged as 'those who are called according to [His] purpose' (8:28). Though clearly it is divine sovereignty and providence that is working out these things for good to the people of God ('according to [His] purpose'), surprisingly, the subject of Paul's sentence in 8:28 is

83 Indeed, we find out later that it is not just the Spirit, but Christ, too, who intercedes for believers (8:34).

84 The love of God towards his children is in no doubt, considering the divine initiatives of Romans 6–8, and in the focused statement of God's plan for them in 8:28–30. Besides, the love of God in Christ for the ones he redeemed is explicitly affirmed in 8:35, 37.

not God, but 'all things' – it is these 'all things' that are co-working! 'All things' have seemingly come to life and are being personified as actively working on behalf of God, for the people of God, for their good. 'To say that all things assist believers is thus – in a *biblical* context – a heightening of the statement that God assists them; for it is to assert not only that He assists them, but also that His help is triumphantly and utterly effective.'[85]

And though the perfecting of this 'good' is, of course, ultimately eschatological – the glorification of believers (8:30, below; and the glorification of God, too, no doubt) – the 'co-working for good' has already begun, in the here-and-now (as the present tense of 'co-work' in 8:28 acknowledges). With that, Paul proceeds to condense the design of God for his children.

> For those whom He foreknew, He also predestined to be conformed to the image of His Son, so that He would be the firstborn among many brothers [and sisters]. And those He predestined, these He also called; and those He called, these He also justified; and those He justified, these He also glorified.
> (Rom. 8:29–30)

It all begins with his gracious election of his people, even as he 'foreknew' them (8:29).[86] To 'foreknow' can mean knowing beforehand (as in Acts 26:5; 2 Pet. 3:17), but a prior knowledge is likely not what is intended here. Rather, the OT sense of 'know' – intimate knowledge and choice (as in Gen. 18:19; Jer. 1:5; Amos 3:2) – is what is at the forefront of the apostle's mind in Romans 8:29, particularly since what is 'foreknown' by God is a personal object (as also in Rom. 11:2; 1 Pet. 1:20): believers

85 Cranfield, *Critical and Exegetical Commentary*, 1: 429 (emphasis original). It is also quite likely that 'all things' are not necessarily 'co-working' with each other, but they are with God himself, the beneficent Father of his children, 'who works all things according to the counsel of His will' (Eph. 2:11).

86 However, it is probably futile and unwise to create a temporal order of the divinely orchestrated events listed in 8:29–30. We are contemplating a rather inscrutable sequence of events that happened in the past, that happen in the present, and that will happen in the future. Propounding a precise timetable for these momentous happenings is not the apostle's goal, though a general movement from eternity past to eternity future is discernible.

themselves, and not something *about* them.[87] 'It highlights his covenantal love and affection for those whom he has chosen.'[88] This intimate knowledge and choice is then the basis of God's predestination of his people (his foreordination of them) to be 'conformed to the image of His Son' (8:29), ultimately a restoration of the *imago Dei* in its fullness, in the model and icon (i.e., 'image', from the Greek *eikōn*; 8:29) of the perfect Man, the Lord Jesus Christ, the *imago Christi*.[89]

This also makes Christ one of the many children of God (i.e., in his humanity; in his deity, he is, of course, *the* Son of God), and thereby he becomes 'the firstborn among many brothers [and sisters]' (8:29). Indeed, it is only with the ongoing conformation of believers to the fullness of the image/*eikōn* of Christ (as they are sanctified) that they become the children of God in its plenary sense and full scope, enjoying all the manifold blessings of siblinghood with Christ.[90]

Because this sanctification-related trajectory of the conformation of God's children to the image of God's Son is pictured in 8:29, the apostle can move, in his summary in 8:30, from predestination → calling → justification → glorification, eliding over sanctification. A remarkable précis this is, indeed, of the development of the children of God, from a time before they existed to a time beyond their earthly existence – all for the sake of being conformed into the image of Christ, the restoration in them of the *imago Dei* that had been defaced at the fall, a reconstitution that ultimately redounds to God's glory, deity's design for creation.[91] And thus will the design of God be accomplished at last – divine glory!

---

87 Moo, *Epistle to the Romans*, 532–3.

88 Schreiner, *Romans*, 453.

89 Jesus Christ is also fully God, of course, but that is an essence unique to the Godhead and utterly unattainable by created beings.

90 Besides 8:29, the notion of believers' conformation to the image of Christ is also found in Matt. 10:24–25; Rom. 6:3–6; 1 Cor. 15:48–49; 2 Cor. 3:18; Gal. 2:20; 4:19; Eph. 4:13, 20–24; Phil. 1:21; 3:20–21; Col. 1:28; 3:4, 10–11; 1 John 3:2. More on this in Chapter 4.

91 In fact, conformation to the image of Christ points to a state *better* than that in the Garden of Eden pre-fall, for at its fulfilment in the eschaton, believers fully conformed to Christ's image (1 John 3:2) will be removed from the very presence of sin. While in the state of innocence (as was Adam once), the situation of humanity could be described as *posse non peccare*, 'possible *not* to sin', and in the current age as *non posse non peccare* ('*not* possible *not* to sin'); in the end, the children of God will be in a state (as is Christ) that is *non posse peccare*, '*not* possible to sin' (see Peter Lombard, *The Four Books of Sentences* 2.19.1; Augustine, *Admonition and Grace* 33). What amazing grace! And it all compounds the glory of God for, without the fall and the redemption therefrom, and without sanctification unto

Overwhelming conquerors (Rom. 8:31–39)

The apostle concludes at last, but what a grand finale it is! Moving away from the distress of self-directed sanctification in Romans 7[92] and moving to the delights of Spirit-directed sanctification in Romans 8, the discussion is broadened here at the end of the large section of Romans 6–8 to anything and everything in life, culminating in a majestic benediction and doxological utterance.

Paul begins his conclusion of Romans 6–8 by raising and answering a question, in parallel to what he had done twice before (see Figure 3.28).[93]

> What, then, shall we say to these things? If God is for us, who can be against us? The One who did not spare His own Son but gave Him over for us all, how will He not also with Him graciously grant us all things?
> (Rom. 8:31–32)

REMAIN IN SIN? NEVER! (6:1–7:6)
'What then shall we say? ... *Remain in sin?* ... May it never be!' (6:1–2a)

LAW IS SIN? NEVER! (7:7–8:30)
'What then shall we say? *Is the law sin?* May it never be!' (7:7)

Conclusion

WHO [WHAT] IS AGAINST US? NO ONE, NOTHING! (8:31–39)
'What then shall we say to these things? ... *Who can be against us?*' (8:31)

Figure 3.28

---

glorification, there would have been attributes of the Trinitarian Godhead and aspects of divine working that would otherwise have never been known.

92 And the discomposure of sin-directed suffering in the middle of Romans 8.

93 That a new section commences in 8:31 is clear from the restatement of the rhetorical query: 'What then shall we say?' that was encountered at the beginning of the major sections of Romans 6–8, in 6:1 and 7:7. And that 8:31–39 is a conclusion of sorts to the larger section Romans 6–8 also seems apparent, with an addition of a clause in 8:31 to that repeated question: 'What, then, shall we say *to these things*?', i.e., to all that has been said thus far. Also, in reply to the question of 'Who [what] can be against us?', rather than give a firm negative as in the similar instances earlier (6:2a; 7:7), here Paul fires off a barrage of more rhetorical questions in 8:32, 33, 34a, 35a, 35b. The answer to these is as decisive as the ones given in prior sections: No one [and nothing] can be against us ... because 'God is for us'!

With God on the side of believers, nothing else matters, nothing can overwhelm, and nobody can defeat them (8:31). For if the God who is for them even gave his own Son for them 'all', how can he not also then provide 'all' things in his grace? (8:32).

The apostle proceeds to make his closing argument for believers' triumph explicit: no one and nothing can oppose the 'elect',[94] because God is the justifier (8:33), and Christ, the resurrected One now at the right hand of God, is the intercessor.

> Who will bring a charge against the elect of God? God is the one who justifies. Who is the one who condemns? Christ [Jesus] is the One who died, but even more, He is the One who was raised, the One who is at the right hand of God, the One who also intercedes for us.
> (Rom. 8:33–34)

This is a picture of a courtroom scene, with the adversary, Satan, bringing a charge against God's people – entirely unsuccessfully![95] Not only is the atoning work of Christ sufficient for their justification by God, Christ's ongoing advocacy also prevails for the flesh-related lapses of sinfulness even while Spirit-directed sanctification is ongoing (until the soon-coming final day of glorification). Therefore, there is *nothing* that can separate God's people from him and from his love for them in Christ.

> Who will separate us from the love of Christ? Trouble, or distress, or persecution, or famine, or nakedness, or peril, or sword? Just as it has been written, 'For Your sake we being killed all the day, we are considered as sheep for slaughter.' But in all these things we overwhelmingly conquer through the One who loved us. For I am

94 These are those whom God 'foreknew', 'predestined', 'called', 'justified' and 'glorified' (8:29–30) – the children of God in union with Christ, baptised unto him and bound to him, the blessed ones who are being sanctified and thus being conformed into the image of their Lord by the Spirit.

95 Elements of the forensic arena echo in 8:1 ('condemnation') and 8:3, 34 ('condemned'/'condemns'). The notion of Christ as the intercessor is also found in Heb. 7:25; 1 John 2:1. Of course, we have already seen another divine intercessor, a divine advocate on retainer, acting on behalf of the children of God: the doctor of believers' sanctification, the Holy Spirit (8:26 employs the same verb, 'interceded', as here in 8:34).

> persuaded that neither death, nor life, nor angels, nor principalities, nor things present, nor things to come, nor powers, nor height, nor depth, nor any other created thing will be able to separate us from the love of God which is in Christ Jesus our Lord.
> (Rom. 8:35–39)

No, no one and nothing – not even angels, demonic powers or death – can separate God's people from his love (8:35, 39), in spite of their going through traumatic situations of all kinds on this side of eternity (8:11, 35–36). And Paul corrals Psalm 44:22 in support (in Rom. 8:36), showing that 'the tribulations which face Christians are nothing new or unexpected, but have all along been characteristic of the life of God's people', and will continue to be so until the final day.[96] Yet, 'in all these things' insalubrious and nefarious, traumatic and lethal, the children of God 'overwhelmingly conquer' through Christ, the lover of their souls and the Saviour of their lives, to whom they are baptised and bound (8:37). To 'conquer' alone would indicate successful passage through these trials, but to '*overwhelmingly* conquer' points out that in and through Christ (and by the power of the indwelling Holy Spirit, all prompted by the love of God the Father), every woe and sorrow of temporal life – 'all these things' (8:37) – is paradoxically and marvellously transformed into 'all things' that devolve into good for the people of God (8:28) to whom God has given 'all things' (8:32). Even the agents and entities of evil are transmuted (unwillingly perhaps) into agents of good! And thus is glory accomplished – for God, for the people of God and even for creation!

96 Cranfield, *Critical and Exegetical Commentary*, 1: 440.

4

Scripture

The prescription

The law of Yahweh is blameless, restoring the soul;
the testimony of Yahweh is reliable, making wise the simple.
The precepts of Yahweh are right, rejoicing the heart;
the commandment of Yahweh is pure, enlightening the eyes.
The fear of Yahweh is clean, enduring for always;
the judgements of Yahweh are true, righteous altogether.
More desirable than gold, even than much fine gold;
and sweeter than honey, even the flow [from] the honeycomb.
Also, Your servant is warned by them;
in keeping them is much reward.
(Ps. 19:7–11)

Kendall Schler, 26, of Columbia, Missouri (USA), was declared winner of the 2015 Go! St Louis Marathon, with 581 female finishers behind her. That may have been the end of the race, but it wasn't the end of the story. In fact, just twenty minutes after the announcement, officials realised that they had been duped. Race results showed her starting the run at 7.00 a.m. with all the rest, but there was no evidence that Ms Schler had crossed any of the six other checkpoints of the race on the way to the end of the 26.2-mile trek. Apparently, she had left the course shortly after the start and then returned sometime past the last checkpoint. US Track and Field officials on the course also never saw Schler among competitors, and certainly not among the leaders of the race at any time.

Besides, there was a suspicious history to this rule breaking. This was not the first time Ms Schler's results had been disputed. She had placed third at the same marathon a year prior amid similar accusations. A few years before that, in the 2012 Roots N Blues 10 km run, she had finished

239th overall; but two years later, she had shot up in rankings, finishing 5th overall in that race – the difference in her final times in those two races was more than twenty minutes, very unusual for a course of that length. All of these swirling clouds of doubt led officials to conclude that Kendall Schler had not finished the 2015 Go! St Louis Marathon legitimately. She is thought to have entered the course after the last checkpoint, pretending to have run the entire 26.2 miles.

There are, of course, rewards for finishing first, besides the fame of breasting the tape. There is also the matter of US$1,500 in winnings, not to mention corporate sponsorship, and qualifying for the Boston Marathon. All of which Ms Schler subsequently forfeited; she was also permanently banned from future St Louis Marathons for what can only be called her lawless manoeuvres.[1]

Rules have to be followed, whether for marathons or mathematics, or for treating melanomas or making mayonnaise. Prescriptions of authorities setting the course of a race or instituting the treatment of a disease are expected to be complied with. And as we saw in Chapter 3, there are rules for Christian conduct also – the most crucial of all prescriptions: the 'righteous requirement' of God, who is the organiser and official of this marathon called life (Rom. 8:4). So how does one go about discovering what this divine demand is, so that one can run the race faithfully and finish the course successfully, following the prescription of God's 'righteous requirement' in the power of the Holy Spirit?

Demand

We resume in Romans 8:3–4, as we examine this issue.

> For what the law was unable [to do], in that it was weak through the flesh, God [did]: sending His own Son in the likeness of sinful flesh and for [a] sin [offering], He condemned sin in the flesh, in order that the righteous requirement of the law may be fulfilled in us who walk not according to the flesh but according to the Spirit.
> (Rom. 8:3–4)

1 Reiss, 'Columbia Woman Caught Cheating'. Ms Schler is not the first to attempt such a coup. The most infamous of them all was Rosie Ruiz, who was stripped of her 1980 Boston Marathon title after allegedly having taken the subway to the finish line!

As we saw in Chapter 3, a double weakness confounds believers (8:3a): the weakness of the flesh that will never follow God's requirements, and the incapacity of God's law that can only condemn those who violate it.[2] But what the law was incapable of doing, God did: Christ took on humanity and in his atoning work 'condemned' (i.e., paid the price for) sin. Thus, the flesh's weakness and the law's incapacity (the actual and deplorable situation of the *past*; 8:3a), in light of God's work in Christ (the wondrous accomplishment of the *present*; 8:3b), are starkly contrasted with the outcome expected in the lives of believers (the potential and divinely intended situation of the *future*; 8:4): the keeping of the law's righteous requirement – its prescription[3] – by those submitting to the Holy Spirit's empowerment, rather than to the flesh's enticement (see Figure 4.1).

PAST (8:3a)	PRESENT (8:3b)	FUTURE (8:4)
'*law* was unable to do'	**Work of God in Christ**	'righteous requirement of the *law* may be fulfilled'
'weak … through the *flesh*'		'in us who walk not according to the *flesh*,
		but [walk] according to the Spirit'

Figure 4.1

Thus is the 'righteous requirement of the law … fulfilled'. This direction for life, God's 'righteous requirement', his gracious call to his people to obey and to align their lives with his will, his divine demand, is discerned from Scripture – from every text thereof, from every pericope in both the Old and New Testaments.[4] Thus, all of Scripture constitutes the singular 'righteous requirement' (or divine demand) of the law, with each pericope specifying components of that singularity, each passage providing a guideline for fulfilling the destiny of those united with Christ (baptised and bound to him) to produce good works, so that God may be glorified. After all, '*every* [text of] Scripture [is] God-breathed

2 This incapacity of law is a function of its essence and nature, not a defect thereof.

3 Since the Holy Spirit, the Healer, is the author of the Scriptures, this 'righteous requirement' is analogous to a prescription from a medical practitioner.

4 Though 'pericope' does have a technical meaning in biblical studies, I employ it in this work (and elsewhere) simply to indicate a slice of text in any genre that is utilised in Christian worship for preaching. It is through pericopes, read and exposited in congregations as the basic units of Scripture, that God's people corporately encounter God's word weekly.

and profitable for teaching, for reproof, for correction, for training in righteousness, so that that the person of God may be capable, fully equipped for every good work' (2 Tim. 3:16–17). How is God's righteous requirement derived from individual pericopes of the Bible? Let me explain with some illustrations from Scripture (and elsewhere).

Voices, kings, animals (1 Sam. 15:1–14)

Take, for instance, the narrative in 1 Samuel 15 (the story of Saul being ordered by God to kill all the Amalekites).[5] The prophet Samuel passes on God's message to King Saul that he should eliminate these peoples (15:1–3).[6] He prefaces it by saying: 'Listen to the *voice* [*qol*] of the word of Yahweh' (15:1). Unfortunately, we do not find 'voice' in most English Bibles; such a literal translation of the Hebrew is rarely found in English versions. The seeming redundancy of 'voice' is swept under the rug in most such translations that essentially have: 'Listen to the word of Yahweh.' Hold that thought.

Saul, as we discover in the story, does not obey:[7] rather than wipe out all the animals and humans as commanded, he saves the good ones of the former and the chief of the latter, likely as trophies for personal enrichment and glory (15:4–9). Indeed, right after the battle, the triumphant regent builds a monument in Carmel to commemorate himself, the bane of the Amalekites (15:12)! Soon after, Samuel confronts Saul about his disobedience (about which God had complained to Samuel in 15:10–11). The king declares that he has done everything that God told him to do (15:13). Whereupon Samuel goes: 'What then is this bleating of the sheep in my ears, and the lowing of oxen which I hear?' (15:14) – the rebellious regent caught red-handed!

However, it is not 'bleating' and 'lowing' in the Hebrew – it is 'voice' (*qol*) again. With this 'voice' (of animals, 15:14) and the earlier 'voice' (of God, 15:1), the author is *doing* something with this narrative, telling readers that *The one committed to God listens to the* voice *of God, not the*

---

5 This has been drawn from my chapter, 'Christiconic View', 43–70.

6 The reason for this severe punishment harks back to the historical treachery of the Amalekites against the children of Israel (Exod. 17:8–16; Num. 24:20; Deut. 25:17–19).

7 And he should have, not only because it was God who commanded him to do so, but also because the injunction was explicit: the word translated 'listen' (15:1) is the Hebrew verb *shm'*, which also means 'obey'.

voice *of worldly seductions.*[8] Again, most English translations render 'voice' in 15:14 as 'bleating' and 'lowing' and thus, combined with the omission of 'voice' in translations of 15:1, the force of the text is almost completely negated! Indeed, 'voice' forms a critical motif in the whole story, the key to determining what the author was *doing* in this pericope. But those missteps catalogued above are a clear indication that Bible translators and scholars do not think in terms of what biblical authors are *doing* with what they are saying.[9] And here in 1 Samuel 15, the thrust of the text is clearly the issue of listening to/obeying God. That is what God is calling his people to do; that is the divine demand of God, his righteous requirement in this pericope.[10]

And all of that was discerned by catching what the author was *doing* with what he was saying. Now for a brief detour into language philosophy to further understand authorial *doing.*

Pragmatics and authors' doings

With the blossoming of language philosophy in the late twentieth century, the understanding of how language works has matured considerably.[11] Communication of any kind – sacred or secular, spoken or scripted – is now being recognised as a communicator *doing* something with what is communicated. Authors, including those of Scripture, *do* things with their words, directing responses from readers. This notion of authors *doing* things with what they say falls into the field of language philosophy called pragmatics.

Pragmatics, studying communication as an event, deals with what authors/speakers *do* with what they write/say.[12] In an event of

8 Just a few chapters before this one, in 6:12, the author had used the verb *g'h*, for 'lowing'. That substantiates his use of *qol* here in 15:14 as the result of deliberate design – he is *doing* something with what he is saying.

9 There is an old adage in the field of medicine: 'Unless you know the existence of a disease, you'll never diagnose it in a patient!' Perhaps there should be a similar one for the field of hermeneutics: 'Unless you know the existence of authorial *doings*, you'll never discern it in a text.'

10 'Voice' shows up, usually correctly translated, later in this pericope (15:19, 20, 22, 24), so all is not lost with the misdiagnosis!

11 This section is modified from Kuruvilla, *Vision for Preaching*, 71–89.

12 I conflate it all into 'what authors *do* with what they say', mixing doing and saying, to cover all bases and for ease of expression. While this phrasing seems to be echoing Speech-Act theorists, there are significant differences. See the discussion in Kuruvilla, *Text to Praxis*, 19–35.

communication for application, what is being conveyed by authors with their words is the pragmatics of the utterance – the *thrust* of what they wrote, i.e., what they are *doing* with what they are saying. To catch what communicators are *doing* takes more than just a dissection of the linguistic, grammatical and syntactical aspects of an utterance, which are the operations of semantics. Semantics, though a necessary foundation of interpretation, does not by itself yield the thrust or authorial *doing* of the text, which is the function of pragmatics. And discerning the pragmatics is essential for arriving at valid application from the text/utterance.

One sees this even in folk tales intended to elicit a response of life change. Take the old one by Aesop about the dog that found a bone. On its way home with its booty, the canine happened to cross a bridge over a stream, and as it looked into the water it spotted 'another' dog with a bone. Well, greed took over, the real animal barked at the virtual one, and thereby lost the bone it had. While the story deals with dogs, bones, bridges, streams and reflections, the thrust of the story is about being content (and the loss one incurs otherwise). This is what the text is all about, this is its thrust, its *doing* with its saying, its pragmatics. And that is what Aesop would want readers to respond to: *One practises the prudence of contentment rather than lusting for the ephemeral.* Indeed, only after grasping this thrust of the text can one ever move to valid application, i.e., application that is consonant with the author's textually projected intent for readers. In other words, if one wants to apply a text, it is not enough to comprehend what authors are saying (the semantics of the text); one must also arrive at what authors are *doing* with what they are saying (the pragmatics of the text). In the fable by Aesop, the semantics dealt with the description of the specific events: the dog-and-bone theatre; but the pragmatics or the thrust of the text was an endorsement of contentment; that was what the whole story was about.

Such an understanding of pragmatics, of what authors *do* with what they say, is critical for the discernment of God's righteous requirement, the Healer's prescription, in biblical pericopes. I submit that without the recognition of authorial *doing*, an appropriate response (i.e., valid application) by the people of God to his divine demand is impossible, and thus interpretation remains abortive and incomplete.

In fact, this is true even for spoken communication intended to direct behaviour. If Jack tells Jill, 'The door is open', whether Jill will respond as Jack intended is entirely dependent upon her catching the pragmatics (thrust or authorial *doing*[13]) of Jack's utterance. Its semantics – the linguistic-grammatical-syntactical analysis of Jack's four-word utterance – though essential, is insufficient, and will get Jill nowhere in terms of application.[14] For a valid response to Jack, the pragmatics of the discourse must be grasped. If they have just had a quarrel in Jack's home, Jill is being told to leave. If they are leaving Jill's home together to go on a date, and Jack notices that her front door is ajar, Jill is being reminded to shut the door. If Jill is about to reveal a juicy bit of company gossip to Jack, her coworker, when she drops into his office, she is being asked to refrain from saying anything, at least until the open-door situation is rectified. What Jack was *doing* with what he was saying in each situation is critical for Jill to grasp, if she is to respond appropriately to Jack with valid application as intended by that speaker.[15]

This is how interpretation of Scripture for application works, too. In the earlier illustration of 1 Samuel 15, unless one catches what the author was *doing* with those wordplays on 'voice', one will not be able to respond appropriately to the demand of that text. The passage is not recommending that readers *Trust God's fairness without doubting* (from God's severe treatment of the Amalekites) or *Watch out for sin's serious consequences* (from the harsh fate of those evildoers). Rather, the authorial *doing* is something to the effect of *Listen to/obey God's voice, not the voice of anyone else or anything else* (from the textual clues dealing with 'voice'). Readers of Scripture are obliged to discern what is being *done* with what was said in the text because that alone reveals authorial direction for application, and thus enables the fulfilment of God's righteous requirement (and thereby the destiny of believers for good works/sanctification, and ultimately the design of God, his glory). The thrust – what the author is *doing* – is, thus, the unified force of a biblical

---

13 I'll be using these synonymous labels rather indiscriminately until we arrive at a more final designation later.

14 The necessity of semantic analysis is obvious: unless the interpreter understands what is meant by 'door' and 'open' and how those words are put together with the article 'the' and the verb 'is' linking subject and predicate, there can be no comprehension of what the author is *doing*. In other words, there is no pragmatics without semantics, but semantics by itself is insufficient for the interpreter to discern the thrust of, and derive valid application for, the particular text/utterance.

15 These open-door 'conversations' were modified from Long, 'The Preacher and the Beast', 7.

passage, the sum of its textual elements, the integration of its pathos and potency, all in one package and calculated to change the lives of readers. So even narratives such as the one in 1 Samuel 15 point out what God's righteous requirement is and how God's people may fulfil it.

The sacrifice of Abraham (Gen. 22:1–19)

Here is another example of authorial *doing* in a narrative, in Genesis 22, that depicts God's righteous requirement.[16]

> Now it happened, after these things, God – He tested Abraham and said to him, 'Abraham!' And he said, 'Here I am!' And He said, 'Take now your son, your only one, whom you love – Isaac – and go forth yourself ...'
> (Gen. 22:1–2)

The account begins with a timestamp: 'And it happened, *after these things*, God – He tested Abraham' (22:1).[17] What exactly were 'these things', and why 'after' them?

In Genesis 12, God spoke to the patriarch for the first time; here in Genesis 22, he speaks to him for the last time. Both addresses contain the same command, found nowhere else in the OT: the Hebrew imperative *lek-lka*, 'go forth yourself' (12:1; 22:2). Both stress a journey, an altar, and promised blessings. In Genesis 12, God commanded Abraham to leave his relatives and his father's house (12:1–3). Yes, Abraham showed faith in stepping out as directed, but he did take along his nephew, Lot, even though the divine word explicitly called for a separation from family ('Go forth yourself from your country, and from your relatives, and from your father's house'; 12:1). Was Abraham thinking of Lot as his likely heir, seeing that he himself was already seventy-five years old, and his wife sixty-five (12:4)?[18]

Soon after, as Abraham enters the Negev, his caravan is hit by a famine (12:9–10), and he promptly decamps to Egypt. Could he not trust God to

16 For further details, see Kuruvilla, 'The *Aqedah*', 489–508; and Kuruvilla, *Genesis*, 250–64.

17 Here I will not make a distinction between 'Abraham' and 'Abram' (as the patriarch was called until his name change in 17:5).

18 In fact, even a quarter century later, Abraham is taken by mirth when God reiterates his promise of an heir (17:17; as also was Sarah, 18:12).

provide? And we know what happened in that land of refuge: Abraham passed off his wife, Sarah, as his sister, lest he get killed by an amorous Pharaoh (12:12–14). But God had promised him seed, so why should Abraham have worried about losing his life before he had had at least one child?

Later, the still childless Abraham tries to assign Eliezer, his steward, as his heir (15:2–3), an attempt that God immediately nixes, correcting the patriarch: 'The one who will come from your body, he – he will inherit' (15:4[19]). Abraham then resorted to a compromise: perhaps the chosen heir 'from [his] body' was to come through the maternal agency of a concubine (16:2). Acting upon this misconception, Abraham fathers Ishmael through Hagar, Sarah's Egyptian maid – another fiasco. Faithlessness constantly seems to characterise Abraham's response to God's promise of an heir.

Then, to make matters worse, in Genesis 20 Abraham *again* palms off his wife Sarah as his sister! This time to a local ruler, Abimelech (20:2), but for the same reason that he had conducted his subterfuge in Genesis 12 – fearing for his own life at the hands of an apparently (to him) concupiscent chieftain (20:11), and again doubting God's promises.

Thus, all along, Abraham is seen rather clumsily stumbling along in his faith in God's word. Genesis 12–20, then, is not exactly an account of pristine faith on the part of the patriarch.[20] And now in our pericope, Genesis 22, the final chapter of the patriarch's story, he is tested. God wanted him to sacrifice his son as a burnt-offering (22:2). What a test (and the man has no idea it is one)!

The father-son relationship is poignantly emphasised in the story: 'father' and 'son' are mentioned fifteen times in Genesis 22:1–20.[21] The readers are never to forget that intimate relationship. Indeed, in the only conversation recorded in the Bible between Abraham and Isaac, the latter's words begin with 'my father' and the former's words end with 'my son' (22:7–8) – this is also Abraham's last word before he prepares to slay

19 The emphasis is evident.

20 Notwithstanding his obedient setting forth in Genesis 12 and his creditable trust in God regarding the extent of his progeny (15:5–6), as well his faith in God's ability to save his kinsman (18:16–33).

21 In 22:2 [×2], 3, 6, 7 [×3], 8, 9, 10, 12 [×2], 13, 16 [×2].

Isaac (*bni*, 'my son', a single word in Hebrew). The narrator is explicitly creating an emotional tension in the story: a father is called to slay the son he loves. Would Abraham trust God now 'after these things' that had transpired in his life (22:1)? Had he learned his lesson? He had and he would.

At the end of Abraham's test, there is a key phrase in the acclamation of the angel of Yahweh: 'Now I know that the *fear of God* is with you' (22:12). Interestingly, the last time 'fear of God' was mentioned in the Abrahamic saga was in 20:11 (in fact, these are the first two occurrences of the phrase in Scripture). There, when Abimelech confronted Abraham with his wife-sister deception, Abraham's excuse was: 'Surely there is no *fear of God* in this place, and they will kill me on the issue of my wife' (20:11). The irony is that Abimelech and his people were actually terror-stricken by the possibility of having sinned against God – they were said to have been 'greatly frightened' (20:8; employing the same root, 'to fear', as in 20:11 and in 22:12). On the other hand, it was Abraham who did not fear God enough to trust deity to take care of him in this crisis (and all his preceding crises).

But that was in Genesis 20. Here, in Genesis 22, Abraham appeared to have learned his lesson, fearing/trusting God as the angel acknowledged (22:12). What had changed the patriarch's attitude between these two chapters, Genesis 20 and 22? It had to have been the crucial event of the intervening chapter, Genesis 21: the birth of the promised heir, Isaac. And, when Isaac is born, three times in two verses God's faithfulness in this matter of promised progeny is established unequivocally: 'Yahweh – He visited Sarah *as He had said*' (21:1a); 'Yahweh did for Sarah *as He had spoken*' (21:1b); 'And Sarah conceived and bore a son … at the appointed time *of which God had spoken to him* [Abraham]' (21:2). This threefold emphatic underscoring of divine promise was an outright rebuke of Abraham's faithlessness thus far: God, ever faithful, *had* done as he had said and as he had promised – surely Abraham could trust him!

And so, in Genesis 22, trust him, the patriarch does. At the end of that traumatic test calling for the sacrifice of this selfsame son, Isaac, the divine declaration, 'Now I know that the *fear of God* is with you' (22:12), gave proof to the fact that Abraham now trusted God enough to obey him without question. 'Genesis 22 may appropriately be read as a, arguably the, primary canonical exposition of the meaning of "one who fears God"', entailing 'obedience of the most demanding kind', grounded in a deep trust in God.[22] Further reinforcing this notion, the Hebrew verb *r'h*, 'to see', echoes through the account (22:8, 13, 14 [×2]). In fact, 'Moriah' (*moriah*, 22:2) is quite likely to be related to this root (shaded in Figure 4.2), and thus it means the 'place of seeing'. Moreover, we have the aphorism in 22:14, 'in the mount, Yahweh – *He will be seen*' (again employing the same root), generating an etiology for what later became the site of the Temple (2 Chr. 3:1).[23] The various uses of *r'h* in the narrative form a chiastic structure, centred on Abraham's exemplary faith in God.

A	God introduces the 'mountain', in the land of 'the place of seeing' (*moriah*, from *r'h*; 22:2)
B	Abraham 'sees' (*r'h*) the 'place' of sacrifice (22:4)
C	Abraham asserts that God 'will see [to it]' (*r'h*; 22:8)
D	**God declares that Abraham 'fears' him (22:12)**
C'	Abraham 'sees' (*r'h*) God's provision of a ram (22:13)
B'	Abraham names the 'place' 'Yahweh will see [to it]' (*r'h*; 22:14a)
A'	Narrator introduces the maxim about the 'mountain', where Yahweh 'will be seen' (*r'h*; 22:14b)

Figure 4.2

This superb play of words and precision of structure in Genesis 22:1–14 strongly emphasise Abraham's faith in a faithful God: he 'sees' (with the eyes of faith) – and God 'sees' (to it).[24] In other words, this narrative defines the meaning of 'fear of God' as obedience and trust that holds back nothing from God, absolutely nothing! Without even scrutinising the details of Abraham's test, the course-correction of his faith and loyalty is clearly depicted in God's pre-test and post-test descriptors of Isaac (see Figure 4.3).

---

22 Moberly, *Bible*, 79, 96. Faith is, of course, an integral part of that 'fear'. Abraham's faith in God is emphasised in 22:5, where Abraham's faith/fear-filled expectation of the outcome of the test is stated: 'I and the lad – we will go … and we will worship, and *we will return*.' God, he was convinced, would work it out somehow – he would 'see' to it (the many wordplays on this verb are noted).

23 Most translations have 'provide' in 22:8, 14a, 14b for the verb *r'h*. That English verb is derived from the Latin root *providêre*, 'to see ahead', aptly fitting the meaning of *r'h* as 'see' (as I have translated it in its various occurrences in this chapter).

24 This rationale is, of course, appropriate for the Temple, where – not very differently – God 'sees [to it]' (i.e., he makes it possible) that his people are found acceptable to him with their sacrifices.

Pre-test:

22:2	'your son, your only one, *whom you love*'

Post-test:

22:12	'your son, your only one'
22:16	'your son, your only one'

Figure 4.3

The trifold description of Isaac in Genesis 22:2 ('your son, your only son, whom you love') was to emphasise that this son, this particular child, was the one Abraham *loved*. And surely it is significant that this is the first time the word 'love' (Hebrew: *'hv*) occurs in the Bible. This love of Abraham for Isaac was a crucial element in this final test of his loyalty to his deity, a filial love that potentially stood in the way of his fear of, and faith in, God. But the stunning subsequent post-test deletion of the phrase, 'whom you love' (pointedly absent twice: in 22:12, 16), was a clear indication that Abraham had passed the fiery inquiry of his priorities. In sum, the harrowing examination proved the patriarch's utter allegiance to God – his unadulterated love for deity over and against anything that advanced a rival claim to that love – i.e., his fear of God.[25] Nothing would stand between Abraham and God. And, in a very clever way, the text confirms this again.

An element of the account that has bewildered interpreters throughout the ages is the disappearance of Isaac from the Abraham stories after 22:16, for the narrative concludes with: 'And Abraham returned to his young men [his servants waiting downhill], and they arose and went together to Beer Sheba; and Abraham dwelt in Beer Sheba' (22:19). Wait, what about Isaac? What happened to him? A strange omission, indeed! In fact, after this narrative, father and son are never shown speaking to each other again in Scripture.[26] After the test, it is as if Isaac has altogether vanished. But the author is *doing* something here. A line had been drawn; the relationship between father and son had been clarified;

25 The equation of 'fear of God' and 'love for God' is not illegitimate: Deut. 6:2, 13 command fear, while the *Shema* calls for love (6:5); Deut. 10:12 and 13:3–4 – each has both elements. Also see Deut. 10:20 with 11:1; as well as Pss. 31:19, 23; and 145:19–20.

26 Though I am certain they did, but behind the text (so to speak) – those are events the inspired author chooses not to mention, for they did not fall within the purview of his theological purpose (his *doings*) for this narrative.

the tension between love (fear) of God and love of son had been resolved. If I may paraphrase: Now *Abraham* so loved *God* that he gave his only begotten son.[27] And to bring that home to readers, father and son are separated for the rest of their days – literarily separated, that is, for the purpose of achieving the narrator's theological agenda: the love/fear of God is to trump every other human allegiance. It is only by discerning this theological thrust, the author's *doing*, or the pragmatics of this pericope, that valid application is possible: God's people must be willing, themselves, to give up everything for God. Anything or anyone that stands between them and their God is an idol![28]

And thus do readers of the Holy Writ comprehend the righteous requirement of God in this pericope, by privileging the text and discerning what the author was *doing* with what he was saying. Such a reading demands respect for the finely granular and brilliantly hued details of the text, all inspired by the Holy Spirit and discerned by an exegetical undertaking that produces tremendous yield for application purposes, furthering the fulfilment of God's righteous requirement.[29]

'Leasters' ministers (Eph. 3:1–13)

Let's examine another text, this time a didactic epistolary pericope, to discern God's righteous requirement therein. But before jumping into the specific passage, Ephesians 3:1–13, it is necessary to look at what has already been talked about in Ephesians 1–2. Ephesians 1:1–14 disclosed

---

27 I am simply trying to be clever with what I call an intertextual pun; no, I do not see any allusion to the atonement in this pericope; neither does the NT make one – in fact, Heb. 11:17 refers to the patriarch's faith (also see Jas. 2:21–24). Granted, Paul seems to be alluding to LXX Gen. 22:12, 16 in Rom. 8:32, but the apostle's studied avoidance here of the potent Greek adjective 'beloved' (*agapētos*, found in LXX Gen. 22:12, 16) is telling. Calvin, on Gen. 22:13, is honest about this widespread and reflexive tendency to link OT texts with NT (atonement) themes: 'I am not ignorant that more subtle allegories may be elicited; but I do not see on what foundation they rest' (*Commentaries on the First Book of Moses*, 571).

28 There is, therefore, no textual reason to move to a typological interpretation of the substitutionary sacrifice of Christ as is commonly undertaken. Instead, this narrative's delicate nuances, intricate detail and carefully negotiated twists and turns, precisely placed in the larger story of Abraham, result in an incisive thrust that powerfully impacts lives both ancient and modern.

29 See Kuruvilla, *Privilege the Text!* For other examples of authors' *doings*, developed pericope by pericope through individual books, see, besides my commentary on Genesis cited earlier, Kuruvilla, *Mark*; Kuruvilla, *Ephesians*; Kuruvilla, *Judges*; Kuruvilla, *1 and 2 Timothy, Titus*; and my commentaries on the Psalter: Kuruvilla, *Psalms 1–44*; Kuruvilla, *Psalms 45–100;* and Kuruvilla, *Psalms 101–150.*

God's preordained, purposeful plan, before the foundation of the world: 'With all wisdom and insight He made known to us the mystery of His will' (1:8–9).[30] What exactly that plan, the 'mystery of his will', was is revealed in 1:10:

> … the administration of the fullness of the consummation of all things in Christ – the things in the heavens and the things on the earth in Him.
> (Eph. 1:10)

This is the key verse of Ephesians (and I suspect, of all of Scripture) that points out God's grand plan for the entirety of the cosmos: 'the consummation of all things in Christ – the things in the heavens and the things on the earth'. This is God's glorious purpose and the direction and trajectory of all creation: 'the consummation of all things in Christ', the redoing, repairing, reworking of all things – now in sick and sinful chaos – into alignment with Christ. One day, in God's grand production, everything is going to be integrated, harmonised and aligned with Christ who becomes the unifying end of the cosmos. Everything, everywhere is headed for this awesome end: to be consummated in Christ for God's glory.[31] But 1:1–14 also told us that this grand plan for the cosmos involves God's people.[32] They were chosen, predestined, adopted, engraced, redeemed, forgiven, claimed and sealed – *blessed* into God's grand plan. The rest of the letter details the roles of the people of God in this great undertaking of God.

Immediately after this 'glory'-laden introduction of 1:1–14 (see 1:6, 12, 14), Paul talks of how Christ has been exalted over every cosmic power

---

30 See Kuruvilla, *Ephesians*, 20–37.

31 This cosmic undertaking of God for his glory forms the arena of all his activities and, therefore, ought to govern how the Bible is read. Such a reading I call a 'consummative-theological interpretation' of Scripture and its metanarrative context, including not only creation, fall and justification, but also sanctification and glorification – the humanity-related aspects of God's grand plan for his glory through the 'consummation of all things in Christ'. *Consummative* thus pertains to God's ultimate goal for the cosmos, and *theological* pertains to how each passage (i.e., pericope) of Scripture propounds a segment of theology intended to govern the lives of the people of God so that they may fulfil their roles in the grand design of God for his glory (more on this below; also see Kuruvilla, *Privilege the Text!* and Kuruvilla, *A Vision for Preaching*).

32 This is clear from the many first- and second-person plural pronouns and verbs in 1:1–14.

as part of this consummation of all things in him – exalted 'far above every rule and authority and power and dominion and every name that is named, not only in this age but also in the one to come. And He put all things in subjection under His feet' (1:21–22). The magnificent blueprint of God *will* be realised: no opposition to this purpose can stand.[33]

Then in Ephesians 2, after detailing mankind's disgraceful past, their engraced present and their glorious future,[34] we are told, in 2:11–22, that as a community, all believing humanity – Gentiles and Jews and Indians and Americans and Britishers and everyone else – has been united in Christ as one organism, the Church universal. Thus, the consummation of all things in Christ involves the Church unified as one believing humanity without distinction, which 'is growing into a holy temple in the Lord … a dwelling of God in the Spirit' (2:21–22).[35] What an amazing and glorious privilege!

With that, we come to Ephesians 3 and encounter a textual phenomenon that looks like a digression. Paul begins the chapter with: '*For this reason I*, Paul, the prisoner …' (3:1). But then he breaks off, to resume only in 3:14, where he repeats his opening phrase as he regains his place: '*For this reason I* bow my knees before the Father …' (3:14). So he had intended to pray in 3:1, but apparently got sidetracked, and finally wound his way back to the prayer trail in 3:14. What happened? Why the intervening section of 3:2–13? On closer examination, we'll find out that it is clearly deliberate, and perfectly placed in the sequence of passages in Ephesians.[36]

> For this reason I, Paul, the prisoner of Christ Jesus for the sake of you Gentiles …
> (Eph. 3:1)

Yes, Paul is in prison when he writes this letter, incarcerated in Rome. Though a prisoner of Caesar, he chooses to label himself the prisoner of Christ Jesus. He is Christ's prisoner first, Caesar's second. Now that's all

33 See Kuruvilla, *Ephesians*, 38–51.

34 See Kuruvilla, *Ephesians*, 52–65. We have examined Eph. 2:1–10 in detail in Chapter 1.

35 See Kuruvilla, *Ephesians*, 66–83.

36 For more details, see Kuruvilla, *Ephesians*, 84–98.

well and good, but one has to admit that Paul is still the prisoner of an earthly ruler. And so, as one reads that half-sentence in 3:1, the situation Paul is in now makes all that he had been saying in the previous two chapters odd and incongruous.

God, Paul had declared earlier, is the deity with a grand plan to consummate all things in the cosmos in Christ (1:1–14). And his Christ is endowed with great power, seated at God's right hand, over everything in the universe, so that every entity is under his feet (1:15–23). And the people he has redeemed for good works that they may be shown off triumphantly by God (2:1–10) possess an incredibly magnificent stature as a church, a holy temple to God, the dwelling of God's Spirit (2:11–22). That's what Paul has been talking about before he arrives at our section. So here is a guy who's been extolling the triumph of the God he serves, the God who has exalted Christ as cosmic lord over every power in every space in every time. Here is a fellow who cannot stop praising God's illimitable, uncontainable power. Here is a chap who is wonderstruck at the privilege of the church that is becoming the temple of God. And this bloke is a prisoner in chains? How can the servant of such a great God who is doing such great things with such great power to accomplish his great plan be a helpless captive in the dodgy dungeons of a puny, pagan despot, Caesar? How is God's grand purpose to consummate all things in the cosmos in Christ ever going to be accomplished if this deity cannot even keep a harmless old geezer out of gaol? Caesar sure looks more powerful than God!

That is why Paul, after writing that half-sentence in 3:1, 'I, Paul, the *prisoner*', broke off and said to himself (in my speculation): 'Wait a moment. I'd better clarify this for my readers. Or they're going to get the wrong idea about God and his grand design.' And so Paul wrote 3:2–13 to explain how this paradox of God working through an imprisoned weakling actually made perfect sense. This is a very relevant question not just for the apostle, but for all believers. For, when you think about it, Paul's captivity reflects the experience of God's people – then, now and always. After having learned in Ephesians 1 that God has blessed them into his grand plan to consummate all things in Christ, they wonder how on earth God is going to accomplish that using them – outnumbered, insignificant, weak and suffering. Like Paul: no money, no influence, no power and, in many parts of the world, like the apostle, no liberty.

But the inspired writer shows readers that that kind of thinking is wrong. Yes, in his current situation in a dungeon, Paul could not be in more impotent, more shameful or more vulnerable a position, at least from a human perspective: the apostle is Caesar's captive, in Caesar's jail, watched by Caesar's guards, under Caesar's control, in Caesar's city. But then Paul goes: 'Yes, I may be subjugated, disenfranchised, insignificant, weak, and suffering. But our God … he's something else, and – guess what? – he's working out his grand plan even through this broken vessel like me.' Look at 3:2–3:

> … you have heard of the administration of God's grace that was given to me for you, that, by revelation, the mystery was made known to me, as I wrote before in brief …
> (Eph. 3:2–3)

This helpless prisoner, Paul, was actually being used by God in his awesome purpose to make known the 'mystery … as I wrote before in brief', i.e., in 1:9–10, about 'the consummation of all things in Christ – the things in the heavens and the things on the earth'. And that was Paul's specific role: he was God's man for the moment, shedding first light on the revelation of this glorious undertaking of God, including the co-opting of Gentiles into God's grand plan that had, until now, been veiled (3:6). That's how Paul had been – and still was being – used by God, to proclaim those amazing truths. And here's the paradox and the irony: this privileged agent of the divine King is a petty arrestee of a human king.

But with this 'digression' of 3:2–13, Paul affirms that despite his being a pitiful, powerless, pathetic prisoner, God was able to use him to achieve his grand plan. Indeed, God's use of Paul is not because the apostle was anything special. Notice how Paul gives himself zero credit for all that God is doing in and through him; catch the preponderance of passive verbs in these verses (italicised):

> You have heard of the administration of God's grace that *was given* to me for you, that, by revelation, the mystery *was made known* to me …
> (Eph. 3:2–3)

> … which, in other generations, *was not made known* to the sons of men, as it has now *been revealed.*
> (Eph. 3:5)

> … of which I *was made* a servant, according to the gift of God's grace that *was given* to me.
> (Eph. 3:7)

> To me, less than the least of all the saints, this grace *was given.*
> (Eph. 3:8)

These passives underscore that it was all God's doing, making them the so-called 'divine' passives. All of Paul's successes were only by God's grace: 'I was made a servant,[37] according to the gift of God's grace that was given to me according to the working of His power' (3:7). He was made a tool of God, an instrument of God in the hands of God, to accomplish the grand plan of God – the consummation of all things in Christ. Paul is arguing here that if God can use him – overwhelmed, powerless, imprisoned – surely this God of such amazing grace can use every other believer in his glorious enterprise, no matter how adverse their circumstances or how dire their situations. Because it is all God's doing, from beginning to end, and entirely of divine grace. Paul's label of himself affirms this truth:

> To me, *less than the least of all the saints*, this grace was given to proclaim to the Gentiles the unfathomable riches of Christ.
> (Eph. 3:8)

'Less-than-the-least' translates a single word in the Greek that Paul has just concocted, *elachistoteros*. As in English, Greek also has trios made up of adjective, comparative and superlative. For example, in English there is short, shorter, shortest and low, lower, lowest. Likewise, less, lesser, least. But Paul here wants to go one more step with less-lesser-least, and so he coins a new Greek word, *elachistoteros*, best rendered 'leaster', thus creating a

37 In the KJV, the Greek *diakonos* is translated 'minister', used in the heading for this section.

quartet: less, lesser, least and … leaster![38] In other words, Paul's 'leasterness' is no hurdle to God using him, even for proclaiming the 'unfathomable riches of Christ'. And if God can use Mr Leaster, surely he can use others of his people, no matter how insignificant, overwhelmed and weak they may be. The lives of God's saints – of each and every believer, even of the 'leaster'[39] – are not negligible factors in God's calculus, but integral components in the divine plan to consummate all things in the cosmos in Christ. That's why Paul concludes this seeming digression of 3:2–13 with 'I ask you not to lose heart at my tribulations for your sake, which is your glory' (3:13). The people of God are not to lose heart at the apostle's tribulations or, for that matter, their own. Hang in there! God is working, and he is bringing glory to his people – *his* glory that is reflected by them.[40]

This is what 3:2–13 is all about. The triumphant status of God's people in Christ trumps their tumultuous station in the world. God can and will use them, no matter what deplorable earthly situation they are in. And therefore, they can remain patient in perseverance! So the divine demand (righteous requirement) of this pericope is a call to the people of God, exhorting them not to lose heart. Whatever their dire circumstances may be, they can rest assured that God is working out his grand plan in, through and with them.

All that to say, whatever the genre of the text of Scripture being considered – and we have looked at narrative and didactic, but this is true also of hymnody, law and prophecy[41]—God's righteous requirement is detailed therein, pericope by pericope, and it is incumbent upon the children of God to align themselves to his will – their duty to their deity.

Duty

I have been making the point that authors *do* things with what they say – the thrust of the text – and that discerning this is essential to determining

38 The superlative 'least' with an added comparative ending, '-er'.

39 Or even of the 'leastest' (my own new word to generate a quintet)!

40 Or 'remanated' by them, to use Jonathan Edwards' terminology.

41 See the interpretation of Psalms 8 and 19 in Chapter 1 as examples; for more, see my commentaries on the Psalms. On the genre of law, see below, as well as forthcoming volumes: Kuruvilla, *Exodus*; and Kuruvilla, *'Applicable', not 'Obeyable'*.

the righteous requirement of God (so that the people of God may fulfil their destiny to do good works and thereby achieve the design of God, his glorification, by the power of the Spirit). Let us carry the notion further.[42]

Pericopes and the world in front of the text

A text is not an end in itself, but is the means to an end, a literary instrument of the author's action of projecting a transcending vision – the *world in front of the text*.[43] Earlier, I utilised Aesop's story of the dog and the bone as an illustration. That uninspired tale projects an ideal world for readers, a world in which inhabitants practise contentment: that's what Aesop wanted his readers to respond to (by being content with what they have). Or in that inspired 1 Samuel 15 narrative discussed earlier, the biblical author pictures an ideal world in which inhabitants listen to/obey the voice of God, disregarding the seductions of all other voices: that's what that writer would want readers to respond to (by being exclusively obedient to the divine voice). In essence, these worlds are the thrusts of those texts, and this is what their authors are *doing* with what they are saying. And readers are being invited to dwell in such ideal worlds, abiding by the demands of those respective worlds. Here's the uninspired Aesop: 'Come, live in this ideal world by practising contentment'; and here's the inspired author of 1 Samuel 15: 'Come, abide in this ideal world of God by obeying only his voice.' Considering the other biblical pericopes we have scrutinised, here's the author of Genesis 22: 'Come, live in God's ideal world by being willing to give up everything to love/fear/trust God totally.' Or Paul in Eph. 3:1–13: 'Come, dwell in this ideal world of God, not losing heart at your difficult circumstances, for God can, and will, use every single one of us, no matter how dire our circumstances, in his grand plan.' And so on. To live in these respective worlds is to abide by the values of those worlds as depicted by/in those particular pericopes. Thus, in texts, a view of life in God's ideal world is portrayed, and a divine invitation to that world is being extended to

42 See Kuruvilla, *Vision for Preaching*, 91–109.

43 This is a modification of Paul Ricoeur's understanding of 'the world in front of the text' ('Naming God', 217). Also see Kuruvilla, *Text to Praxis*, 19–35; and Kuruvilla, *Privilege the Text!*, 33–65, from where some of the figures below have been adapted.

readers. And as readers and God-followers inhabit that world – that is to say, as they live according to the righteous requirement of God proposed therein – they are becoming citizens of God's world, and microcosms of the divine kingdom are being instantiated.[44]

In fact, *all* texts and utterances – inspired or otherwise – intended to direct application function in this manner by projecting ideal worlds.[45] For instance, if our favourite protagonists, Jack and Jill, are in a lift together and Jill says to Jack, 'Hey, you are standing on my foot!' the *semantic* meaning (what Jill is saying) describes the spatial location of Jack's foot upon the lower limb of Jill, while the *pragmatic* meaning (what Jill is *doing* with what she is saying – the thrust of her utterance) seeks the relocation of Jack's foot from that traumatic situation upon Jill's anatomy. Actually, what Jill was *doing* with what she was saying was projecting an ideal world in which no one is ever stationed upon her lower extremities to cause her distress. And Jill's desire was for Jack to inhabit such an ideal 'nobody-ever-standing-on-Jill's-foot-to-cause-her-pain' kind of world. And that inhabitation could be accomplished only by Jack conforming to the requirement of that world – removing the burden of his foot off Jill's, thus alleviating her agony, for in Jill's projected ideal world nobody stands on her foot to cause her pain.

Likewise for Scripture. Because it is intended for future application for sanctification by God's people, the interpretation of Scripture cannot cease with the elucidation of its semantics (its linguistic, grammatical and syntactical elements), but must proceed further to discern its pragmatics, the *world in front of the text* (the thrust of the text, what the author is *doing*). And thus, this projected ideal world forms the intermediary between text and application and enables one to respond validly to the text. When the text is rightly applied, its readers are, in effect, inhabiting the world it projects, because they are now living by the righteous requirement of God, as found in that particular pericope.[46] So here is

44 Returning to medical analogies, this ideal world may be likened to a healthy world, wherein life is lived according to the Healer's prescription.

45 Of course, uninspired texts have no authority upon the faith and practice of the people of God.

46 For all practical purposes, these elements – pragmatics, thrust of the text, and *world in front of the text* (i.e., what its author is *doing*) – may be considered equivalent.

our expanded mode of interpretation of the biblical text to derive valid application, as depicted in Figure 4.4.[47]

Figure 4.4

The biblical canon as a whole projects a single *world in front of the text* – God's ideal world, individual segments of which are portrayed by individual pericopes, each with its own thrust or divine demand. Taken together, the integrated composite of all these segments makes up the canonical projection of God's ideal *world in front of the text* – the plenary canonical world (the consolidated and singular righteous requirement of God[48]) (see Figure 4.5).

PERICOPE	SEGMENT OF IDEAL WORLD	*RIGHTEOUS REQUIREMENT* CANONICAL WORLD
Pericope 1	Segment 1 of Canonical World	
Pericope 2	Segment 2 of Canonical World	
Pericope 3	Segment 3 of Canonical World	
Pericope 4	Segment 4 of Canonical World	Plenary Canonical World
Pericope 5	Segment 5 of Canonical World	
…	…	
Pericope *n*	Segment *n* of Canonical World	

Figure 4.5

Thus, each pericope of Scripture is God's gracious invitation to mankind to live in his ideal world by abiding by the thrust of that pericope – i.e., the righteous requirement (or divine demand) of God's ideal world as called for in the world-segment projected by that particular pericope. And as God's people accept this divine invitation, pericope by pericope they are progressively and increasingly inhabiting this ideal world and abiding by divine demand, fulfilling God's righteous requirement. One pericope at a time, the various aspects of Christian life, individual and

47 'World' in the figure is specifically the *world in front of the text*.

48 As implied in Romans 8:4 by *dikaiōma*, 'righteous requirement', a singular noun.

corporate, are gradually being brought into alignment with the will of God for the glory of God – God's world is coming to pass, it is being actualised, and 'real-ised', as his 'righteous requirement' is progressively being fulfilled.

Pericopal theology, God's righteous requirement

For each pericope, then, its particular world-segment is what the author wants us to catch; this is what he would want us to respond to: to the thrust of that text, God's righteous requirement and his divine demand, that details how things should be in his ideal world. Those who seek to abide in that ideal world of God must therefore adopt this world's precepts, priorities and practices, as proposed in that particular pericope.

Because this world speaks of God and how he relates to his creation, and bearing as it does direction for life change, this projected world may rightly be called 'theology'.[49] Thus, the segment of this ideal world that each pericope projects is the theology of that pericope or pericopal theology.[50] So: *Pericopal theology is the theology specific to a particular pericope – representing a segment of the plenary world in front of the canonical text that portrays God and his relationship to his people (the righteous requirement of God) – which functions as the crucial intermediary in the move from text to application.* Living by the theology of the pericope, God's people accept God's gracious invitation to inhabit his ideal world, and thereby they align themselves to the divine demand of that ideal world – i.e., to the righteous requirement of God.[51]

So any interpretation of Scripture geared for application must discern the theology of the pericope under consideration, elucidating what that specific text affirms about God's relationship with humankind, and this

49 'Theology is, and always has been, an activity of what I call the "imaginative construction" of a comprehensive and coherent picture of humanity in the world under God' (Kaufman, *Essay on Theological Method*, ix). See Kuruvilla, *Vision for Preaching*, 91–109.

50 For distinctions between pericopal theology, biblical theology and systematic theology, see Kuruvilla, *Privilege the Text!*, 113–16.

51 All the terms that have been used here to label the thrust of the text are virtually synonymous. One might conceive the difference between the singular 'righteous requirement' and the plurality of pericopal theologies only in that the entire canon represents the singular 'righteous requirement' (or divine demand) of God, divided among the pericopes of Scripture. On the other hand, each portion of the canon has a particular pericopal theology. 'Righteous requirement' is the whole, and pericopal theology indicates each individual part. Nevertheless, I shall use both terms (and divine demand) somewhat interchangeably.

species of theology forms the basis of the subsequent move to derive application. Biblical interpretation that does not discern this crucial intermediary, pericopal theology, is *de facto* incomplete, for without it valid application can never be arrived at. So, in this conception, there is a twofold aspect to the interpretive transaction: the discernment of the theology of the pericope – i.e., the move from text to theology (the theological move) – and the discovery of how the latter may be applied in real life – i.e., the move from theology to application (the applicational move) (see Figure 4.6).

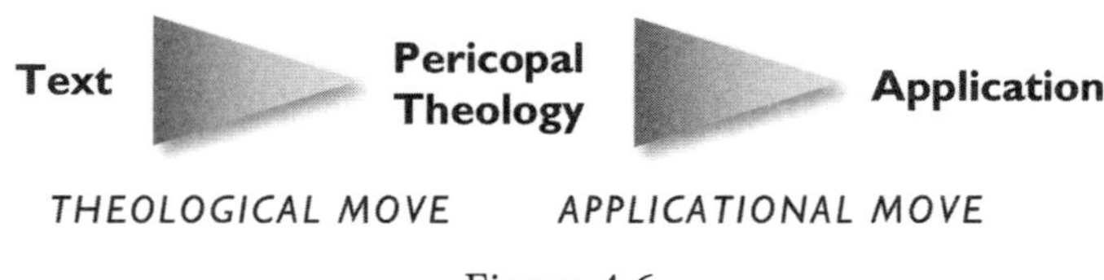

Figure 4.6

Pericopal theology, thus, helps to bring that specific portion of the biblical text to bear upon the situation of its readers, thereby aligning congregation to canon, God's people to God's word. Pericope by pericope, the community of God is thus increasingly oriented to the will of God as it progressively inhabits the projected canonical world of God, thus fulfilling the righteous requirement of God. And, thereby, gradually, God's ideal world comes to be.[52]

One should not construe divine demand and God's righteous requirement as merely a litany of dos and don'ts that a capricious God burdens people with.[53] Instead, God's call to be aligned with his demand and to fulfil his requirement is a gracious invitation to his people to inhabit his ideal world, and to enjoy its fullness of blessing, in his presence. This is what they were created for and this is the only way to be

52 If the reader is wondering about preaching at this point, that would quite appropriate, because in the corporate context of the Church, it is preaching of scriptural pericopes that gradually discloses this world. Thus, sermon by sermon, week by week, the inhabitation of God's ideal world – i.e., the alignment of God's people to divine demand and to pericopal theology, the fulfilment of God's righteous requirement – is being facilitated by the preacher. In fact, the two moves pictured in Figure 4.6 are the very same moves I employ in preaching and the pedagogy of preaching. For more on this facet of ministry, see my *Vision for Preaching* and my *Manual for Preaching*.

53 In fact, there is no compulsion to obey, although there are strong incentives to do so, both positive and negative (hence my use of 'divine *demand*').

satisfied, fulfilled, blessed. It is a divine offer that should capture humanity's imaginations and set afire their affections for God's ideal world, as the divine kingdom is unveiled pericope by pericope. This is the world God would have, and this is the kind of people God would have in his world.

Christological and christiconic

Every child of God rightly has the innate sense that the Bible is about Christ, the God-Man, i.e., Scripture is christological. The question, though, is *how* Scripture is christological. Let me suggest how the approach to textual interpretation detailed above comports with the christological nature of God's word and how it coheres with God's design to glorify himself through the good works he destined for humankind.[54]

As we have seen, Scripture, interpreted pericope by pericope, is God's gracious call to his people to live with him in his ideal world, abiding by its values and his 'righteous requirement' (Rom. 8:4). Since only one Man, the Lord Jesus Christ, perfectly met every aspect of God's will, being without sin (2 Cor. 5:21; Heb. 4:15; 7:26), one can say that this Person, and this Person alone, has perfectly inhabited God's ideal *world in front of the text*. That is to say, Jesus Christ alone has comprehensively abided by the theology of every pericope of Scripture, exhaustively fulfilling the totality of God's righteous requirement (and divine demand).[55] Thus, each pericope of the Bible, propounding pericopal theology, is actually portraying a characteristic of Christ's perfect human life, depicting what it means to perfectly fulfil, as he did, the particular call of that text – the righteous requirement of God as found in that pericope. The Bible as a whole, the collection of all its pericopes, then, portrays what a perfect human looks like, exemplified by Jesus Christ, God incarnate, the perfect Man: the plenary image of Christ. By him alone is God's world perfectly

54 For some of the differing ways in which Scripture is construed as christological for preaching purposes, see Gibson and Kim (eds), *Homiletics and Hermeneutics*. For my view therein, see 'Christiconic View', 43–70 (and for my responses to the other contributors, see 30–4, 111–12, 150–3). Also see Kuruvilla, 'Christiconic Interpretation', 131–46; and Kuruvilla, *Vision for Preaching*, 131–48.

55 This is an integral extension of the doctrine of Christ's impeccability, of course. But the fact that he atoned for humanity's failure to meet God's righteous requirement also means that Christ, in God's eyes, fulfilled it (see Matt. 5:17). He alone, in a manner of speaking, is perfectly healthy, having fully kept the Healer's prescription for righteousness.

inhabited and by him alone is God's righteous requirement perfectly met. So much so, the composite and canonical *world in front of the text* (i.e., the integration of all the world-segments of individual pericopes = the integration of the theologies of all the pericopes = God's singular righteous requirement) is the 'image' of Christ, the perfect Man, with each pericope being a pixel of that image, or a facet of Christlikeness. And thus, the written word of God in its entirety depicts the plenary image of the incarnate Word of God. Scripture *is* christological! (See Figure 4.7.)

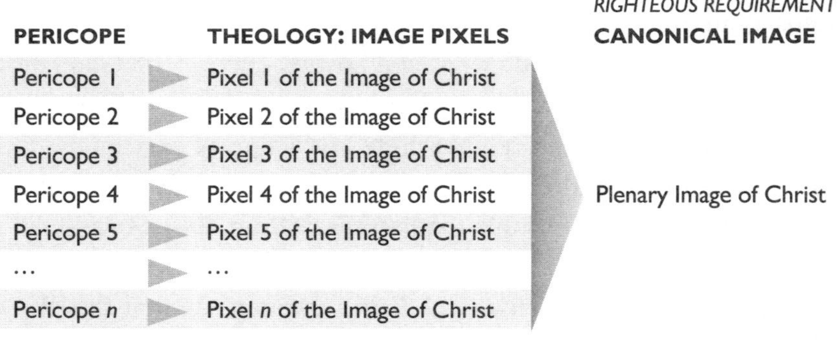

Figure 4.7

So, pericope by pericope (or pixel by pixel), as God's people are aligned to the image of Christ displayed in each pericope, they become progressively more Christlike. After all, that is God's ultimate goal for his children, to be 'conformed to the image [Greek *eikōn*] of his Son' in his humanity (Rom. 8:29[56]). This interpretive modality of discerning the righteous requirement of Scripture is, therefore, called a *christiconic* hermeneutic.[57] Paul declared: 'We proclaim Him, instructing all people and teaching all people with all wisdom, that we may present all people mature in Christ' (Col. 1:28).[58] Indeed, 'God has destined all his children to the end that they be conformed to Christ.'[59] That, I submit, is the

56 Also see 1 Cor. 15:49; 2 Cor. 3:18; Gal. 2:20; 4:19; Eph. 4:13–16, 20–24; Phil. 1:21; Col. 1:28; 3:10–11.

57 Kuruvilla, 'Christiconic Interpretation', 131–46; and Kuruvilla, *Privilege the Text!*, 238–68.

58 I.e., 'the building up of the body of Christ, until we all attain to the unity of the faith, and of the knowledge of the Son of God, to a mature person, to the measure of the stature of the fullness of Christ' (Eph. 4:12–13).

59 Calvin, *Institutes*, 702 (3.8.1).

primary function of God's word: the word of God is the instrument of God to conform the people of God into the image of the Son of God by the power of the Spirit of God.[60]

In accomplishing this conformation of his people to the image of Christ, God is restoring the *imago Dei*, the image of God in humanity, that was defaced by the fall.[61] After all, God intends for mankind to 'share his holiness' (Heb. 12:10), as they are conformed to the image of God in Christ once again, partaking of the 'divine nature' (2 Pet. 1:4). That is why, as regards sanctification – i.e., the impartation of the image of Christ to the believer on this side of eternity – the NT consistently points to Jesus as an example.[62] Calvin would heartily concur:

> Christ, through whom we return into favor with God, has been set before us as an example, whose pattern we ought to express in our life ... What can you require beyond this one thing? For we have been adopted as [children] by the Lord with this one condition: that our life express Christ, the bond of our adoption. Accordingly, unless we give and devote ourselves to righteousness, we not only revolt from our Creator with wicked perfidy but we also abjure our Savior himself.[63]

Yet, Vanhoozer is right about this mimetic development of Christlikeness: 'For those who by faith through the Spirit have been united to Christ, putting on Christ is not a fiction (what *if*) but a reality (what *is*) ... Disciples do not act like Christ in order to approximate an exemplar *outside* them. Rather, disciples put on Christ *from the inside out*.'[64] Sanctification is a gradual *becoming* of what one actually *is* in position – united with Christ: baptised to him and bound to him. That is to say,

60 That empowerment of the Holy Spirit was discussed in Chapter 3.

61 See Chapter 1 of this work.

62 See Matt. 10:38; 11:29; 20:26–28; Mark 10:42–45; Luke 22:24–27; John 13:12–17, 34–35; 15:12–13; Rom. 6:10–11; 15:2–3, 7; 1 Cor. 11:1; Eph. 5:2, 25, 29; Phil. 2:4–11; Col. 3:13; 1 Thess. 1:6; Heb. 12:3; 1 Pet. 2:18–24; 4:1; 1 John 2:5–6; 3:3, 16. This, of course, is not to assert that Jesus Christ is *only* an example or a model. It is because he is incarnate God and Saviour of humanity that he can be, among other things, exemplary to this race.

63 Calvin, *Institutes*, 686–7 (3.6.3).

64 Vanhoozer, 'Putting on Christ', 161 (emphases original).

becoming Christlike is the manifestation of the life of the Lord Jesus Christ who is already indwelling the Christian by his Spirit; it is not a fictional simulation, but a factual actualisation. By meeting divine demand pericope by pericope, i.e., the righteous requirement of God, the child of God becomes progressively more Christlike. Clement of Alexandria, a second-century church father, declared: 'He [Christ] it is who is the spotless image. We must try, then, to resemble Him in spirit as far as we are able … to be as sinless as we can.'[65]

One might liken recurrent encounters with the biblical text for conformation to Christlikeness with hypothetical multiple weekly visits to a doctor.[66] Say you are visiting me, a dermatologist (my other job), this week. I might tell you how to take care of your dry skin. Next week, if you return, I might advise you on how to take precautions in the sun. The week after that, you might be given recommendations regarding your moles. After that, I'd offer tips on how to care for your hair. Then, your nails.[67] Et cetera. As you follow my recommendations, your dermatological status is being improved week by week, and you are well on your way to developing perfect skin! After several weeks of this, you might decide to visit your cardiologist. The first week she might advise you on controlling your blood pressure. The week after that, how to maintain an exercise regimen. Then, how to control your cholesterol with diet and a prescribed statin. And so on, week by week, until you attain a perfect cardiovascular state. You might then move on to an endocrinologist, and onward to a gastroenterologist, and later, a nephrologist, and so on, slowly and steadily being perfected in physical health.

So also for Scripture transforming our lives unto the perfection of spiritual health. Week by week, pericope by pericope (and, no doubt, sermon by sermon), as the people of God are aligned to God's righteous requirement in those particular pericopes, and as they sequentially inhabit those pericopal segments of the *world in front of the text* (i.e.,

65 Clement of Alexandria, *Christ the Educator*, 5–6.

66 Indeed, if preaching of pericopes is in view, such an encounter with the biblical text is actually occurring weekly in an ecclesial situation, with the body of Christ gathered for worship, under the ordained pastoral leader, the doctor of souls (or the one who is the 'curator' [related to 'cure'] of spiritual health). See my *A Vision for Preaching*, where these facets of preaching are discussed.

67 Skin, hair and nails comprise the domain of a cutaneous specialist.

pericopal theology), they are being gradually and increasingly molded into the image of Christ, the only one who fully kept God's will, the perfectly healthy One. Thus is God's righteous requirement fulfilled and thus is God glorified. What he had designed for his created ones to do, and what they failed to do post-fall, he now accomplishes in those he brought into union with Jesus Christ, as Christlikeness is imparted, inculcated and imbued in them, by the power of the Spirit and through the agency of Scripture.

> We all, with faces having been unveiled – reflecting, as in a mirror, the glory of the Lord – are being transformed [into] the same image from glory to [more] glory, exactly as [by empowerment] from the Lord, the Spirit.
> (2 Cor. 3:18)

In sum, the incarnated Word, the Lord Jesus Christ, portrayed in the inscripturated word, is the summit of revelation, and the one into whose image mankind is to be conformed, in the power of God's Spirit, for the glory of God. Therefore, the role of pericopes is to demonstrate facets of Christlikeness and, to the extent that one lives in obedience thereunto, to apply divine demand and thus fulfil God's righteous requirement pericope by pericope, from every text of Scripture, to that extent one has become more like the perfect Man, the Lord Jesus Christ. Thus is Scripture christological – in a *christiconic* fashion.

Excursus on the law

If divine demand, God's righteous requirement, is found in every pericope of the Bible, then it must be present in the law genre of Scripture, particularly in the Pentateuch. Does that mean that Christians have to obey the Mosaic Law in this current dispensation? How can it be valid for God's people today, and how does it conform them to Christlikeness?[68]

As was discussed in Chapter 2, all of the seemingly negative remarks made of the law by the apostle in Romans can be explained by seeing

68 The lack of space precludes a fuller treatment here of biblical law in the life of the Christian, for which see Kuruvilla, *'Applicable', not 'Obeyable': Biblical Law and the Christian* (forthcoming).

'law' as a shorthand for 'law's *condemnation*'. Indeed, there are several positive remarks made of the law in Romans (2:12–13, 17–18, 20, 25–27; 3:21, 31; 7:12, 14, 16; 8:4; 13:8–10); Paul actually cites the law to make his points both in this letter and elsewhere (7:7; 13:8–10; 1 Cor. 9:8–9; 14:21; Gal. 5:14; Eph. 6:1–3; 1 Tim. 5:18).

In Romans 10:4 ('Christ is the *telos* [the Greek term] of the law, unto righteousness for everyone having faith'), the Greek word *telos* could conceivably mean 'end' as in 'termination', suggesting that the Mosaic Law is no longer applicable, but the context dictates otherwise. In Romans 9–11, Paul's major concern is the salvation of his fellow Israelites. After contrasting the Gentiles' attainment of righteousness by faith in Christ with the Jews' failure to arrive at righteousness by works (9:30–33), the apostle, adducing his concern for the salvation of the latter group, asserts that faith in Christ is what provides justificatory righteousness, for Christ *fulfilled* [he is the *telos* of] the law perfectly, and his righteousness is now credited to believers by faith (10:1–4). Therefore, 'fulfilment' to translate *telos* fits the context better. The church fathers quite uniformly read *telos* (= Latin *finis*) this way.[69] Calvin explains: 'For as [Christ is] the *finis* of the law, so is [he] the head, the sum, in short the fulfillment, of all spiritual doctrine.'[70] After all, Christ, as the perfect Man, is the one who met all of God's demands and the entirety of his righteous requirement. Cyril of Alexandria is explicit:

> We distinguish Christ as the fulfilment of the law and the prophets and quite rightly … Indeed, how could anyone doubt it? … [Christ] said, 'I have not come to abolish the law but to fulfil [Matt. 5:17].' For just as many colours being added at the right time [later] does not at all destroy a preliminary drawing of a picture – rather brings [it] into clearer vision – even so, in the same manner, we say the shadows of law are not overthrown, rather are fulfilled as it moves on the way to the truth.[71]

---

69 See Badenas, *Christ the End of the Law*, 7–37.

70 *Commentary on 2 Cor. 1:19* (my translation from the Latin).

71 *Commentary on Romans* on 10:4 (my translation from the Greek). That Jesus' 'fulfilment' of the law (Matt. 5:17) did not mean that he was 'abolishing' it is obvious: in the very next verses, he asserts that the law is permanent and unfailing not even by 'an iota or a serif' until 'all is performed', even as he abjures those who disregard the performance of these laws,

God's righteous requirement and divine demand are never annulled, only better portrayed with Christ, the perfect human who fulfilled them comprehensively and exhaustively (thereby rendering shadows and outlines with colour and clarity, so to speak). This is to assert that law also remains, like the rest of Scripture, 'God-breathed and profitable for teaching, for reproof, for correction, for training in righteousness, so that the person of God may be capable, fully equipped for every good work', thereby conforming God's people to Christ who are bringing glory to God by their good works (2 Tim. 3:16–17).[72] And if Christ's *eikōn* is the model for humanity of all time, then all are called to obey the law (and every other portion) of the inspired Holy Writ.[73]

The Reformers agreed that law was valid for believers, labelling its role for them as its 'third use', its moral aspect. Calvin called this the law's 'principal use', the maintenance of the morality of God's people, and the 'best instrument' for comprehending 'what that will of the Lord is which they aspire to follow'.[74] This theologian was not alone in his positive assessment of the law. Concurring with him was the Lutheran statement of faith, the Formula of Concord (1577):[75]

> We believe, teach, and confess that the preaching of the Law is to be urged with diligence, not only upon the unbelieving and impenitent,

even 'one of the least of these commandments'. In the same breath, Jesus lauds 'the one who keeps and teaches' the law as 'great in the kingdom of heaven' (Matt. 5:18–19). The same Greek verb in 5:17, *pleroō*, 'fulfil', is employed in Rom. 8:4 of the people of God 'fulfilling' God's 'righteous requirement'. Clement of Alexandria, quoting Rom. 10:4 called Christ, 'the fullness [*plērōma*] of the law' (*Stromata* 4.21 [my translation from the Greek]). Origen declared: 'For Christ is the *finis* of the law: this is the perfection of the law, and righteousness is Christ' (*Commentary on Romans*, 8.2; my translation from the Latin translation by Rufinus [ca. 400]). So also Aquinas: 'And to be noted, *finis* does not always signify consumption, but sometimes perfection: accordingly, the *finis* of the law is Christ' (*Catena Aurea on Matthew* 10.7; my translation from the Latin).

72 For good works abounding to God's glory, see Chapter 3.

73 Gal. 3:23–26 suggests a change in the role of the law in the current post-cross dispensation, asserting that law's function as a pedagogue to lead a non-Christian to justification has, for the believer in Jesus Christ, now become moot. Note that it does not declare that the law is *in toto* abolished in all its functions or that it has no role in sanctification. In Eph. 2:15 (as also in Col. 2:14) the 'nullifying the law of commandments in decrees' is undoubtedly referring to the condemnation of the law, i.e., the enmity abolished 'in Christ Jesus', 'by the blood of Christ' (Eph. 2:13), 'in Himself' (2:15), 'through the cross', 'in Himself' (2:16), and 'through Him' (2:18). See Kuruvilla, *Ephesians*, 66–83; and Kuruvilla, 'From "Far" to "Near"', 67–86.

74 Calvin, *Institutes*, 1: 418 (2.7.12).

75 Of course, the Lutheran understanding of 'Law' is not restricted to the genre of law in Scripture, but that does not affect the argument here.

> but also upon true believers, who are truly converted, regenerate, and justified by faith. For although they are regenerate and renewed in the spirit of their mind, yet in the present life this regeneration and renewal is not complete, but only begun, and believers are, by the spirit of their mind, in a constant struggle against the flesh, that is, against the corrupt nature and disposition which cleaves to us unto death. On account of this ... it is needful that the Law of the Lord always shine before them ... Thus the Law is and remains both to the penitent and impenitent, both to regenerate and unregenerate men, one [and the same] Law, namely, the immutable will of God.[76]

Christians were to 'daily exercise themselves in the Law of the Lord', and the law was to be 'diligently urged upon them without ceasing', because it was 'a mirror in which the will of God, and what pleases Him, are exactly portrayed'.[77] Thus the law is to be obeyed. Rightly, therefore, Cranfield decries ...

> that modern version of Marcionism which regards the law as a disastrous misconception on the part of religious [people] from which Jesus desired to set us free ... [or] the view that the law was an unsuccessful first attempt on God's part at dealing with [a hu]man's unhappy state, which had to be followed by a second (more successful) attempt (a view which is theologically grotesque, for the God of the unsuccessful first attempt is hardly a God to be taken seriously).[78]

Yes, the law is still valid. Paul's own words in Romans 3:31 attest to this truth: 'Do we inactivate the law through faith? May it never be! Rather, we uphold the law.' All that to say, there is no indication anywhere in Paul (or elsewhere in the NT for that matter) that divine law – God's righteous

76 'Formula of Concord', Epitome: Article VI, The Third Use of the Law. Affirmative Theses 2–3, 6. This article's Negative Thesis 1 called any teaching that the law *not* be urged of believers 'a dogma and error injurious to, and conflicting with, Christian discipline and true godliness'.

77 'Formula of Concord', Solid Declaration Article VI. The Third Use of the Law.

78 Cranfield, 'St. Paul and the Law', 67–8 (this was already cited in Chapter 2).

requirement – is annulled, abrogated or abolished.[79] If this is the case, then how then do Christians today apply the Mosaic Law?

I suggest that a distinction – admittedly artificial, but practically useful – be made between the 'obeyability' of texts and the 'applicability' of texts. Every pericope of Scripture that promulgates a law is 'obeyable' if its explicit stipulation can be put into practice straight away, without any hermeneutical operation being undertaken to enable its relevance in future time and/or distant space to the one 'obeying' it.[80] Levirate marriage? Well, I need to marry my sister-in-law if my brother dies. Cultivate particular plants in particular seasons? Yes, get the fertiliser ready. Do things with ephods, altars and Urim and Thummim? Sure, let's engage in some future-gazing. Stone that rebellious child? Right, hand out the rocks. And so on. On the other hand, 'application' calls for more hermeneutical labour, particularly in answering the question: How is the ancient text of law to be made relevant to the modern 'applier' living in a different age and in a different arena? Or, what is the author of that text *doing* with what he is saying?

The laws of the Torah are uniquely and exquisitely contextual (indeed, so also are the pericopes of the rest of biblical literature), documents addressed to particular peoples, billeted in a particular geographical

---

79 The argument that 'ceremonial' and 'civil' laws of the OT are context-specific and not for modern application, while 'moral' laws are not context-specific and therefore are for current application is gravely problematic. One cannot distinguish with any clarity between these three categories of law in Scripture – one could argue that they are *all* moral! The Bible sees its law as a monolithic unit, without distinctions: God's people are 'obliged to obey the whole law' (Gal. 5:3) and are guilty of its violation even if they 'keep the whole law but stumble in one [point thereof]' (Jas. 2:10). Jesus himself declared that guilt would be incurred by the one 'who sets aside one of the least of these commandments' (Matt. 5:19). It certainly does not make much sense to accept Lev. 19:18 ('love your neighbour as yourself') but disregard 19:19 ('[with] a garment of two kinds of fabric [you] shall not cover yourself'). The fact is that 'law' as used by Paul extends even beyond the Pentateuch: he appeals to the 'law' in 1 Cor. 14:21 but cites Isa. 28:11–12; he explains he is dealing in Rom. 3:10–18 with 'whatever the law says' (3:19), but has just quoted from the Psalter (5:9; 10:7; 14:1–3; 36:1; 53:1–3; 140:3), Proverbs (1:16), and Isaiah (59:7–8). In Ps. 119, the notion of *torah*, a designation used twenty-five times in that chapter, is not limited to the Pentateuch, but broad enough to encompass the universal laws of God that govern the cosmos (see 119:89–91) and every instruction for how humankind should live in the kingdom of God. Also, we saw in Rom. 8:4 that the 'righteous requirement of the law' is an emphatic singularity (indicated by the singular Greek word, *dikaiōma*).

80 The issue of the authority of every text of the Bible over the Christian I take for granted; this is an emergent property of the canonical Scriptures that the Church considers normative for God's people. But I also argue that every pericope of Scripture, by virtue of incorporation into the canon, bears a divine demand and carries an inherent imperative, regardless of genre (as we have already seen).

location, sojourning in a particular era, maintaining a particular cultic organisation, constrained by a particular culture and supporting a particular political configuration. None of those laws are directly relevant to a Christian living in Louisville, Kentucky, USA, in 2025 (or in another space and another time). What can one do to overcome this 'distanciation'?[81] As I have already described in this chapter, the interpreter should first discern what the author is *doing* with what he is saying – the thrust of the text, the theology of the pericope – and then 'apply' that thrust to contemporary life. In other words, 'obeyability' (direct and straightforward[82]) is to be distinguished from 'applicability' (indirect, via discernment of pericopal theology[83]). As we have just seen, each pericope of Scripture (in every genre of Scripture) is God's gracious invitation to mankind to live in his ideal world by abiding by the theology of that pericope, i.e., the righteous requirement of God's ideal world as called for in that pericope. And as mankind accepts that divine invitation, pericope by pericope God's people are progressively and increasingly inhabiting this ideal world, adopting its values and abiding by its requirements. More importantly, the people of God, pericopal pixel by pericopal pixel, are being conformed into the image of the Son of God, the only one who comprehensively and perfectly fulfilled God's righteous requirement, his divine demand all throughout Scripture – a christiconic hermeneutic for application. For God's ultimate goal is to conform his children into the *eikōn* of his Son, Christ (Rom. 8:29).

For instance, Deuteronomy 22:12 and Numbers 15:37–41 command the wearing of tassels on the four corners of an Israelite's cloak. It appears that in the ancient Near East, tassels on the corners of garments were symbols that signified the special status of their wearers as gods or kings. It is conceivable, then, that obedience to the commandments of Yahweh was also inextricably bound up with the special status of the children

81 A characteristic property of a written text that is seemingly orphaned from the circumstances of its provenance. See Ricoeur, 'Hermeneutical Function', 131–44.

82 Impossible to undertake for the genres of Scripture that are not laws or imperatives. How does one directly and straightforwardly 'obey' a story or a song?

83 As was demonstrated, it is possible to 'apply' texts from any genre of Scripture indirectly, by discerning pericopal theology. For more on the pericope-by-pericope practicalities of this operation, see my commentaries on Genesis, Judges, Psalms, Mark, Ephesians, 1 Timothy, 2 Timothy and Titus (and a forthcoming volume on Exodus).

of Israel as God's special possession: Exodus 19:4–6; Deuteronomy 4:20; 7:6–8; 26:16–18 – all link this singular standing with God to his having brought them out of the land of Egypt. Incidentally, the tassel commandment in Numbers 15:37–41 also makes an explicit connection with the Exodus.[84] Thus the tassel, as an extension of the garment hem – usually the most ornate part of a Near Eastern garment – was considered an important social statement, a visible marker of special standing before God. The blue colour required made this undertaking quite exclusive, the dye's production being extremely expensive. That is to say, garments of that colour signified a certain nobility of status before deity.[85] However, even a poor Israelite could afford to have at least four threads of blue in the tassel (Num. 15:38). This, therefore, would serve as a marker and reminder to the children of the Hebrew nation, one and all, of their unique place before God and the resulting obligation to obey him – the 'obeyable' sense of the text. The pericopal theology of the passage underscores that each person in the community of God be constantly marked and reminded of their standing before God and the lofty moral obligations that accrue therefrom – the 'applicable' sense of the text. In the specific application of this pericopal theology in contexts and circumstances where such garments and unique colours do not signify the same honour, one might decide to wear or place in view a visual remembrancer of a different kind to bring to memory believers' peculiar and particular standing before God (perhaps with a wall plaque, a lapel pin or any number of other tangible objects; see Figure 4.8, below, for a layout of this move from text to pericopal theology to application).[86] And thus, abiding by the divine demand of that law, the children of God (of all time and in every place) become more Christlike, as they interpret the law as being 'applicable' via pericopal theology, but not necessarily 'obeyable'.

And this goes for law in the NT, as well. Consider the example of Ephesians 5:18 – 'Be not drunk with wine.' While this textual fragment

84 Bertman, 'Tasseled Garments', 128.

85 See Milgrom, 'Of Hems and Tassels', 61–5. He also suggests that the blue tassel denoted elements of the priesthood as well, in accordance with God's declaration that Israel was a kingdom of priests (Exod. 19:6). Also see Goodnick, 'Tassel and the Blue Cord', 103n12.

86 Dorsey, 'Use of the OT Law', 13–15.

is not a pericope or even a full sentence in the Greek,[87] focusing on this half-sentence that is an imperative (i.e., a law) is profitable for the purpose of illustration. The command calls for the people of God not to be drunk with *wine*. The thrust of the text across time and space, pericopal theology, is concerned with drunkenness with *all alcoholic drinks*, thus prohibiting drunkenness with *vodka*, *beer*, *Scotch* or one's libation *du jour* (or even with future alcoholic concoctions that are yet to be conceived, compounded and consumed; see Figure 4.8, below). If this verse fragment were a complete pericope, what the author of Ephesians might have been *doing* would be projecting a segment of God's ideal *world in front of the text* in which God's children refrain from intoxication with alcoholic beverages of any kind – the divine demand, so to speak, of this morsel of text. And if they so refrained, they would be moving one more step closer to Christlikeness. This is the difference between 'obeyability' (not getting drunk on *wine*) and 'applicability' (not getting drunk on *any alcoholic beverage*[88]). Such a confusion of (or non-distinction between) 'obeyability' and 'applicability' – the way I am defining those terms – is widely prevalent in circles of biblical interpretation and pulpits of biblical preaching, and such unclarity creates problems galore and perplexities endless. All that to say, Scripture is not written *to* us – it is not 'obeyable'; but it is written *for* us – it is 'applicable'.

Or take 1 Peter 2:17 (or a snippet thereof): 'Honour the king.' This law is not 'obeyable', because I, living in the United States in 2025, am not the subject of a monarch. But it is 'applicable', because what Peter is *doing* with 'king' encompasses all supreme governmental authorities, whether they be presidents, prime ministers, pharaohs, emirs, kaisers or tsars. They, too, are deserving of honour, as Scripture commands, and as I obey that divine demand I become more Christlike.

87 And neither does the pericope from which this five-word slice is extracted deal primarily with drunkenness.

88 One could hypothetically broaden this pericopal theology to 'not getting intoxicated *on any drug*', thereby including as its specific application addictive substances that are ingested, inhaled or injected. However, in light of the focus of the text of Eph. 5:18 on 'filling' (a fluid-related phenomenon), and its emphasis upon the contrast between the results of Spirit-filling ('speaking … singing … making melody …' – all vocal; 5:19) and the implied equally vocal manifestations common with the abuse of alcohol, it seems judicious to restrict the breadth of pericopal theology to 'alcoholic beverages'. No doubt, there is a degree of interpretive freedom here.

So here we are, with the texts of 'law' discussed above, showing the movement from text to pericopal theology to possible application, to illustrate the distinction between 'obeyability' and 'applicability' (see Figure 4.8).

	'OBEYABILITY'		'APPLICABILITY'
	Text	***Pericopal Theology***	**Application**
Deut. 22:12 **Num. 15:37–41**	'tassel'	*visual markers of status before God*	wall plaque, lapel pin ...
Eph. 5:18	'wine'	*all alcoholic beverages*	vodka, beer ...
1 Pet. 2:17	'king'	*all rulers*	prime ministers, presidents ...

Figure 4.8

'A law reflects the mind, the personality, the priorities, the values, the likes and dislikes of the Lawgiver. Each law issued by God to ancient Israel [and indeed, every divine demand, explicit or implied, in every pericope of every genre Scripture, to every reader of the OT and the NT] reflects God's mind and ways, and is therefore a theological treasure' to be valued, understood and applied as the righteous requirement of a holy deity (2 Tim. 3:16–17).[89]

In sum, every genre, narrative, didactic, hymnic, prophetic and even legal, bears the Lawgiver's righteous requirement in each of its pericopes. And it is the role of every pericope of Scripture to portray what this divine demand is (the theology of the pericope, what happens in God's ideal world, in his kingdom – the righteous requirement of God), so that God's children might be aligned to it in the power of the Spirit, thus becoming progressively sanctified, becoming Christlike, holy as God, their Father, is holy.[90] And through such a christiconic reading that

89 Dorsey, 'Law of Moses', 332.

90 This will of God expressed in each pericope is a gracious invitation extended by God to his children, offering them the possibility of living in his way in his ideal world. Yet, it should not be forgotten that although it is an invitation that can be refused, repudiation of that loving call of the Father comes with grave consequences. However one conceives of God's invitation, the prescriptive and normative nature of the requirements of the Lawgiver should not be forgotten. Hence, the gracious invitation is also a divine demand – not peremptory, not capricious, not tyrannical, but merciful, tender and gracious, promulgated for the good of this loving Father's children.

promotes faithful obedience and sanctification of the people of God, God is glorified as they manifest his holiness, imaging Christ to the world, as Jesus himself declared in John 15:8: 'By this is My Father glorified, that you bear much fruit and become My disciples.'

Trinitarian interpretation

Such a christiconic hermeneutic is also Trinitarian in concept and function. Looking at the three entities that ground such interpretations – text, pericopal theology and application – each is particularly related to a specific Person of the Trinity. The text inspired by God the Holy Spirit (2 Pet. 1:21) depicts Jesus Christ, God the Son, to whose image mankind is to conform (Rom. 8:29); and in so being conformed, the will of God the Father is being done and his kingdom is coming to pass (Matt. 6:10).[91] (See Figure 4.9.)

Figure 4.9

And thus, the alignment of the people of God to the righteous requirement of God from the word of God transforms believers into the image of the Son of God, in the power of the Spirit of God, for the glory of God. Pericope by pericope, habits are changed, dispositions are created, character is built, the *Christicon* is formed pixel by pixel as good works are performed, and humans are becoming what they were designed by God to be – glory-givers to God.

> To this [end] we pray always for you, that our God may consider you worthy of [your] calling and fulfil [your] every desire of goodness and the work of faith with [His] power, by which the name of our

91 Of course, the arrival of this divine kingdom in all its fullness and glory will have to await the Second Advent of Christ, but until that macrocosm is established, microcosms (in the form of Christians, both individual and corporate) are instantiating, actualising and 'real-ising' the ideal world of God. For where there are citizens, there is a kingdom.

> Lord Jesus may be glorified in you, and you in Him, according to the grace of our God and the Lord Jesus Christ.
> (2 Thess. 1:11–12)

It was to such teaching – to God's 'righteous requirement' and for it to be 'obeyed' (in the production of good works, implied in 2 Thess. 1:11 in 'desire of *goodness* and the *work* of faith') – that the people of God were 'handed over'.

> But thanks [be] to God that [though] you were slaves of sin, yet from the heart you obeyed unto the teaching to which you were handed over, and having been freed from sin, you were enslaved to righteousness.
> (Rom. 6:17–18)

This is the responsibility of believers, their sanctification in the power of the Spirit, all because of their relationship to God in Christ, united to him – baptised into him and bound to him. Thanks be to God, indeed! But is there more to relationship with God and responsibility to God? There is!

Relationship precedes responsibility

In Scripture, relationship to God is always followed by responsibility to God. That is to say, when individuals come into relationship with God, God always gives them guidance as to how they should then live – i.e., in accordance with the 'righteous requirement' in his word, as we have seen. After all, this was exactly the situation that Adam and Eve were in, in the Garden: created in relationship to God, with a responsibility to him (which, of course, they failed to fulfil).[92] Thus, God's design, all along, has been to direct the behaviour of those who are already his children, for

92 Indeed, such a theme of relationship leading to responsibility resonates through the Pentateuch (and the rest of the OT). God elected a people; *then* he required of them obedience to his will. Notable is the fact that the Ten Commandments (responsibility) was prefaced by an announcement of relationship: 'I am Yahweh your God, who brought you out of the land of Egypt, out of the house of slavery' (Exod. 20:2). Therefore, 'Thou shalt …' and 'Thou shalt not …' *Because* they were in relationship to a holy God (a relationship inaugurated prior to the giving of the Mosaic Law), God's people were responsible to be as holy as their God was. Lev. 20:26 has God declaring: 'You are to be holy to Me, because I, Yahweh, am holy, and I have set you apart from the peoples to be mine.' Likewise, 18:2–4 (among others), affirming relationship as the basis for responsibility: 'I am Yahweh your God … You

the sake of his glory. A relationship with God – initiated by a unilateral divine act of grace and apprehended by humans by faith – always precedes the responsibility of the people of God to accede to the will of God to be as holy as God.[93] Indeed, even in the Decalogue the 'love' for the people of God to their deity is equated to their obedience – this God is the one 'showing lovingkindness to thousands, *to those loving Me and to those keeping My commandments*' (Exod. 20:6). Indeed, to love God primarily means to serve him loyally in obedience.[94]

There is a widespread misunderstanding in Christendom, even within evangelicalism, that love towards God is something of the heart, private, sappy and sentimental. But an examination of '[covenantal] love' (Hebrew: *'ahav*) in the ancient Near East convincingly demonstrates that at its core such a love is an unsentimental relationship between the lesser party and the greater party in the covenant. On the part of the greater party (usually a suzerain or a ruler), it involves his faithful, loving beneficence towards his people, the lesser party (vassals or subjects); on the part of the latter, it is their reciprocal faithful, loving service to the former. This was the understanding of 'love' in the milieu of the people of God of the OT. No wonder that corpus clearly considers 'love' and 'obedience' as parallel notions:[95]

> 'Know that Yahweh, your God, He is God, the faithful God, keeping His covenant and His lovingkindness to those who *love Him* and those who *keep His commandments*.'
> (Deut. 7:9)

> 'You shall *love Yahweh* your God, and *keep His mandate, and His statutes, and His judgements, and His commandments* all [your] days.'
> (Deut. 11:1)

---

shall do my judgements and keep my statutes, to walk in them. I am Yahweh your God. So you shall keep my statutes and my judgements … I am Yahweh.'

93 This is a *practical* sanctification, of course, not a *positional* sanctification that, in Christ, has been completely and perfectly accomplished for every child of God at the instant of union with Christ. Also not to be forgotten, this responsibility is graciously empowered by God the Holy Spirit (as we have already seen and will see again).

94 As Levenson shows in his magisterial work, *Love of God*, from which I have borrowed liberally for the following discussion.

95 As we already saw with Exod. 20:6; besides the verses noted below, also see Deut. 10:12; 11:13, 22; 19:9; 30:20.

> 'I command you this day to *love Yahweh* your God, to walk in His ways, and to *keep His commandments and His statutes and His judgements*, that you will live and become numerous, and that Yahweh your God will bless you …'
> (Deut. 30:16)

And there is ample NT attestation to this notion:[96]

> 'If you love Me, My commands you will keep … The one who has My commandments and keeps them, this is the one who loves Me; and the one who loves Me will be loved by My Father, and I will love him and will manifest Myself to him … If anyone loves Me, My word he will keep; and My Father will love him and We will come to him and We will make our abode with him.'
> (John 14:15, 21, 23)

> By this we know that we love the children of God, when God we love and his commandments we do. For this is the love of God, that his commandments we keep.
> (1 John 5:2–3)

'If we put all this together, we come up with an identification of the love of God with the performance of his commandments. Love, so understood, is not an emotion, not a feeling, but a cover term for acts of obedient service' – a posture of loyal and committed obedience of vassal towards suzerain.[97] In other words, 'covenantally conceived, love is defined, first and foremost, by a set of deeds. The deeds are not dependent on emotion: whether or not individuals feel a sentiment that they name as "love," they are always obligated to serve their lord.'[98] This is why love can be commanded, as the *Shema* does:

96 Particularly in Johannine literature; beyond what is noted here, see John 15:10, 12; 1 John 2:3–5; 3:22–24; 4:21 and 2 John 6.

97 Levenson, *Love of God*, 4. This does not rule out affect in such a relationship (as Hosea and Song of Songs attest; and see below for God's emotional attachment to his people), but that is secondary to the primary sense of 'love' as commitment and faithfulness in obedience and service. To be clear, Levenson does not comment on New Testament declarations; those are my additions. But the complementarity of the assertions of this corpus to those of the Old Testament are obvious.

98 Levenson, *Love of God*, 60.

> You will love Yahweh, your God, with all your heart and with all your soul and with all your strength.
> (Deut. 6:5)

In sum, the 'love of God' is primarily service, and the misinterpretation of love as simply romantic or erotic 'has left [us] with scant resources with which to understand the love of vassals for their lords'.[99] There is, of course, no doubt about God's 'love' for his people, expressed both in his own abiding by his covenantal obligations to them and in his emotional affect for them – his lovingkindness.[100] And as for the reciprocal emotional affect of God's people for their deity, as they serve him and experience his steadfast lovingkindness, how can they *not* love him? Levenson asserts: 'The love owed by the covenantal vassal to his lord (or by the subject to his king) is both active and affective … By contrast, where love is understood as primarily a sentiment, the dimension of deeds and of the service that the deeds bespeak is lost or radically transformed. And when that happens to any form of love, love is eviscerated and lightened beyond recognition, and its days become numbered.'[101] That is quite an indictment. But that's where the world is today and, sadly, the Church as well!

All that to say, a loving relationship with God should result in the keeping of his commandments, his 'righteous requirement' (Rom. 8:4). And it is the role of each pericope of Scripture – *every* pericope of Scripture – to spell out what divine demand is, so that the children of God might fulfil them, abiding by his commandments, and be holy, as God, their Father, is holy (their destiny for a new life of good works). And it is through this obedience that God is glorified as his people manifest his holiness and represent him to the world in their good works

99 Levenson, *Love of God*, 22. The conscription of love solely to emotions is, apparently, a modern phenomenon. Levenson refutes the exclusivity of love-as-romantic by pointing to the relationship between parents and children – also labelled 'love'. 'In this case, it seems to me, we are more likely to speak of actions than affects', parental care for their children, and filial undertaking of household responsibilities, et cetera (*Love of God*, 19). Not surprisingly, the parent-child relationship frequently describes the filiation between God and his people (Deut. 6:5; 8:5–6; 11:13; 14:1; 32:6; et cetera).

100 For the latter, in Deut. 7:7, God's 'love' translates *chashaq* – a word that has erotic connotations (Gen. 34:8; Deut. 21:10–14; also see Deut. 10:15; Ps. 91:14) – and the next verse, Deut. 7:8, employs the traditional verb for '[covenantal] love', *'ahav*, a deliberate parallelism to demonstrate that the relationship involves not only action but also affect.

101 Levenson, *Love of God*, 91. Strong words, but, tragically, true!

(God's design for his glorification by his people). As Jesus said (and as we have seen):

> 'In this way, let your light shine before people, in such a way that they may see your good works, and glorify your Father, the One in heaven.' (Matt. 5:16)

Coworkers in sanctification

This discussion of practical, ongoing sanctification of God's people, their conformation to Christ's image, and their responsibility to apply Scripture and to approximate such Christlikeness, should not be misconstrued as a sort of do-it-yourself lifting up of oneself by one's own theological bootstraps while attempting to fulfil God's righteous requirement.[102] Hardly! The gradual, progressive conformation to the image of Christ in this life (and ultimate conformation in the next) is a matter of God's grace mediated by his Spirit (as we have seen in Chapter 3) – notwithstanding the component of human responsibility to obey divine demand. On this, I echo Wright:

> Everything ... about moral effort, about the conscious shaping of our patterns of behavior, takes place simply and solely within the framework of grace – the grace which was embodied in Jesus and his death and resurrection, the grace which is active in the Spirit-filled preaching of the gospel, the grace which continues to be active by the Spirit in the lives of believers. It is simply not the case that God does some of the work of our salvation and we have to do the rest. It is not the case that we begin by being justified by grace through faith and then have to go to work all by ourselves to complete the job by struggling, unaided, to live a holy life.[103]

With Christ, all things have been made anew: sinners have been justified, sin expiated, forgiveness gained and reconciliation with God accomplished for those who believe in Jesus Christ as their only God and

102 Bryan Chapell labels such an approach '*sola bootstrapsa*' (*Christ-Centered Preaching*, 289)! See Kuruvilla, 'Christiconic View', 43–70; and Kuruvilla, *Manual for Preaching*, 80.

103 Wright, *After You Believe*, 60.

Saviour; they are now united with Christ, baptised into him and bound to him. And eternal condemnation for disobedience to divine demand is no more their lot, for Jesus has made atonement for sin (Rom. 8:1). Indeed, his ministry before the Father continues for those ones he redeemed – his intercession for them (Rom. 8:34; Heb. 7:25) and his advocacy on their behalf (Heb. 9:24; 1 John 2:1).

But this newness of creation that Christians are in union with Christ, and the forgiveness of sin they therefore enjoy, does not negate the reality of God's call in each pericope of Scripture for them to discharge their responsibility to love and to fear and to serve him, to fulfil his righteous requirement to glorify God: relationship with God precedes, but also mandates, responsibility towards God. Therefore, in the mercy and grace of the heavenly Father, there is yet another aspect of the work of Christ that enables this sanctification of God's people: Christ's sending of the Holy Spirit (John 14:16; 15:26; 16:7) that unites the children of God with Christ (see Chapter 2). Indeed, the Saviour's work was accomplished *so that* the Father's will (his 'righteous requirement') may be fulfilled by his Spirit-indwelt and Spirit-empowered children:[104]

> God … sending His own Son in the likeness of the flesh of sin and for [a] sin [offering], He condemned sin in the flesh, in order that the righteous requirement of the law may be fulfilled in us who walk not according to the flesh but *according to the Spirit*.
> (Rom. 8:3–4)

And so the children of God thenceforth commit to walking, not according to the dictates of the evil flesh (that is itself subservient to sin), but according to the direction of the divine Spirit. That it is the Holy Spirit who gives one the ability to obey God is well established by the OT.[105] As well, in the NT, there is Jesus' declaration that 'apart from Me you are not able to do anything' (John 15:5).[106] All attest to the working

104 Also see Rom. 6:4, 6; 7:4; Eph. 2:10; Titus 2:14; 3:4–8, all of them bearing *hina* ('in order that') clauses, pointing to the purpose of salvation: sanctification unto good works (for the glory of God).

105 See Deut. 30:6; Jer. 31:31–34; Ezek. 36:26–28; 37:1–28; et cetera.

106 Also see 1 Cor. 4:7; 2 Cor. 3:5; 4:7; 8:1 with 8:7 (the grace of God becomes the Macedonians' own work of grace); 12:9–10; Gal. 6:3; Eph. 4:7; 1 Thess. 5:24; 1 Pet. 4:10–11; et cetera.

of God through his Spirit in and with the work of his children.[107] Thus God is able both to command what he wills (his righteous requirement) and to give what he commands (his empowerment to fulfil that righteous requirement).[108] With the indwelling of the Holy Spirit a new life is begun, and the believer is enabled to fulfil the righteous requirement of God (Rom. 8:3–4), the divine demand of God in every part of Scripture.

Though the obedience of God's people is a consequence of deity's own gracious operation in them through his Spirit, there are also benefits that accrue to them because of God's pleasure in the worthy lifestyles of his children that glorify him.[109] Jesus explicitly affirmed that obedience would bring blessing:[110]

> 'Blessed are those who hear the word of God and keep it.'
> (Luke 11:28)

Any positive consequence from behaviour that is divinely prescribed and spiritually empowered is, in the end, an act of God's grace – a divine 'blessing'.[111] Even the experience of God's love is contingent upon an obedient walk with God. Jesus declared: 'If you keep My commandments, you will remain in My love' (John 15:10[112]). Besides, there are eternal rewards for obedience (and loss thereof for disobedience).[113]

---

107 See Ezek. 36:27; Eph. 2:10; 3:16; Gal. 2:20; Phil. 2:13; 4:13; Col. 1:9–11; Heb. 13:20–21.

108 That was Augustine's oft-repeated prayer to God: 'Grant what you command and command what you will' (*Confessions* 10.29, 31, 37; my translation from the Latin).

109 For divine pleasure in human obedience (of believers), see Heb. 13:20–21; also Rom. 12:1–2; 14:18; 2 Cor. 5:9; Eph. 5:10; Col. 3:10; Heb. 13:16; 1 John 3:22. Such a life is one that is lived 'worthy of the gospel of Christ' (Phil. 1:27), 'worthy of the Lord' (Col. 1:10), 'worthy of the God who calls you into His own kingdom and glory' (1 Thess. 2:12; also see Rom. 16:2; Eph. 4:1). This is, as we have seen, to 'walk' in 'good works, that God prepared beforehand' (Eph. 2:10), and not 'walk' in trespasses and sins (2:1–2).

110 Also see John 13:17.

111 See, for instance, the promises of peace for Christians adopting certain kinds of behaviours: Rom. 8:6; 2 Cor. 13:11; Gal. 6:16; Phil. 4:6–7. On the other hand, there are also consequences for the children of God who disobey: 'For the ones the Lord loves, He disciplines, and He scourges every child whom He receives' (Heb. 12:6).

112 Also see 1 John 2:5; 4:12. Thus, God's love is unconditionally extended from the divine donor's side, but only conditionally experienced from the human recipient's. The exhortation in Jude 21 to believers to 'keep yourselves in the love of God' is telling; it implies that one *can* exclude oneself from the experience of divine love!

113 See, for gain of rewards, Matt. 6:1–4; Rom. 14:10–12; 1 Cor. 3:13; 4:5; 9:24; 2 Cor. 5:10; Col. 3:22–25; 2 Tim. 2:5; Jas. 5:7–11; and for loss of rewards, 1 Cor. 3:15; 10:4–5; 1 John 2:28; et cetera.

But though it is all of grace from beginning to end, yet with that divine engracing there is also Christian responsibility as has oft been noted here. How practical sanctification unto Christlikeness is both a function of divine sovereignty and human responsibility is an inscrutable question. And, as in most aspects of spirituality that necessarily involve the Holy Spirit, there is an uncommon reticence exhibited by Scripture as to how exactly this happens – Wallace calls it 'a studied reserve on the *method* of sanctification. That is, the biblical authors speak positively about the ministry of the Spirit but typically refrain from telling how that ministry is to be implemented into the believer's life.' He speculates that this approach may reflect Jeremiah 31:31, 34 that has Yahweh promising that his people will not have to teach one another or exhort one another to know Yahweh. 'This new covenant mentality of what might be labelled a "soft mysticism" is prevalent in the NT.'[114] Perhaps this biblical reluctance for prescription is also because of the impossibility of providing specifics for application for every possible individual in every possible congregation in every possible age in every possible place.[115] Wright's words are wise: 'We are here, as so often in theology, at the borders of language, because we are trying to talk at the same time about "something God does" and "something humans do" as if God were simply another character like ourselves, as though (in other words) the interplay of God's work and our work could be imagined on the model of two people collaborating on a project. There are mysteries here …'[116] Indeed!

The bottom line in this divine-human coworking for sanctification is that the child of God is never to attempt obedience with self-resources:

---

114 Wallace, *Greek Grammar*, 639 (emphasis original). After all, 'the wind bloweth where it listeth, and thou hearest the sound thereof, but canst not tell whence it cometh, and whither it goeth' (John 3:8 KJV).

115 Indeed, offering specifics for application is, therefore, the responsibility of the leaders, the shepherds of the flock and disciplers of the growing. For such a conception as it relates to preaching, see Kuruvilla, *Vision for Preaching*.

116 Wright, *After You Believe*, 97. As Gal. 4:19 indicates, the maturation of Christians is the process of Christ being 'formed' in them, a work empowered by the Holy Spirit (3:3). Indeed, believers are to 'work out [from the Greek *katergazomai*]' their own salvation, acknowledging, at the same time, that it is God who is at 'work [from *energeō* – a *divine* work] in you, both to will and to work [also from *energeō* – a *human* work] for His pleasure' (Phil. 2:12–13; notice the common root in all three Greek verbs, *-erg*, from *ergon*, 'work'). A mystery, for sure!

that would be a self-exalting, flesh-driven, merit-attempting, grace-rejecting, faith-negating obedience to divine law – the legalism Paul so often excoriated. Utterly futile. Instead, the 'obedience of faith' or 'faithful obedience' (Rom. 1:5; 16:26[117]) that God expects of his children is a God-glorifying, Spirit-empowered, merit-excluding, grace-accepting, faith-exercising endeavour (see Figure 4.10).

Legalistic Obedience	'Faithful Obedience'
Self-exalting	God-glorifying
Flesh-driven	Spirit-empowered
Merit-attempting	Merit-excluding
Grace-rejecting	Grace-accepting
Faith-negating	Faith-exercising

Figure 4.10

In sum, obedience to God can only be accomplished by God's power. The Holy Spirit now indwells believers, graciously enabling them to overcome the flesh and meet God's 'righteous requirement' as we have seen in Romans 8:3–4. As Augustine said, 'Law [or "righteous requirement"] was given so that grace may be sought; grace was given that the law may be fulfilled.'[118] So, Christian life, in its entirety, is a function of divine grace, designed to bring glory to God, as deity had intended from the creation of humankind. This lifelong process includes the Father's choice of men and women to become a holy people in the Son (justification), their empowerment by the Spirit to live lives that are Christlike producing good works (sanctification) and, one day, the consummation of their transformation into the image of Jesus Christ (glorification), as God is himself glorified throughout this process. And so with the author of Hebrews one can affirm that God is the one equipping his children to *do* his will, even as God himself is *doing* it all (13:20–21) – that is how God is pleased and that is how God is glorified: 'Now may the God of peace … equip you with every good thing to *do* his will, [He] *doing* in us what is pleasing before him, through Jesus Christ, to whom be glory forever. Amen.'

117 For more on 'faithful obedience'/'obedience of faith', see Kuruvilla, *Privilege the Text!*, 195–204.

118 *On the Spirit and the Letter* 19.34 (my translation from the Latin).

Conclusion

We all, with faces having been unveiled –
reflecting, as in a mirror, the glory of the Lord –
are being transformed [into] the same image
from glory to [more] glory,
exactly as [by empowerment] from the Lord, the Spirit.
(2 Cor. 3:18)

From [divine] *Glory* [lost] *to* [divine] *Glory* [regained] – that is the story of mankind. Of course, God's intrinsic glory is never lost or regained; rather, it is humanity's capacity to glorify God that has undergone these momentous changes of loss and regain. Chapter 1 of this work ('Sin: the disease') detailed how, at the creation of this race, deity's glory was the intent of God (Design). To glorify God by being like him, a form of imitation or following as the OT frequently asserts, was what was planned for humans.[1] However, humanity utterly failed in this endeavour, with the calamity of the fall of the first pair, man and woman (Deviance). The

1 For following Yahweh, see Num. 14:24; 32:11–12; Deut. 1:36; 13:4; Josh. 14:8–9, 14; 1 Sam. 12:14; 1 Kgs. 11:6; 14:8; 18:21; 2 Kgs. 23:3. Perhaps reflecting this OT emphasis, in the Gospels the command, quite frequently, is to follow Jesus; Matt. 8:22; 9:9; 10:38; 19:21 (among others); also see 1 Pet. 2:2. For imitating God/Christ, see Matt. 5:44–48; Luke 6:36, 40; John 13:15–16; 17:11, 21; Rom. 15:1–3, 5; 2 Cor. 8:9; Eph. 5:1–2; Phil. 2:4–11; Col. 3:13; 1 Thess. 1:6; 1 Pet. 1:15; 4:1; 1 John 2:6; 3:16. All this is in addition to the numerous exhortations of Scripture to follow/imitate deity, though not using mimesis language (e.g., Lev. 19:2; Job 23:11; Isa. 52:12; Matt. 10:38; 20:26–28; John 13:12–17; et cetera). Such imitation or mimesis is not to assert that the children of God are to do as Christ did (as in the common slogan 'WWJD?'). The fact is that this is a mimesis not precisely of Christ but one of Christlikeness, simply because we have no historical data about Christ doing those things as required in the many pericopes of Scripture. However, there can be no doubt that the 'righteous requirement' of God was met by Jesus Christ: for one, he is impeccable; for another, his righteousness is credited to believers and God considers that these redeemed ones have (vicariously) fulfilled his divine demand and righteous requirement: in Christ, it is as though they have not sinned. That too, reinforces the notion that Jesus Christ fulfilled all that God requires of humanity; that is why his atonement was acceptable to God for the sins of that race. As was noted in Chapter 2, such a life change by mimesis is a living out of the reality of who the child of God actually *is*, in Christ, by virtue of being baptised unto him and bound to him. Luther was right: 'It is not the imitation that makes sons, but the sonship that makes imitators' (*Lectures on Galatians 1519, Chapters 1–6*, 263 [on Gal. 3:13–14]).

blight of this disease affected the entirety of the race, rendering humans incapable of glorifying God and thereby 'divesting themselves' of God's reflected glory upon them and through them to the rest of creation.

> The eating from this tree [of the knowledge of good and evil] was the symptom of their [of the first pair of humans] disobedience and the breaking of the command given by God; and through their guilt they consequently divested themselves of the glory surrounding them, rendering themselves unworthy of such wonderful esteem.[2]

If God's original plan was to undergo fruition, he would have to work a miracle, given the absolute inutility of the raw material – fallen humans – he had on hand. And so, a miracle he did work. Chapter 2 (Salvation: the cure') detailed the therapeutic mission God undertook (Deliverance), as incarnate God, Jesus Christ, saved those who had faith in his redemptive work, curing them of the bane of sin, baptising them to himself in the Spirit, and binding them to himself in an espousal. The goal of this deliverance was that these saved people of God would henceforth live new lives of good works, thus exhibiting holiness in every aspect of their being (Destiny). Here, too, an imitation is implicit – an identification with Christ in his death and resurrection 'so we too may walk in newness of life' (Rom. 6:4).

> [A] man who could be seen was not to be followed; God was to be followed – but he couldn't be seen. So in order to present human beings both with one who could be seen by human beings and with one whom human beings might properly follow, God became a human being.[3]

However, the deliverance of humanity has not yet been consummated: the child of God, though saved, still possesses the flesh, that immoral, incorrigible and irredeemable entity totally opposed to God and his

2 Chrysostom, *Homilies on Genesis* 16.5, in *Homilies on Genesis 1–17*, 216.

3 Augustine, 'Sermon 371: On the Lord's Nativity', in *Part III: Sermons 341–400*, 313. This statement is also cited in Aquinas, *Summa Theologica* 3.1.2.

holiness and serving the false authority personified as 'sin'. Chapter 3 ('Spirit: the healer') explained how the presence of the indwelling, lifegiving Spirit in believers now creates a grievous angst (Discord): the child of God wants to follow the true authority, God who healed them, but the pull of the flesh continues to seduce. This chapter also explored the role of the Holy Spirit (Doctor) in guiding and empowering believers to overcome this treacherous undertow of the flesh, and thus to keep the 'righteous requirement' of God – the expected and intended outcome of God's salvific work (Rom. 8:3–4). In other words, the Holy Spirit, the divine healer, aids the children of God to give glory to God (as they achieve their destiny of good works/holiness in all of life).

> He [Christ] justly puts Himself forward here as a pattern [Latin: *exemplum*], to the imitation of which all the godly may be conformed … We must always keep this conformity between the Head and the members before our eyes, not only that believers may endeavour to form themselves to the pattern of Christ, but that they may trust to be reformed daily for the better by His Spirit so that they may walk unto the end in newness of life.[4]

But what exactly is the 'righteous requirement' of God? Chapter 4 ('Scripture: the prescription') pointed out that the word of God is the source of deity's requirement (Demand) – guidelines for the godly walk along the road to glorifying God, i.e., prescriptions for spiritual health.[5] Scripture, then, spells out the answer to the question, 'Now that we are

4 Calvin, *The Gospel According to St John*, 98 (on John 15:10–11).

5 Östborn helpfully points out that the root of the Hebrew *torah* is *yrh*, 'cast' or 'throw', with hands, ostensibly (see in Job 30:19; 1 Sam. 20:36). In fact, Prov. 6:13 uses the participle of *yrh* with the sense of 'pointing' (with fingers). The *hiphil* form of *yrh* is *horah*, 'to instruct' (Exod. 35:34; Mic. 3:11), an extrapolation of the stretching out of one's hand/fingers as if to point. It stands to reason that *torah*, the noun derived from *yrh*, is also linked to this sense of 'pointing' or 'indicating', and thus it is functionally related to 'instructing' (see Östborn, *Tōrā in the Old Testament*, 7–9). That is exactly what the Torah, the word of God, does through its Author, the divine Doctor – it guides the people of God in the way they should go. It is not accidental, then, that early Christians were referred to as those of 'The Way' (Acts 9:2; 16:17; 18:25; 19:9, 23; 22:4; 24:14, 22), followers of a leader who himself claimed to be the 'way' (John 14:6). Or that a major metaphor for following/imitating God is to 'walk': Hebrew *hlk* (Gen. 5:22–24; 17:1; Deut. 5:33; 8:6; Pss. 1:1; 84:11; 119:1; et cetera) and Greek *peripateō* (Rom. 6:4; 8:4; 2 Cor. 5:7; Eph. 5:2; Col. 1:10; 1 Thess. 2:12; 4:1; et cetera).

saved, how then shall we live?' (Duty). This too is a form of imitation, for it is to the image of Christ that the children of God are being gradually conformed (Rom. 8:29). Calvin agreed: 'Christ, through whom we return into favour with God, has been set before us as an example [Latin: *exemplar*], whose pattern we ought to express in our life ... What can you require beyond this one thing? For we have been adopted as [children] by the Lord with this one condition: that our life express Christ, the bond of our adoption.'[6] This is the call of Scripture: to be conformed to the pixels of the image of Christ as depicted in its pericopes (pericopal theology).

> On the day called Sunday, all who live in cities or in the country gather together to one place, and the memoirs of the apostles or the writings of the prophets are read, as long as time permits; then, when the reader has ceased, the presider [i.e., the one presiding, the leader] verbally instructs and exhorts to the imitation [Greek: *mimēseōs*] of these good things.[7]

And by aligning their lives to the theologies of each pericope of the word of God, the people of God are being progressively conformed to the image of the Son of God, by the power of the Spirit of God, for the glory of God! Thy Kingdom come!

Now to the One who is able
to keep you unfallen and to stand [you] before his glory
blameless [and] with exultation,
to the only God our Saviour, through Jesus Christ our Lord,
be glory, majesty, power and authority,
before all ages, and now, and unto all ages.
Amen!
(Jude 24–25)

6 *Institutes*, 686–7 (3.6.3; this was cited earlier in Chapter 4).

7 Justin Martyr, *First Apology* 67, in *Ante-Nicene Fathers*, 2: 65.

Bibliography

Auden, W. H., *For the Time Being* (New York: Random House, 1944).

Augustine, 'Sermon 371: On the Lord's Nativity', pp. 312–15 in John E. Rotelle (ed.), *Part III: Sermons 341–400*, vol. 10 of *The Works of Saint Augustine*, trans. Edmund Hill (New York: Augustinian Heritage Institute, 1995).

Badenas, Robert, *Christ The End of the Law: Romans 10.4 in Pauline Perspective*, Journal for the Study of the New Testament Supplement Series 10 (Sheffield: JSOT Press, 1985).

Barclay, William, *Flesh and Spirit: An examination of Galatians 5:19–23* (Nashville: Abingdon, 1962).

Beale, G. K., *Union with the Resurrected Christ: Eschatological New Creation and New Testament Biblical Theology* (Grand Rapids: Baker, 2023).

Bertman, Stephen, 'Tasseled Garments in the Ancient East Mediterranean', *Biblical Archaeologist* 24 (1961): 119–28.

Best, Ernest, *A Critical and Exegetical Commentary on Ephesians* (International Critical Commentary. Edinburgh: T. &. T. Clark, 1998).

Bhopal, Raj S., *Concepts of Epidemiology: Integrating the ideas, theories, principles, and methods of epidemiology*, third ed. (Oxford: Oxford University Press, 2016).

Boulet, Jacques E. J., 'The Biblical Hebrew *Beth Essentiae:* Predicate Marker', *Journal for Semitics* 29.2 (2020): 1–27.

Brown, DeNeen L., '"You've Got Bad Blood": The Horror of the Tuskegee Syphilis Experiment', *The Washington Post*, 16 May 2017, https://www.washingtonpost.com/news/retropolis/wp/2017/05/16/youve-got-bad-blood-the-horror-of-the-tuskegee-syphilis-experiment/ (accessed 24 May 2024).

Brueggemann, Walter, *Genesis* (Atlanta: John Knox, 1982).

Calvin, John, *Commentaries on the First Book of Moses Called Genesis: Volume 1*, trans. John King (Grand Rapids: Eerdmans, 1948).

——, *The Gospel According to St John 11–21 and the First Epistle of John*, trans. T. H. L. Parker, Calvin's Commentaries (Grand Rapids: Eerdmans, 1959).

——, *Institutes of the Christian Religion*, The Library of Christian Classics 20, ed. John T. McNeill, trans. Ford Lewis Battles (Philadelphia: Westminster, 1960).

Campbell, Constantine R., *Paul and Union with Christ: An exegetical and theological study* (Grand Rapids: Zondervan, 2012).

Cassuto, Umberto, *A Commentary on the Book of Genesis: Part I from Adam to Noah: Genesis I–VI 8*, trans. Israel Abrahams (Jerusalem: Magnes, 1961).

Chapell, Bryan, *Christ-Centered Preaching: Redeeming the expository sermon*, second ed. (Grand Rapids: Baker, 2005).

Chrysostom, John, *Homilies on Genesis 1–17,* The Fathers of the Church, trans. Robert C. Hill (Washington, D.C.: Catholic University of America Press, 1986).

Clement of Alexandria, *Christ the Educator*, trans. Simon P. Wood (Washington, D.C.: The Catholic University of America Press, 1954).

Clines, David J. A., 'The Image of God in Man', *Tyndale Bulletin* 19 (1968): 53–103.

Clinton, Bill, 'Tuskegeee Public Health Study Apology' (Washington, DC: White House, 1997), https://www.c-span.org/video/?c4584112/bill-clinton-apologizes-tuskegee-experiment (accessed 24 May 2024).

Conant, T. J., *The Meaning and Use of Baptizein* (New York: American Bible Union, 1868).

Congress of the United States, 'National Research Act (Public Law 93–348)', pp. 342–54 in *United States Statutes at Large, 1974, Volume 88, Part 1* (Washington, D.C.: United States Government Printing Office, 1976).

——, 'Quality of Health Care – Human Experimentation, 1973: Hearings before the Subcommittee on Health of the Committee on Labor and Welfare, United States Senate, Ninety-Third Congress, First Session, 7–8 March, 1973' (Washington, D.C.: United States Government Printing Office, 1973).

Cotter, David W., *Genesis*, Berit Olam: Studies in Hebrew Narrative and Poetry (Collegeville, MN: Liturgical Press, 2003).

Cranfield, C. E. B., *A Critical and Exegetical Commentary on the Epistle to the Romans*, 2 vols, International Critical Commentary (Edinburgh: T. & T. Clark, 1979).

——, 'St. Paul and the Law', *Scottish Journal of Theology* 17 (1964): 43–68.

Denninger, David, 'The Creator's Fiat and the Creature's Witness: A Literary Study of the Structure, Dynamics, and Meaning of Psalm 19', Ph.D. diss. Trinity International University, 1996.

Dorsey, David A., 'The Law of Moses and the Christian: A Compromise', *Journal of the Evangelical Theological Society* 34 (1991): 321–34.

——, 'The Use of the OT Law in Christian Life: A Theocentric Approach', *Evangelical Journal* 17 (1998): 1–18.

Dumbrell, William J., 'Genesis 2:1–17: A Foreshadowing of the New Creation', pp. 53–65 in *Biblical Theology: Retrospect and prospect*, ed. Scott J. Hafemann (Downers Grove: InterVarsity, 2002).

Dunn, James D. G., *Romans 1–8*, Word Biblical Commentary 38A (Dallas: Word, 1988).

Editors, 'An Immoral Study', *St Louis Post-Dispatch*, 30 July 1972.

Edwards, Jonathan, *Two Dissertations: Dissertation I: Concerning the end for which God created the world*, in Paul Ramsey (ed.), *Ethical Writings. WJE Online Vol. 8*, http://edwards.yale.edu/archive?path=aHR0cDovL2Vkd2FyZHMueWFsZS5lZHUvY2dpLWJpbi9uZXdwaGlsby9nZXRvYmplY3QucGw/Yy43OjUud2plbw==#nlink209 (accessed 9 October 2023).

Emmrich, Martin, 'The Temptation Narrative of Genesis 3:1–6: A Prelude to the Pentateuch and the History of Israel', *Evangelical Quarterly* 73 (2001): 3–20.

Ferguson, Sinclair B., *The Holy Spirit*, Contours of Christian Theology (Downers Grove: InterVarsity, 1996).

'Formula of Concord', Solid Declaration Article VI. The Third Use of the Law. https://bookofconcord.org/solid-declaration/ (accessed 17 August 2023).

——, Epitome: Article VI, The Third Use of the Law. Affirmative Theses 2–3, 6, https://bookofconcord.org/epitome/ (accessed 17 August 2023).

——, Epitome: Article VI, The Third Use of the Law. Negative Theses 1, https://bookofconcord.org/epitome/ (accessed 17 August 2023).

Fowl, Stephen E., *Ephesians: A commentary*, New Testament Literature (Louisville: Westminster John Knox, 2012).

Fretheim, Terence E., 'Is Genesis 3 a Fall Story?', *Word & World* 14 (1994): 144–53.

Gibson, Scott M. and Matthew D. Kim (eds), *Homiletics and Hermeneutics: Four views on preaching today* (Grand Rapids: Baker, 2018).

Gonzalez, Rudolph D., 'Romans 6:1–14: The case for a chiastic Q&A', pp. 71–84 in Mikeal C. Parsons and Richard Walsh (eds), *'A Temple Not Made with Hands': Essays in honor of Naymond H. Keathley* (Eugene, OR: Pickwick, 2018).

Goodnick, Benjamin, 'The Tassel and the Blue Cord', *Jewish Biblical Quarterly* 21.2 (1993): 99–108.

Hamilton, Victor P., *The Book of Genesis Chapters 1–17*, New International Commentary on the Old Testament (Grand Rapids: Eerdmans, 1990).

Heller, Jean, 'Syphilis Victims in U.S. Study Went Untreated for 40 Years', *The New York Times*, 26 July 1972, https://www.nytimes.com/1972/07/26/archives/syphilis-victims-in-us-study-went-untreated-for-40-years-syphilis.html (accessed 24 May 2024).

Hodge, Charles, *On the Epistle to the Romans*, rev. ed. (Philadelphia: Alfred Martien, 1873).

Iyengar, Sheena, 'How to Make Choosing Easier', https://www.ted.com/talks/sheena_iyengar_how_to_make_choosing_easier/transcript?language=en (accessed 19 January 2024).

Jones, James H., *Bad Blood: The Tuskegee syphilis experiment* (New York: The Free Press, 1981).

Justin Martyr, *First Apology*, pp. 7–70 in Alexander Roberts and James Donaldson (eds), *The Ante-Nicene Fathers*, 10 volumes (Edinburgh: T. & T. Clark, 1885–1887).

Kaufman, Gordon D., *An Essay on Theological Method*, third ed. (Atlanta: American Academy of Religion, 1995).

Kitz, Anne Marie, 'Demons in the Hebrew Bible and the Ancient Near East.', *Journal of Biblical Literature* 135.3 (2016): 447–64.

Kuruvilla, Abraham, *1 and 2 Timothy, Titus: A theological commentary for preachers* (Eugene, OR: Cascade, 2021).
——, *'Applicable', not 'Obeyable': Biblical law and the Christian* (In preparation).
——, 'The *Aqedah* (Genesis 22): What Is the Author *Doing* with What He Is *Saying*?', *Journal of the Evangelical Theological Society* 55 (2012): 489–508.
——, 'Christiconic Interpretation', *Bibliotheca sacra* 173 (2016): 131–46.
——, 'Christiconic View', pp. 43–70 in Scott M. Gibson and Matthew D. Kim (eds), *Homiletics and Hermeneutics: Four views on preaching today*, p. 43–70 (Grand Rapids: Baker, 2018).
——, *Ephesians: A theological commentary for preachers* (Eugene, OR: Cascade, 2015).
——, *Exodus: A theological commentary for preachers* (In preparation).
——, 'From "Far" to "Near"! A Pericopal Theology Guide to Preaching Ephesians 2:11–22', *Journal of the Evangelical Homiletics Society* 20.2 (2020): 67–86.
——, *Genesis: A theological commentary for preachers* (Eugene, OR: Resource Publications, 2025).
——, *Judges: A theological commentary for preachers* (Eugene, OR: Cascade, 2017).
——, *A Manual for Preaching: The journey from text to sermon* (Grand Rapids: Baker, 2019).
——, *Mark: A theological commentary for preachers* (Eugene, OR: Cascade, 2012).
——, *Privilege the Text!: A theological hermeneutic for preaching* (Chicago: Moody, 2013).
——, *Psalms 1–44: A theological commentary for preachers* (Eugene, OR: Cascade, 2024).
——, *Psalms 45–100: A theological commentary for preachers* (Eugene, OR: Cascade, 2024).
——, *Psalms 101–150: A theological commentary for preachers* (Eugene, OR: Cascade, 2024).
——, *Text to Praxis: Hermeneutics and homiletics in dialogue*, Library of New Testament Studies 393 (London: T. & T. Clark, 2009).
——, *A Vision for Preaching: Understanding the heart of pastoral ministry* (Grand Rapids: Baker, 2015).

Labuschagne, C. J., 'Significant Compositional Techniques in the Psalms: Evidence for the Use of Number as an Organizing Principle', *Vetus Testamentum* 59 (2009): 583–605.
Lee, Stan, *Amazing Fantasy 15* (New York: Marvel Comics, 1962).
——, *Amazing Spider-Man 149* (New York: Marvel Comics, 1975).
——, *Amazing Spider-Man 181* (New York: Marvel Comics, 1978).
Levenson, Jon D., *The Love of God: Divine gift, human gratitude, and mutual faithfulness in Judaism* (Princeton: Princeton University Press, 2016).
——, *Sinai and Zion: An entry into the Jewish Bible* (Minneapolis, MN: Winston, 1985).
——, 'The Temple and the World', *Journal of Religion* 64 (1984): 275–98.
Long, Thomas G., 'The Preacher and the Beast: From Apocalyptic Text to Sermon', pp. 1–22 in Richard L. Eslinger (ed.), *Intersections: Post-critical studies in preaching* (Grand Rapids: Eerdmans, 2004).
——, 'The Use of Scripture in Contemporary Preaching', *Interpretation* 44 (1990): 341–52.
Luther, Martin, 'Lectures on Galatians 1519, Chapters 1–6', pp. 151–441 in Jaroslav Pelikan (ed.), *Luther's Works, Vol. 27: Lectures on Galatians* (St Louis: Concordia, 1964).
Magner, Lois N. and Oliver J. Kim, *A History of Medicine*, third ed. (Boca Raton, FL: CRC Press, 2018).
Mathews, Kenneth A., *Genesis 1–11:26*, New American Commentary 1A (Nashville: Broadman and Holman, 1996).
Milgrom, Jacob, 'Of Hems and Tassels', *Biblical Archeology Review* 9 (1983): 61–5.
Moberly, R. W. L., *The Bible, Theology, and Faith: A study of Abraham and Jesus*, (Cambridge: Cambridge University Press, 2000).
Moo, Douglas J., *The Epistle to the Romans*, New International Commentary on the New Testament (Grand Rapids: Eerdmans, 1996).
Morrison, Patt and Nancy Heffernan, 'Iranian's Suicide Solves Suitcase Mystery: Husband Joins Smuggled Bride in Death', *Los Angeles Times*, 12 January 1985, https://www.latimes.com/archives/la-xpm-1985-01-12-mn-9507-story.html (accessed 26 April 2024).
National Transportation Safety Board, *File No. 1-0016: Aircraft Accident*

Report, Eastern Air Lines, Inc., L-1011, N310EA, Miami, Florida, December 29, 1972. National Transportation Safety Board Aircraft Accident Report Number AAR-73-14, (Washington D.C.: National Transportation Safety Board, 1973).

Nygren, Anders, *Commentary on Romans*, trans. Carl S. Rasmussen (Philadelphia: Muhlenberg Press, 1949).

O'Brien, Peter T., *The Letter to the Ephesians*, Pillar New Testament Commentary (Grand Rapids: Eerdmans, 1999).

Östborn, Gunnar, *Tōrā in the Old Testament: A semantic study* (Lund, Sweden: Håkan Ohlssons, 1945).

Ouro, Roberto, 'The Garden of Eden Account: The Chiastic Structure of Genesis 2–3', *Andrews University Seminary Studies* 40.2 (2002): 219–43.

——, 'Linguistic and Thematic Parallels Between Genesis 1 and 3', *Journal of the Adventist Theological Society* 13.1 (2002): 44–54.

Palumbo, Donald, 'The Marvel Comics Group's Spider-Man Is an Existentialist Super-Hero; or "Life Has No Meaning Without My Latest Marvels!"' *Journal of Popular Culture* 17.2 (1983): 67–82.

Porta, Miquel (ed.), *A Dictionary of Epidemiology*, sixth ed. (New York: Oxford University Press, 2014).

Porter, Stanley E., 'A Newer Perspective on Paul: Romans 1–8 Through the Eyes of Literary Analysis', pp. 366–92 in M. Daniel Carroll R., David J. A. Clines and Philip R. Davies (eds), *The Bible in Human Society: Essays in honour of John Rogerson*, Journal for the Study of the Old Testament Supplement Series 200 (Sheffield: Sheffield Academic Press, 1995).

Rad, Gerhard von, *Genesis*, trans. John H. Marks, rev. ed. (Philadelphia: Westminster, 1972).

Reiss, Aaron, 'Columbia Woman Caught Cheating in St. Louis Marathon', *Columbia Missourian*, 17 April 2015, https://www.columbiamissourian.com/sports/columbia-woman-caught-cheating-in-st-louis-marathon/article_97866362-07f3-5e96-a106-95d8b515d830.html (accessed 14 May 2024).

Richardson, Niall, 'The Gospel According to *Spider-Man*', *The Journal of Popular Culture* 37.4 (2004): 694–703.

Ricoeur, Paul, 'The Hermeneutical Function of Distanciation', pp. 131–44 in Paul Ricoeur (ed.), *Hermeneutics and the Human Sciences: Essays on language, action and interpretation*, trans. John B. Thompson (Cambridge: Cambridge University Press, 1981).

——, 'Naming God', *Union Seminary Quarterly Review* 34 (1979): 215–27.

Sawyer, Vincent S., 'In Christ: The Life of Victory', *Calvary Baptist Theological Journal* 3 (1987): 55.

Schreiner, Thomas R. *Romans*, Baker Exegetical Commentary on the New Testament (Grand Rapids: Baker, 1998).

Strack, Hermann L. and Paul Billerbeck. *Kommentar zum Neuen Testament aus Talmud und Midrasch: Book I: Das Evangelium nach Matthäus* (Munich: C. H. Beck, 1926).

Tannehill, Robert C., *Dying and Rising with Christ: A study in Pauline theology* (Berlin: Verlag Alfred Töpelmann, 1967).

Temple, William, *Nature, Man, and God* (Edinburgh: T. & T. Clark, 1940).

Uniform Law Commission, 'Uniform Determination of Death Act', https://www.uniformlaws.org/committees/community-home?CommunityKey=155faf5d-03c2-4027-99ba-ee4c99019d6c (accessed 26 April 2024).

Vanhoozer, Kevin J. 'Putting on Christ: Spiritual Formation and the Drama of Discipleship', *Journal for Spiritual Formation and Soul Care* 8 (2015): 147–71.

Wallace, Daniel B., *Greek Grammar Beyond the Basics: An exegetical syntax of the New Testament* (Grand Rapids: Zondervan, 1996).

Walsh, Jerome T., 'Genesis 2:4b–3:24: A Synchronic Approach', *Journal of Biblical Literature* 96 (1977): 161–77.

Wells, Robert E., *Is a Blue Whale the Biggest Thing There Is?* (Morton Grove, IL: Albert Whitman & Co., 1993).

Wenham, Gordon J., *Genesis 1–15*, Word Biblical Commentary 1 (Nashville: Thomas Nelson, 1987).

Westermann, Claus, *Creation*, trans. John J. Scullion (Philadelphia: Fortress, 1971).

Westminster Assembly, *The Larger Catechism Agreed Upon By the Assembly of Divines at Westminster* (Philadelphia: D. Hogan, 1814).

Wijdicks, E. F. M., 'The Diagnosis of Brain Death', *New England Journal of Medicine* 344.16 (2001): 1215–21.

Wolde, Ellen van, 'The Text as an Eloquent Guide: Rhetorical, Linguistic and Literary Features in Genesis 1', pp. 134–51 in L. J. de Regt, J. de Waard and J. P. Fokkelman (eds), *Literary Structure and Rhetorical Strategies in the Hebrew Bible* (Assen, Netherlands: Van Gorcum, 1996).

Wright, N. T., *After You Believe: Why Christian character matters* (New York: HarperOne, 2012).

Index of authors

Index of Scripture references

Exodus

Leviticus

Numbers

Deuteronomy